Mere Churchianity

Church and the Threat it Poses to the Body of Christ

John Hampton

Unless otherwise stated, Scripture quotations are from the Holy Bible, New International Version. Copyright © 1973, 1978, 1984 International Bible Society. Used by permission of Hodder and Stoughton Publishers (UK) and The Zondervan Corporation (US)

ISBN-10: 1530493536
ISBN-13: 978-1530493531

To Liz

Table of Contents

Section 3. Church Finance: Feeding the Monster

Section 4. Church Structure: Body Building

Conclusion to Part 2. Jesus and his Bride: The State of the Union

Part 3: Where do we go from Here?

Section 1. Staying on Message

Section 2. Ground Zero

ACKNOWLEDGMENTS

What started as a collection of thoughts around eighteen years ago has slowly evolved into the book you are now holding. Writing *Mere Churchianity* has been a distinctly on-off affair, with life supplying a succession of diversions and distractions (as it does to all of us), and there were many times when I doubted that I could bring the book to completion.

The fact that it has, indeed, reached the finish line is due in no small part by my collaborator and travelling companion — my wife and editor, Liz. Her proofreading skills along with her insights have been invaluable; having someone both available and prepared to act as a sounding board has been a hugely important factor in 'smoothing out the wrinkles', as she puts it. Through long months and years she has faithfully read and annotated draft after draft, whilst at the same time she has tirelessly kept things going on a multitude of other fronts to enable me to write. If it wasn't for her contribution — not least her questions — this would be a very different book indeed. It speaks volumes for her character that, despite my suggestion on more than one occasion that her name should appear on the cover alongside my own, she has declined. But this book is as much hers as it is mine.

I'd also like to say a big thank you to our children, Ashley, Stephanie, Kristina and Jordan, whose encouragement to finish writing this book carried me through the many periods during which I wondered if I could keep going. Each of them has been, at different times and often unknowingly, a lens through which I've been able to observe many aspects of current church life; periodic accounts of their own experiences, as well as those of their friends, have helped me find the energy to press on, increasingly convinced of the existence of a wider audience who might benefit from at least some of the things I've committed to paper. The driving force behind this book is the conviction that the next generation should not continue to miss out on the kind of body life God desires for them... and indeed, what He has always intended for all His people from the very beginning.

I have gathered a garland of other men's flowers, and nothing is mine but the ribbon which binds them.

Michel de Montaigne

PREFACE

Standing on the Barricades

The great Christian revolutions come not by the discovery of something that was not known before. They happen when someone takes radically something that was always there.

H. Richard Niebuhr

Leipzig is situated a couple of hours drive to the south of Berlin in the former East Germany. Most people, if they know anything about the city, will be aware of its role in the political upheaval of the late eighties and early nineties—the mass rallies held here in 1989 are now recognized as having made a significant contribution to the collapse of the Berlin Wall and communism in general.

The most iconic image of those rallies has to be the candle-lit marches involving tens of thousands of people walking around the city ring proclaiming, 'Wir Sind das Volk': *We are the people*—the anthem of ordinary men and women risking their lives in an effort to throw off their ideologically-driven leaders. As I write this, the city is preparing to celebrate the twenty-fifth anniversary of that epoch-defining, peaceful protest. Leipzig is truly a modern-day Jericho: the people marched around the city with the result that the Berlin Wall—like the walls of its biblical counterpart—came 'tumbling down.'

What I hadn't realised until my family and I moved here fifteen years ago, was the fact that Leipzig and its environs had been at the centre of a much earlier and even more significant revolution half a millennium before our arrival. At that time, the region found itself a hotbed of religious upheaval, the eye of a particularly violent theological storm—one which would radiate from here and buffet the whole world.

Half-way between Leipzig and Berlin lies the town of Wittenberg, best known as the cradle of the Reformation and the birthplace of Protestantism. One of the first things I wanted to do when we arrived in Germany was to visit Martin Luther's church and stand in front of the door to which he had nailed his *Ninety-five Theses* five hundred years earlier. To my disappointment, I discovered that the original wooden doors had burnt down two and a half centuries ago and had eventually been replaced by two bronze doors upon which the *Theses* had been embossed. Despite this, it was a powerful, almost overwhelming experience to stand at the very spot where the history of the Western Church had been irrevocably changed. I was particularly struck by the fact that such a relatively small document could have such a profound effect, not only on the Church but on the whole world. Luther himself remarked, 'I would never have thought that such a storm would rise from Rome over one simple scrap of paper.'

What I've written here is considerably longer than *The Ninety-five Theses*, but—despite my secret hopes—I have to acknowledge that realistically it is extremely unlikely that it will ever have quite the same impact as Luther's writings... Even so, I'd like to think that what I've articulated in the following pages has something to do with issues that are as fundamental today as those Luther addressed so long ago—or dare I say it—even more so, for as vital as Luther's reforms were, *I am convinced they didn't go far enough.* Luther identified some of the symptoms of a sick body but not the underlying disease; he reformed both the theology and the practices of the church to some extent but, as John Nelson Darby, one of the founders of the Plymouth Brethren, put it, 'The Reformation did not directly touch the question of the true character of God's church.'

The main purpose of this book is very much concerned with addressing this question: that is, defining what we mean by 'the church'. This is possibly more important than ever before, since, as we shall discover, there is a growing disillusionment with the church, not just amongst unbelievers, but within the Christian community itself. The reason for this dissatisfaction resides, I believe, in the fact that we do not have a coherent understanding of what the church is in the first place. I'd like to illustrate this by way of the following personal experience:

An assistant pastor once asked me what I looked for in terms of church, fellowship and so on. I replied that I simply wanted to follow God, grow to love Him more and continue to be transformed into His image—and that I wanted to do this in the company of other Christians who had the same goal, since we better attain these things through one another's presence and encouragement in our lives. The response was un-expected, to say the least:

'But that isn't church!'

When I reflected on the conversation afterwards, I found it disconcerting that the priority of the person with whom I had been talking *didn't* appear to be about encouraging people to love God and follow Him; rather the priority seemed to be the institution of the church itself. The comment, *'But that isn't church!'* caused me to question his understanding of church as opposed to mine: the more I pondered this, the more I realised that the reason we found ourselves talking at cross purposes was due to the fact that, whilst we were both using the word *church*, we were talking about two very different things: he, like most people, was talking about *church-as-a-thing-in-itself*—something which I will define in due course—whereas I was talking about the *ekklesia*. And there, in a nutshell, lies the problem which confronts all of us and with which this book is concerned.

Returning to the October Revolution of 1989—whilst both the citizens of Leipzig and the world's press continue to remember the events of that time, there is another revolution taking place. However, since it is taking place within the Christian community rather than in the wider world, it is generally unrecognized and largely unreported as a result. It is a slow-burning revolution which has been smouldering for some years, but one which is increasing in strength. A softly spoken refrain is growing in volume, rising up from many of those within the Western church, the anthem of the *ekklesia*:

Wir Sind Gottes Volk—We are God's people.

In the same way that ordinary East Germans had had enough of their communist oppressors, many Bible-believing Christians, to speak plainly, have had their fill of church;

increasingly, some of them have decided to throw off the yoke of those who—even though they ought to have known better—have sought to control rather than disciple them. But rather than stage a revolt in an attempt to overthrow 'the system', the action that many have taken is simply to leave the church, while others are considering whether to follow suit. Sadly, however, this has not led the vast majority of these refugees to some sort of Promised Land, but rather to a wasteland, a spiritual desert. Even then, and as we shall see, for many of those who have chosen self-imposed exile, remaining outside their comfort zone is evidently preferable to a return to the church.

I believe it was Michelangelo who was once asked how it was that he could sculpt a horse from a block of marble. He replied, 'It's simple. I take the block and chisel off everything which doesn't look like a horse.' *Mere Churchianity* is an attempt to do something similar: like the sculptor, I've taken the monolith of *church-as-a-thing-in-itself* and I have attempted to chisel off everything which doesn't look like Christ's body in order to reveal his beautiful Bride. In so doing, like one of those faces to be found in the mass demonstrations on Leipzig's ring-road, I hope to play my small but useful part in helping to set her free.

Woe to you who are complacent in Zion.

Amos 6:1

INTRODUCTION

CRISIS? WHAT CRISIS?

Not Even Wrong

To look at something as though we had never seen it before requires great courage.

Henri Matisse

Nobel-prize winning Physicist, Niels Bohr, once gave an address to a gathering of philosophers in Copenhagen on the subject of Quantum Theory. At the end of his address, he was disappointed to find that there were no questions forthcoming. Remarking on this to two of his colleagues, he said, 'Those who are not shocked when they first come across quantum theory cannot possibly have understood it. Probably I spoke so badly that no-one knew what I was talking about.' [1]

My subject here is not Physics, but rather the church — or more precisely, *church-as-a-thing-in-itself* — but if by the time you reach the final page you, like Bohr's philosophers, have no questions, if you're not at the very least *troubled* by the implications of *church-as-a-thing-in-itself...* then I too will have failed in my attempt to adequately convey just what is at stake — because if the thesis which I present is correct, then the implications are of vital importance.

Wolfgang Pauli, another great physicist who was almost as famous for his rudeness as for his science, supposedly said of a student's research paper: 'Not only is it not right, it's not *even* wrong!' I believe that church as many experience it today is, like that physics paper, so far off base that 'it's not even wrong.' My contention is that our concept of church has been distorted so radically, that far from being at least in the right ball park, there is no ball park even in sight... and as a result, many of us have found ourselves playing almost a different sport altogether.

There's a saying in business that *your system is perfectly designed to yield the results you've been getting;* in other words, if we keep doing what we've been doing, we will keep getting what we've been getting. Of course, it might well be that as far as your church situation is concerned, you feel that 'what you've been getting' is fine, in which case all is well and good. If you're happy with the way things are then there isn't perhaps any reason to continue reading other than curiosity as to where all this might be heading. I suspect, however, that there are many people reading this who are *not* entirely happy with the situation in which they find themselves; on the contrary, when it comes to their church life, they're asking themselves:

Is this as good as it gets?

By this, I don't mean to endorse or even suggest the idea that believers should act like spoiled or selfish children, people who simply expect to be spoon fed instead of taking at least some responsibility for their own spiritual growth. Rather, I mean to suggest that for many, church does not satisfy a deep, legitimate yearning for God.

In any other area of life, if the prevailing state of affairs was as dysfunctional as it appears to be within large sections of the church, questions would be asked; perhaps a form of soul-searching or self-analysis would take place as a result. But due to a number of factors—including a mindset which regards any suggestion for reform as a criticism and thus inherently unchristian—too often little or nothing is done to rectify the situation.

Some say that things *are,* in fact, changing all the time and that there's good reason to hope that the church will sort itself out one of these days. Indeed, on the face of it, all sorts of new things *are* happening; generally speaking, however, these are simply cosmetic: they do not deal with the underlying, deep-seated issues that I wish to discuss in this book.

In the meantime, the fact is that more often than not the new way of doing things is, in reality, simply the old way of doing things in disguise. The supposedly new ideas, presented in a succession of programmes which we have seen come and go in many of our churches over the years, are simply a case of the same fifty-two cards in the deck being reshuffled and dealt out once more; they are merely attempts to freshen things up when current programmes start to feel stale, rather than being activities inspired by the Holy Spirit. I constantly hear and read about the next wonder-method that will revolutionise the church and its impact on the nations, but all that really happens is that the church furniture gets moved around. However, since the changes are embellished with slogans like, 'For Such a Time as This' (often with the word 'fire' added in there somewhere) it seems that no-one notices that, in real terms, it's business as usual. Meanwhile, as Alexander Solzhenitsyn put it, the world is perishing at one thousand times the rate at which the church is getting its act together… if 'fire' *is* relevant, it is only insofar as we are fiddling while the world burns.

If I might borrow from the discipline of Science one more time, then it's worth considering the words of Thomas Kuhn: in his book, *The Structure of Scientific Revolutions*, Kuhn described how science progresses when the burden of evidence against an existing model becomes so great as to make continuing support for it unsustainable, to the point that the current model is finally abandoned in favour of a new one; he coined the phrase *paradigm shift* in order to describe the process of change. My hope is that this book will act as a catalyst for the same sort of paradigm shift; a paradigm shift not in the area of science, of course, but in terms of our understanding of what Christ meant when he described his body—the *ekklesia*—because, unless there's a radical change in our thinking, it seems reasonable to assume things will continue to be 'not even wrong' pretty much indefinitely.

This brings me to my central proposition:

I contend that the generally accepted understanding of Christ's *ekklesia*—which is almost exclusively translated in our Bibles as 'church'—is flawed at a fundamental level; that *church*, as we commonly understand the term, is largely a man-made structure without a solid scriptural foundation. I am absolutely convinced that if someone with no preconceived ideas regarding the church were to open the Bible, he or she would not be able to arrive at a picture of the body of Christ which looks *remotely* like that which exists today.

In Song of Songs 8:5 we read:

'Who is this coming up from the wilderness
leaning on her beloved?'

If we agree, as some have suggested, that Solomon's words paint a picture of the church leaning upon Jesus, then since Jesus is the Word of God, we ought therefore to find that the church is supported by Scripture in the same way that the woman is supported by her beloved. I will, in the pages that follow, hold our idea of church against the plumb line of Scripture where we will discover that the church is certainly leaning, but it is leaning *away* from the Word rather than upon it. By this, I mean that much of what the church does is neither guided nor sanctioned by these same scriptures and therefore does not necessarily have God's approval. One might say:

The church is leaning despite the fact it has little or no
Invisible means of support.

In the following couple of chapters, I'd like to present a largely personal and admittedly subjective perspective on the subject of *church*—but one which I am confident will resonate with many of those who read it. I will then move on to what I hope is a more objective analysis, one which examines in some detail the supposed scriptural basis for church as we understand it. This will, in turn, lead us to the following crucial consideration:

In what could be the greatest irony of all,
Is it possible that Church itself is not biblical?

PART 1

ROOTS AND FRUITS

Multitudes of Christians within the church are moving toward the point where they may reject the institution that we call the church. They are beginning to turn to more simplified forms of worship. They are hungry for a personal and vital experience with Jesus Christ. They want a heartwarming personal faith. Unless the church quickly recovers its authoritative biblical message, we may witness the spectacle of millions of Christians going outside the institutional church to find spiritual food.

Billy Graham
World Aflame, 1965

1

A VIEW FROM THE PEW:

Never has so much had to be said by so Many to so Few

My God Doesn't Plod

If you have raced with men on foot and they have worn you out, how can you compete with horses?

Jeremiah 12:5

A friend of ours was talking with her home group leader about her frustrations with their church. Whilst recognising the legitimacy of some of the concerns she was raising, at one point the leader pleaded, 'But can't you just plod along with the rest of us?' Shocked and surprised, our friend replied, *'My God doesn't plod!'* Our friend's experience is, sadly, far from unique.

One of my greatest passions in life has been to travel and in this respect my wife, Liz, and I have been very fortunate; due to our ongoing careers in teaching, not only have we lived in several parts of England, but we have also been able to live and travel in many parts of the world, including Africa and Japan. As a result, we've found ourselves in a variety of churches, not only worshipping alongside Baptists, Methodists and Anglicans, but also Charismatics, Free Evangelicals and many others besides. Regrettably, however, I cannot begin to number how many frustrated and dispirited Christians we've encountered on our travels over the years, from all sorts of backgrounds — including those who attend self-styled 'cutting-edge' churches.

Of course, in the interests of fairness and objectivity, it needs to be recognized that amongst this number, there were individuals with a variety of personal issues: those with an axe to grind, some agenda to pursue, or some perceived grievance, to name a few. But at the same time, it's also important to emphasize that a substantial proportion of those disaffected with the church — in my experience at least — are not by nature malcontents: rather, they are people who simply want to move on in God yet find *church,* of all things, blocking their path.

I've met enough people from different denominations and different countries to be utterly convinced that there are multiplied thousands of Christians scattered around the world who desperately want to restore the joy of their salvation (Psalm 51:12). But, for the vast majority, attending church fails to provide the very thing which Christians hunger for the most: to find themselves in the presence of God. A. W. Tozer drew attention to this unmet desire decades ago:

> 'This hunger must be recognized by our religious leaders. Current evangelicalism has...laid the altar and divided the sacrifice into parts, but now seems satisfied to count the stones and rearrange the pieces with never a care that there is not a sign of fire upon the top of lofty Carmel.' [1]

Instead of encountering God, many find themselves merely encountering their fellow men, many of whom are as desperate and frustrated as they are; they have been sidetracked into attending shallow, man-orchestrated and earth-bound meetings which involve only a token attempt to allow for divine involvement (if that) and which have little or no impact on their spirituality or on their daily lives. If anything, rather than bringing people closer to God, church draws them away from Him.

Most of those who find themselves jaded by their circumstances make the decision to endure the situation nevertheless; some remain with the hope that perhaps they can effect change from the inside, whilst others resign themselves to stay in fellowship at all costs, even if change isn't likely. Still others feel that the only way to be heard — the only way to get the attention of their leaders — is to walk away. Of great concern is the possibility that some of these people end up not only walking away from church but drifting away from God Himself.

Exodus II
Evidence that demands a verdict

Of course, it could be said that I'm overstating the situation, or that I'm building a case based upon anecdotal evidence alone. Twenty years ago, for example, I found myself sitting in a Sunday service led by a pastor who would almost certainly take issue with some, if not most of the things I've just written. During the service he attempted to encourage the congregation by claiming that the number of Christians in the UK was at an all-time high, although where he had obtained his figures was not made clear. But I asked myself then, as I do now, how such a statement — if indeed his information was correct — isn't more of an indictment of British Christendom than it is a reason to celebrate. One has to wonder what sort of claim this is when an apparently greater number of believers than ever before are presiding over the evident moral and spiritual collapse of their country. Surely, if anything, it should be viewed as a cause for concern rather than complacency and it is surely a far cry from the legacy of those such as John Wesley and George Whitfield — two men of times gone by who really *did* make an impact both spiritually and morally — and who genuinely contributed to a cause for celebration.

One can of course argue about statistics, about how many are in fact being added to or lost from our number, about whether Christianity in the West is growing or shrinking, and so forth; but what seems to be certain is the diminishing overall *impact* Christianity is having on the surrounding culture. I cannot see anyone making a case for Britain having become *more* Christian, however one defines this, and it begs the question:

If numbers *are* rising, then where's the fruit?

Not only does such misguided optimism as that exhibited by the pastor disguise the true situation, but the associated triumphalism can encourage a dangerous complacency, one which can only serve to strengthen the devil's agenda; while we are sleeping our enemy is indeed busy sowing weeds amongst us (Matthew 13:25).

It's time to rouse ourselves and begin to ask some difficult but necessary and long overdue questions. If the body really *is* being properly fed and exercised, as some suggest, then why is so much of it flabby and out of shape, as evidenced by a steady stream of articles and reports in the media proclaiming that Christianity is on the retreat? Figures recently published in *The Telegraph* suggest that Christianity is declining fifty per cent faster in the UK than previously thought; indications are that within a few decades practicing Muslims will outnumber their Christian counterparts in England,[2] a picture mirrored in the US where Hispanic Americans—traditionally Catholic—are turning to Islam in increasing numbers.[3]

Of course, one shouldn't believe everything one reads; some might argue that the media and its atheist-driven agenda are deliberately painting a picture which is much darker than the actual situation. But what happens when we're confronted with facts and figures generated by respected Christian organisations which depict an equally, if not more, damning state of affairs?

According to research published on the website of the *Evangelical Alliance*, between 2000 and 2013 the Catholic, Methodist and Presbyterian churches in Britain experienced a decline in membership of thirteen, fifteen and twenty per cent respectively.[4]

As far as the Church of England is concerned, things are equally bleak, if not more so: according to its own figures, in the past 40 years, the number of adult churchgoers has halved, while the number of children attending regular worship has declined by four fifths. The average age of a C of E congregant is 61, and at a synod recently held by the Church, it was suggested that the latter will no longer be 'functionally extant in twenty years' time'... a euphemism for the fact that most of these congregants will no longer be alive by then.[5] All indications are that, like a dinosaur, the Anglican Church is heading for extinction.

While the mainline denominations in particular appear to be creaking and groaning along, with some seemingly staggering on their last legs, there can be no disputing the apparent rude health of the Pentecostals and some other new church groups, all of which are presently experiencing significant growth in the UK and elsewhere. However, upon closer inspection, we discover that this growth is not necessarily purely from conversions but involves other factors, such as the impact of immigrant communities who bring their faith with them. Rising attendance in the newer churches is also due to transfer growth—Christians joining from other churches. Indeed, I believe it's possible that the success of some of our larger churches may well derive from what might be described as 'supermarket syndrome': people transferring their allegiance at the expense of smaller, 'corner-shop' churches, some of which may face closure as a result.

In the meantime, should any Charismatics or Pentecostals feel immune from the ills which have beset their 'old school' colleagues, they need to recognize that they too are infected with the same disease—the precise nature of which will be expounded upon in this book—and that they face the same fate. It is sobering to remember the spiritual vitality enjoyed by the Methodist Church at its outset and to recall the impact it had on Britain and beyond in the early days; and yet one can see a time in the not-too-distant future when the Methodists will nevertheless find themselves circling the wagons before waving a final goodbye.

The prognosis for North America is equally bleak: statistics commissioned by Christian author Ken Ham show that two-thirds of young people in evangelical churches in the US will leave when they move into their twenties.[6] In *Already Gone: Why Your Kids Will Quit Church and What You Can Do to Stop it*, Ham writes:

> 'Like the black plagues that nearly wiped out the general population of Europe, a spiritual black plague has almost killed the next generation of European believers. A few churches are surviving. Even fewer are

thriving. The vast majority are slowly dying. It's a spiritual epidemic, *REALLY*. A wave of spiritual decay and death has almost entirely stripped a continent of its godly heritage, and now the same disease is infecting North America.'[7] (Emphasis in original)

Perhaps the statistic which should cause the most concern is one from a report by *Tearfund* published in 2007 which identified four people groups in particular that the church in the UK is failing to attract. And which group is at the head of the list?

Christians.

The survey reports that, 'the ratio of de-churched (people who have a personal relationship with God that have stopped going to Church), to regular attenders is about 2:1.' [8] It turns out that there are twice as many Christians who have left the church compared to those who still attend. Instead of a minority, these 'black sheep' — so often written off by others as loners and rebels — actually constitute a silent majority, a widely scattered flock without a shepherd. First, the world turned its back on the church and now many Christians are doing the same, participants in a modern day *diaspora*.

The *Tearfund* report also revealed that the experience of church is so negative for the 'de-churched', that 82% of those who leave are either 'not likely' or 'not very likely' to return. It's important to note, however, that according to the report, *it is not Christ but the Church that many Christians in the UK reject.*

If these figures are indeed accurate — that there are without doubt many sincere Christians who are dissatisfied with their respective church situations to the degree that many of them leave with no intention of returning — then the obvious question is *why*?

From Great Expectations to Bleak House
The descent from being the apple of God's eye to merely a cog in the machine

Many Christians have, at some time or other, experienced the same wonder that David expressed as he contemplated God's love for us:

> 'When I consider your heavens,
> the work of your fingers,
> the moon and the stars,
> which you have set in place,
> what is mankind that you are mindful of them,
> human beings that you care for them?'
>
> *Psalm 8:3-4*

David's awe is palpable... 'When I consider your heavens, the work of your fingers, the moon and the stars, which you have set in place...' His words reflect our own astonishment when confronted with the truth: *that we are valued by the Creator of the cosmos*: '...what is mankind that you are mindful of them, human beings that you care for them?'

But it doesn't stop there. Elsewhere, David reminds us that God isn't simply interested in us collectively, but is concerned for each of us as individuals; he is mindful of *me*, knowing each one of us better than we know ourselves. Further on in Psalms, we read:

> 'For you created my inmost being; you knit me together in my mother's womb...When I was woven together in the depths of the earth, your eyes saw my unformed body. All the days ordained for me were written in your book before one of them came to be.'
>
> *Psalm 139:13 -16*

And the Good News keeps on coming. I defy anyone to compose a more attractive, compelling and hope-filled message than that found in John 3:16:

> 'For God so loved the world that he gave his one and only Son, that whoever believes in him shall not perish but have eternal life.'

Not only does God *know* each one of us, as Psalm 139 suggests, but we come to the realisation whereby each of us can say, 'He *loves* me, "warts and all"; *He died for me.'*

In John 10:3 we read that, '[Jesus] calls his own sheep by name and leads them out.' Being called by name, by Jesus — *a human being cannot experience a greater sense of significance than this*. At whatever point in our life or in whatever way we recognize we are saved, the effect of this knowledge can be breathtaking, making it possible for us to experience 'the peace of God, which transcends all understanding' (Philippians 4:7).

But sadly, for many of those newly born into the kingdom, their ability to continue living in the good of this knowledge becomes increasingly difficult.

A significant proportion of those who accept Christ start out with a burning desire to know more about God, a natural outcome of which is to find others with whom they can fellowship and share their passion; they join a church as the next step in their faith journey... and yet several years later they find themselves desiring to be anywhere other than in church. All too often the initial glow wears off: there is a gradual loss of Holy awe and of the sense of one's significance in the eyes of this infinite God. Where there once was passion there is now passivity; where there should be inspiration there is inertia. For some, accepting Christ and subsequently joining a church has represented the ultimate bait-and-switch, and these same people might be forgiven for feeling that John Newton's words in *Amazing Grace* have been reversed...*I once was found but now feel lost...* One of the consequences is that, in the US, 'On any given Sunday there are 7 million people sitting in the pews who report that they are on the way out the door, never to return.' [9]

The obvious question becomes: *What happened?* What happened to the sense of that special relationship with God and the desire to deepen it in the company of others? If Jesus values us, to the degree that he's prepared to die for us, then *why can church make us feel the exact opposite?* How do people make the transition from feeling that they, as individuals matter to God, to feeling that... well... they are simply one member of a larger group... a face in the crowd? How could it be possible that the same God who calls us by name would set up something whereby so many end up feeling anonymous, our presence only recognized or acknowledged when a job needs doing?

❖   ❖   ❖

Ticking all the wrong boxes

Therefore, since we are receiving a kingdom that cannot be shaken, let us be thankful, and so worship God acceptably with reverence and awe, for our "God is a consuming fire."

Hebrews 12:28-29

There's a story about John Wayne's role as the centurion at the foot of the cross in *The Greatest Story Ever Told*: supposedly, Wayne's delivery of the line, 'Truly, this man was the son of God', was regarded as lacking sufficient emotion by the director who, after calling 'cut' said:

'Say it with *awe* John.'

'*Gotcha*', growled the Duke.

Action was resumed and Wayne looked into the camera and drawled:

'*Awww*, truly, this man was the son of God.'

('Cut!')

There's a reason for relating this story as I hope you will see in a moment; however, it needs to be made clear regarding what I'm about to say that I am not suggesting that the church today is doing nothing of value; there are, of course, all sorts of positive things happening in many an individual church. But even then, the fruit of their endeavours can subsequently be lost—as the following example illustrates:

A city-wide worship event recently organized by a local church featured an internationally renowned worship leader. The meeting was a tremendous blessing to everyone present, there being a deep sense within many that they had genuinely encountered God. However, when the pastor of the host church stood up to close the meeting immediately after the worship had ended, I was dismayed to realise that he had decided to use this particular opportunity to spend a good five minutes describing current renovations to the building and asking for volunteers to help lay a new carpet during the coming week. I was not alone in walking away sad and perplexed that the glory found in the presence of God could so easily have been dismissed for the sake of apparently more pressing matters.

Like John Wayne, the pastor seemed to be lacking in awe: instead, he seemed more concerned with maintaining the building rather than welcoming the One for whom—ostensibly—it had been acquired. By his actions the pastor had, in one sense, managed to snatch defeat from the jaws of victory, something which increasingly seems to be a metaphor for the church at large.

One of the most soul-destroying experiences of church life that I have ever had to endure occurred during my tenure as a member of a church council. There was to be a review of the state of our church, and one evening the council was presented with a document containing dozens of tick-boxes, each box relating to a specific aspect of the church; the intention was to go through each box, one by one.

Before we even got started on agreeing which particular box to tick (a depressing prospect in itself), there was — literally—a five-minute debate about whether to use red or green ink for certain answers. I'd had a hard day at work and this felt like it had more to do with the meeting I'd just left than with the Good News of Jesus Christ. As I sat there in total despair, I imagined a cartoon strip depicting God and His angels staring down in incredulity, with a voice from heaven saying in a disbelieving tone, 'They're arguing about the *colour of the pen* now!'

In, *Of God and Men,* A.W. Tozer understood all too well both the causes and the consequences of this mindset:

> 'When religion loses its sovereign character and becomes mere form spontaneity is lost, and in its place come precedent, propriety, system—and the file-card mentality. Back of the file-card mentality is the belief that spirituality can be organized. Then is introduced into religion those ideas which never belong there— numbers, statistics, the law of averages, and other such natural and human things. And creeping death always follows.' [10]

Five years previously, Liz and I had found ourselves in a different part of the world, in yet another church; we attended a series of training sessions prior to becoming cell group leaders within what was — by English standards — a very large fellowship. During one such training session a graph was presented to the packed hall via the ubiquitous overhead projector; the graph illustrated the degree to which the Holy Spirit would be present in cell meetings depending on how 'effectively' the meetings were led. Now, I defy anyone to come up with a more disturbing example of presumption — of organising God out of His own church. I was taken aback by the audacity of attempting to predict just how, when or why God's Spirit would be present in our meetings. There was no room for grace, no room for God to be in control — it was apparently all dependent on man's ability to orchestrate or even manipulate the Spirit (as if he could).

What I sorely wanted to do — but to my regret, I lacked the courage — was to walk to the front and say something along the following lines:

'I'm leaving now. However, before I go, I think there are a couple of axes missing from this graph.'

I wanted to pick up a pen (the colour didn't matter) and draw a cross — *the* Cross — in the middle of the chart.

Scenarios such as these — which are played out in our churches on a regular basis — illustrate the very real danger that, in the middle of everything, *God Himself can often be forgotten.* When people met Jesus two thousand years ago, they met God in human form, walking in His own creation; and, as if that wasn't incredible enough, through his own sacrifice, this God has made it possible for us to be his *friends* (John 15:14-15). And yet — almost as astonishing — somehow the reality of this message so often gets lost in all the 'stuff of church'. Amongst other things this means that, for many, their Christian experience boils down to the routine of obligatory Sunday attendance and the associated boredom; this in turn perpetuates a kind of downward spiral, ultimately contributing to the spiritual decline of God's people, both individually and corporately.

I'm a Christian—Get me out of here

To sit in a cold church, looking at the back of people's heads, is perhaps not considered the most exciting place to meet new people and hear prophetic words.

George Carey

I recall one particular Sunday service some years ago: during a particularly lengthy sermon which had followed a seemingly endless succession of church notices, I found myself thinking about Blaise Pascal. Pascal was not only a mathematical genius but he was also a deeply spiritual man. During the evening of November 23, 1654, he experienced a mystical vision that lasted two hours and which he called a 'night of fire'. Immediately afterwards, he wrote, "Fire. The God of Abraham, the God of Isaac, the God of Jacob. Not of the philosophers and intellectuals...The God of Jesus Christ." The impact on Pascal was so profound that he sewed the paper on which these words were written into his clothing, where they remained until his death.

As I sat there, I found myself marvelling at the difference between Pascal's experience and my own at that moment and I couldn't help wondering what on earth had gone wrong. Can we really believe that the same God who spoke into existence the sun, moon and stars—the same God who created the vast number of different and complex life forms on our own planet—intends us to sit through and endure the predictable, turgid meetings which are standard fare in so many of our churches? One has to wonder, if a pastor was 'reduced to the ranks' and made to sit in the pews alongside everyone else (and not only forced to sit through the notices and the sermons, but to also carry out the tasks assigned to them) would he or she survive their own church? To his credit, Martyn Lloyd-Jones made the following admission:

> 'I didn't realise how boring church was until I sat at the back.'

The tedium which I experienced that Sunday morning isn't only confined to meetings—in many churches it infects the whole way of thinking. Consider the following passage from a best-selling book on church growth:

'The boundaries of the city's neighbourhoods should be carefully marked on the map, or maps, of the region. Use 1/16" bendable red chart tape for this purpose, carefully pressing it over the streets which mark the edges of each area. As you do so, put a 1/4" round sticker in each neighbourhood, with a number written on it. Create a list of these numbers, designating it with the commonly used name for that territory: e.g., "Woodlands, Section 1."' [11]

It's actually not so much that for many, church is boring, but that church is *passionless*, concerning which Mike Yaconelli had this to say:

'The most critical issue facing Christians is not abortion, pornography, the disintegration of the family, moral absolutes, MTV, drugs, racism, sexuality, or school prayer. The critical issue today is dullness. We have lost our astonishment. The Good News is no longer good news, it is okay news. Christianity is no longer life changing, it is life enhancing. Jesus doesn't change people into wild-eyed radicals anymore. He changes them into "nice people."' [12]

Outside of the main event—the Sunday service—individual believers settle down to become part of a religious society; one with its own jargon, its own accepted modes of behaviour, its own internal politics, its own key players and its own rising stars... in other words, it starts to look and feel just like any other worldly fraternity or organisation. But can this really be the 'abundant life' which John 10:10 describes? When I compare what I read in the Bible to how it's all outworked in many of our churches... it almost seems like two different religions.

Weighed and Found Wanting
Losing hearts and minds

Anyone who has engaged in an *Alpha Course* or who is at least familiar with it will recognize the following question:

Christianity: Boring, Untrue or Irrelevant?

Of course, no serious believer I know would concede that any of these charges accurately describes his or her own faith. But I'm curious as to why Nicky Gumbel would ask this question in the first place. What if the question was changed to read:

Church: Boring, Untrue, and Irrelevant?

That would be an entirely different matter — and I suspect Gumbel asked his particular question because most non-believers mistakenly equate *Church* with Christianity. Our failed ecclesiology has been a major factor in helping to misrepresent the Christian faith to the rest of humankind, contributing to the low view that the latter takes of both Christians and the Christian faith itself. The result is that Christianity has become progressively marginalised, a sideshow in the eyes of many, causing millions of people to reject, not simply the church, but the Good News itself.

How differently Christianity was perceived in the beginning compared to today. For instance, in Acts 5:13-14 we read:

> 'No one else dared join them, even though they were highly regarded by the people. Nevertheless, more and more men and women believed in the Lord and were added to their number.'

In sharp contrast, we find that rather than being respected, many Christians are increasingly looked upon as a laughing stock, a group of delusional people whose irrelevance grows daily. In their book, *The Millennials*, co-authors Thom and Jess Rainer present the results of a survey of people born in the US between 1980 and 2000. The Rainers comment:

> 'Christianity is not the belief of the vast majority of this generation. And they believe the American church to be one of the least relevant institutions in society.' [13]

Meanwhile, on the other side of the Atlantic, John Stott claimed that, 'One of the major reasons that people reject the Gospel today is not because they perceive it to be false but because they perceive it to be trivial.'[14] It's no longer the case that no-one dares to join us:

They just can't be bothered.

One thing can be assumed with absolute confidence: God is not the author of all this. He is 'a consuming fire' and whatever else we can say about Him, one thing is certain: *He is never boring*. But if God is clearly not responsible for this mind-numbing state of affairs, then who is?

Exit Wounds

Every day people are straying from the church and going back to God.

Lenny Bruce

Despite significant differences relating to certain aspects of theology and regardless of individual or denominational church practices — such as the style of worship, the format of meetings and so on — all the churches I've ever attended have appeared to demonstrate some remarkably similar (and not altogether positive) characteristics. Reflecting on my experiences down the years, I have come to realise that — regardless of denominational stripe — at grass roots level, 'church life' has always felt fundamentally the same.

Part of the human condition is that those who lead, in whatever context, usually have a vision that almost always places them at the centre of it. This is true in any sphere of life and, sadly, it would appear that Christians are as susceptible to this as anyone else; this would account for the fact that a universal feature of each and every church to which I've belonged is the existence of a small group of people — sometimes just one person — orchestrating or directing everything. At the same time, other than by responding to requests from the latter to fill whatever 'holes' exist in order to help keep the church ticking over, the vast majority have little or no opportunity to contribute in the way they feel called.

Sooner or later, a piece of paper with a question along the lines of, 'In what ways do you see yourself serving the church?' is passed before one's eyes; yet absent from the same document are words to the effect of, 'How can we best serve you in order to help you grow?' Some will argue that the act of serving the church in *any* capacity encourages spiritual growth, and whilst there is certainly a measure of truth in this, if the primary — if not the *only* — avenues of service available are those tasks deemed by the church to be necessary, then the prospect of marked spiritual progress is doubtful. It's my observation that a passion for serving where God has led your heart is much more likely to promote growth than being made to feel that one's primary role is that of a pawn—available to be used as and when others decide, often being asked to fulfil a duty for which one has no calling, and by implication, little or no motivation. A great many Christians find no place to exercise their gifts, which are parked for the foreseeable future; instead, they are given tasks to carry out which simply perpetuate the very structures that fail to feed them.

Too often church members are subtly encouraged to defer to the vision of the leadership while little or no attention is given to their own. Wherever I've been, the views and opinions, the dreams and visions of the many are constantly subordinated to those of the few, despite the fact that—as others have said—the best way to kill someone with a dream is to give them a different one. In the meantime, the personal sense of their significance as a child of God slowly diminishes; whereas God loves us unconditionally, many feel they are only valued for what skills or time they can offer in terms of helping maintain the machinery of church. God sees us as His children: *church* sees us primarily as resources. The following story from *Classic Christianity* by Bob George illustrates this perfectly. A well-known local businessman had responded to an altar call at George's church and he and George had gone forward:

> 'We were both in tears as we stood before the pastor. "Bob, this is tremendous!" the pastor exclaimed, "this man is one of the most brilliant businessmen in our city! He's wealthy, he's talented, and we need to put him to work! I want you to see that Mac is totally involved in what you're doing. We want to take full advantage of what he can do." I will never forget Mac, his eyes full of tears, speaking with a sincere, trembling voice: *"Pastor, I don't need a job. I need the Lord."'* [15]

Evidently the pastor was interested in Mac merely for the skills he possessed... Mac, on the other hand, simply wanted the Lord. Not only was that true of Mac, I believe it's true for everyone.

People don't want to be part of someone else's project – they want Jesus.

In sharp contrast to the life many experience in the church, Jesus offers us this invitation:

'Come to me, all you who are weary and burdened, and I will give you rest. Take my yoke upon you and learn from me, for I am gentle and humble in heart, and you will find rest for your souls. For my yoke is easy and my burden is light.'

Matthew 11:28-30

While the burden to which Jesus was referring was the burden of the Law, placed upon ordinary men and women by their religious leaders, today many rank and file Christians have to carry the weight of *church*. Similar to the Law, the church carries its own expectations and demands, not to mention the guilt put upon individuals by their own leaders.

American preacher Billy Sunday commented that Christianity means a lot more than church membership, and I remember once asking an elder why his church felt the need for just such a membership. His reply spoke volumes:

'So we know who we can discipline.'

I think it's safe to say that, as far as most people are concerned, this is hardly an incentive to sign up. More importantly, the elder's comment should prompt us to ask:

Is this really the best we can do with the Good News of Jesus Christ?

Is this the primary reason as to why God elects people to His *ekklesia* — so that they can be disciplined? It all sounds light years away from the God of Psalm 8 and John 3:16. No wonder people are leaving the church in droves.

For some, a day arrives when yet another sermon on serving the church represents the straw that breaks the camel's back, and they make the choice to step out from under it all... they make the decision to stop being a beast of burden. Tired of church-by-numbers, worn out from constantly sacrificing their own visions on the altar of someone else's; frustrated with repeatedly failing to encounter God one Sunday after another, and disillusioned because their desire to grow in God is continually stymied by the demands of church as an institution with all its attendant needs, increasing numbers of Christians of all ages are evidently finding that they simply can't endure the routine any longer. They are no longer prepared to live with the level of dissonance they experience, with the result that people are quitting church in increasing numbers and — whether one agrees with it or not — turning to DIY Christianity. More and more people are taking responsibility for their own spiritual well-being rather than handing this over to a 'chosen few' who, more often than not, fail to equip those of whom unquestioning obedience is demanded. Arthur Wallis noted:

> 'God's heart must be grieved when he sees the gifts that he has liberally bestowed on his people finding no room for expression in the local church where they primarily belong. The consequence has been that gifted men and women have sought avenues of service outside the church, to its further impoverishment.' [16]

As mentioned earlier, while some denominations or individual churches can point to increased growth, the overall trend is nevertheless downwards: of particular concern is the steady, silent exodus of older, more seasoned Christians — people who have so much to offer their respective fellowships. Thus, whilst great show is made of new arrivals entering our churches through the front door, much less noticeable are the many others who are slipping quietly out of the back door, with leaders apparently unable to prevent the haemorrhage.

Time for a Reality Check

However beautiful the strategy, you should occasionally look at the results.

Winston Churchill

One only has to consider the experience of many individual Christians to recognize that something clearly isn't working:

passion for God and zeal for His kingdom are continually quenched in many people's lives as they work through the endless cycle of programmes and initiatives always inspired by someone else and never themselves, whilst at the same time fulfilling the practical responsibilities that are typically expected of church members: meeting and greeting, organising or serving refreshments, car park and Sunday school supervision, to name just a few. As a result, many feel spiritually stifled and oppressed and once again, *church* is often the culprit. In *Who's Feeding Whom?* Theologian and Church historian Meic Pearse summarises the predicament perfectly:

> '...the energies and giftings of Christians will either be suffocated, or they will find an outlet, and it is rather too much for leaders to assume the ability to determine, on the one hand, whether those giftings will be allowed to function or not and, on the other hand, to decide exactly how they will be used. Those who do not fit the leaders' plans will either be smothered into silence, and probable spiritual lethargy, or they will find some other outlet for their energies, usually by creating trouble, which may give the leaders all sorts of opportunities to condemn such people for their wickedness, but will do little to advance the kingdom of God. The only other option is that they will leave the church. That may appear an attractive possibility if all leaders want is a docile fan club, but again it does little to advance the kingdom or equip the saints.' [17]

It seems patently clear that the church at large has a serious problem on its hands and it affects far too many people for us to simply ignore the situation; unfortunately, however, it's been my experience that there are many who would rather ignore it and indeed try to avoid any discussion concerning this problem.

This attitude of denial is all rather reminiscent of Hans Christian Andersen's fairy tale, *The Emperor's New Clothes*, which inspired the title for Wayne Jacobsen's, *The Naked Church*. In Andersen's tale, the Emperor is persuaded by a pair of fraudsters that they have tailored for him attire of the highest quality but which can only be seen by people of high intellect and social standing. To the irredeemably stupid, so they suggest, the clothing appears to be invisible. Of course, there is no clothing at all, and when the king eventually ventures out in public he is completely naked. No-one dares to point out the obvious for fear of appearing an idiot, but they all join in the illusion instead—until, that is, a young boy speaks up and states what everyone can clearly see. Jacobsen draws an analogy between Andersen's deluded Emperor and his complicit subjects, and the situation we find in the church today: namely, that the church has a serious and highly visible problem on its hands but due to a combination of tradition, vested interests and other influences, no-one is prepared to admit it.

Rather than the Emperor's New Clothes, sometimes people use the phrase, 'the elephant in the room' in order to describe circumstances where everyone knows there's a problem but pretend it doesn't exist. In terms of the present discussion concerning the problems facing the church, I'd like to offer the following analogy:

> There is a large, pink elephant in the room, but since people have chosen to wear rose-tinted spectacles, they can't see it.

Nevertheless, and regardless of whether it makes people uncomfortable or not, the 'problem of church' (as Emil Brunner called it) must be confronted, because instead of the oil of gladness, there is a spirit of heaviness resting upon many of God's people. We cannot continue to sweep this whole thing under the carpet—because whether we want to admit it or not, rather than being a potential antidote for the spiritual malaise which the statistics suggest is only too real, the church *itself* often seems to be a large part of the cause.

Multitudes of Christians are, in effect, being asked to plod when they should be running with horses. With little hope for meaningful change on the part of those whose experience this is, for some—in significant enough numbers that ought to cause the rest of us to sit up and take notice—they feel that their only option is to vote with their feet.

Of course, the dilemma confronting those who leave is: *What happens next?* This is something I will address in the final part of the book, but before that, we need to both identify and examine the factors which have helped create this disturbing state of affairs in the first place.

Has it ever occurred to you that one hundred pianos all tuned to the same fork are automatically tuned to each other? They are of one accord by being tuned, not to each other, but to another standard to which each one must individually bow. So one hundred worshippers meeting together, each one looking away to Christ, are in heart nearer to each other than they could possibly be were they to become 'unity' conscious and turn their eyes away from God to strive for closer fellowship. Social religion is perfected when private religion is purified. The body becomes stronger as its members become healthier. The whole church of God gains when the members that compose it begin to seek a better and a higher life.

A.W. Tozer
The Pursuit of God

2

CHURCH-AS-A-THING-IN-ITSELF:

A Case of Mistaken Identity

Busy but Barren
Fruitless Exercise

As anyone in many of today's churches will tell you, there is a veritable *smorgasbord* of activities on offer with which to fill one's entire calendar, and the list is exhausting just to consider, let alone participate in. Apart from Sunday church and midweek meetings, there are Men's Meetings, Women's Meetings, Singles' Meetings, Married Couples' Meetings, Youth Groups and church picnics, along with barbecues, bowling, bingo, and all sorts of other organized social events... there is the opportunity to clamber on board a dizzying merry-go-round of meetings, conferences and Bible weeks, and some people's lives do indeed revolve around a never-ending cycle of church functions such as these.

But are the results, in terms of spiritual growth, commensurate with the amount of time and energy dedicated to all of these programmes? Whilst no-one would deny that there are people who *are* growing spiritually within their respective churches, we must be careful not to fall into the trap of assuming *post hoc ergo propter hoc* – that is to say, we must be careful not to assume a causal connection, mistaking evidence of God's grace in people's lives as proof that what *we* are doing is actually effective and directly related to that growth...

thankfully, God often blesses us despite our faulty theology. And whilst we may point to those who do appear to be benefiting from participation in the various church activities that exist, there are equally many, if not more, whose fire or passion is waning, if not already completely extinguished, despite — or perhaps *because* of — all that's on offer. This fact was clearly illustrated to me several years ago during an event which ironically became known as...

The Weekend of Joy

The order for rejoicing and dancing has come from our warlord.
Genesis, 'Supper's Ready'

One evening, the pastor of the church my family and I were attending remarked that many in the congregation were lacking spiritual fervour. I agreed, observing that there wasn't a lot of joy in evidence.

'That's it!' he exclaimed, 'We need more teaching on Joy!' I suggested that joy was perhaps something more caught than taught and gently tried to put it to him that, since there didn't appear to be much in the way of spiritual passion or joy evident in his own life, then perhaps it was hardly surprising that there was a corresponding lack amongst his own congregation.

However, I must have been too careful about my choice of words, because the pastor didn't seem to register what it was I was trying to say; instead, he had the bit between his teeth and was off and running. In the weeks that followed he began outlining a plan, and eventually an announcement was made that on a weekend in the not-too-distant future a guest speaker was to be flown in to preach on 'Joy'. The entire weekend would consist of sermons, group discussions and so on, with lunches and even a talent show thrown in — all with the subject of *Joy* as the focus.

As is the norm when such events are decided upon, the organisational wheels immediately began to turn: volunteers were recruited to arrange the catering, with people assigned to shop, bake and cook; evening activities were devised and rehearsed and lists were drawn up for a host of other logistical needs. The church swung into action.

Eventually the weekend arrived. The visiting speaker's sermons were quite interesting, and more importantly, he struck me as a Godly man. But the real fun started after his first sermon: we were split into discussion groups and, as fate would have it, I ended up in the same group as the guest speaker. He started off the discussion with a question which, although innocent and well-meaning, in effect lit the blue touch-paper:

'In what ways could you find yourself experiencing more joy as a Christian?'

I doubt very much whether the response that followed was quite what he was hoping for: one person after another complained that there simply just wasn't enough *time* to experience joy since the church itself demanded so much time and energy — all the planning and preparation for this very weekend being a case in point. The irony — that here were people too busy preparing for teaching on *Joy* to actually have an opportunity to experience it — seemed lost on them. The demands of 'the church' itself were taking precedence over the very people who were supposed to constitute it.

Eventually, having sat through a litany of complaints, I decided to speak up. It was a bad mistake:

'Do we really *need* all the cooking, the dishwashing, all the work that's gone into this weekend', I asked, 'and which — if I'm hearing correctly — is defeating the very purpose for which the weekend was originally intended? It seems to me that we can make things as easy or as hard for ourselves as we want; if our guest really has something to say that we need to hear and which, after all, is the main point of this whole exercise — couldn't we all just have brought a packed lunch, sat in the park and listened to him speak?'

I sat back, not entirely sure what sort of response my comments would elicit. Even then, I was totally unprepared for what followed; whereas the speaker's question had aroused a chorus of self-pity, my question more or less turned the group into a snarling lynch mob:

'How selfish!' exclaimed one person in shocked tones.

'What if everyone thought like that?' someone else demanded.

'*Someone's* got to do these things!' declared another.

Those present seemed completely unaware of any contradiction between their responses to my suggestion and their complaints to the visiting speaker only a few moments earlier, and since it was evident that any attempt to pursue the point would clearly be an exercise in futility, from that point on it seemed more prudent to keep quiet.

The reason for the inclusion of this story is that *The Weekend of Joy* illustrates a deeper, more fundamental predicament: it neatly encapsulates the whole problem of *church-as-a-thing-in-itself.*

The Map is Not the Territory:
'The view that an abstraction derived from something is not the thing itself; confusing models of reality with reality itself.'

In *The Misunderstanding of the Church,* the eminent Swiss theologian Emil Brunner wrote the following:

'The *Ekklesia* of the New Testament, the fellowship of Christian believers, is precisely *not* that which every "church" is at least in part—an institution, a something. The body of Christ is nothing other than a fellowship of persons...that which they have in common is precisely no "thing", no "it", but a "he", Christ and His Holy Spirit...the Body of Christ [the church] has nothing to do with an organisation and has nothing of the character of the institutional about it. This is precisely what it has in mind when it describes itself as the Body of Christ.' [1]

The *ekklesia* is populated by flesh and blood individuals filled with the Holy Spirit whom Jesus has called out of the world and into his kingdom. His flock is essentially a fellowship of all those who believe he is the Christ, the Messiah, and although the Christian community started out as such, as time has gone on the *ekklesia* has been allowed to mutate into a very different thing—*the church.*

How were God's people exposed to such grievous bodily harm? I believe a valuable clue in our search for a credible explanation is provided in the following observation by Dr Michael Ramsey, the hundredth Archbishop of Canterbury:

> 'The mistake of ecclesiasticism throughout the ages has been to believe in the Church as a kind of thing-in-itself.' [2a]

If Ramsay's claim is correct then *all the problems we have identified thus far, plus many more besides, would flow naturally from this initial error.*

Dr Ramsey goes on to say:

> 'The apostles never regarded the Church as a thing-in-itself. Their faith was in God, who had raised Jesus from the dead, and they knew the power of his resurrection to be at work in them and their fellow-believers despite the unworthiness of them all.' [2b]

If I may, I'd like to slightly modify Ramsay's statement in order to make the following extremely important differentiation: the real problem is not that we have come to regard church *as* a kind of thing-in-itself, since this implies that *church* could be 'done' properly — that there is a correct version of *church* to be had, so to speak. Rather, the truth is that *church* is something that ought not to exist *at all* as an idea or concept; indeed, as we shall see, the word itself is not derived from *ekklesia* but from an entirely different Greek word and one not found in the biblical text. The result has been that *church* is an abstraction, a formalisation of *ekklesia* which Jesus never intended. The real problem, then, is not so much that we have come to regard church *as* a thing-in-itself, but that church *is* a thing-in-itself.

Before I continue, this seems the appropriate moment to make the following clarification:

Throughout this book I will sometimes refer to *the church* rather than *the ekklesia* despite the fact that the word *church* is a misnomer. I hesitate to do this for the simple reason of not wanting to reinforce the use of the very term I'm trying to eradicate. However, in practical terms its continued use is unavoidable: to exclusively use the correct word *ekklesia,* or even substitute it with *congregation*, for example, would in certain contexts be awkward and disrupt the flow of the narrative — the following paragraphs are a case in point. More importantly, to persist in using an alternative term could potentially cause confusion and thereby obscure any point I am attempting to make.

The continued inclusion, then, of what I will show to be a highly problematic word, is a deliberate strategy and one which seems to be the most sensible method of conveying my meaning — a decision which will hopefully make increasing sense as the book progresses.

Returning to the issue of church being a *thing-in-itself*: at some point in history, I believe that God's people, the *ekklesia*, began to take their eyes off God and fix them upon 'church'; this in turn caused Christ's body to assume an identity that God had not sanctioned, and one which was and continues to be quite separate from the people themselves. One could say that,

> There has been a change in focus from the Lord of the church onto the Church of the Lord.

Somewhere along the line we confused the vertical with the horizontal. This shift in our attention caused a subtle and deadly switch to take place in our understanding of what Jesus meant by his *ekklesia*, causing the latter to undergo the transition to *church-as-a-thing-in-itself*, and in so doing it became a man-made, disembodied version of the actual body of Christ.

Onward Christian Soldiers, Marching as to... Where?

Turn around when possible

In *Mere Christianity*, C.S. Lewis wrote:

> 'Enemy-occupied territory — that is what this world is. Christianity is the story of how the rightful king has landed, you might say landed in disguise, and is calling us to take part in a great campaign of sabotage.' [3]

During the last war, some of the road signs in the south of England were deliberately turned around to point in the wrong direction in order to confuse any enemy group that might land. I mention this with C.S. Lewis' words in mind, and I wonder if it isn't *our* plans that have been sabotaged by the enemy instead? As Christians—a band of brothers marching through hostile territory—I wonder whether the signs we've been following for the last two thousand years or so have been switched by our foe such that they're directing us up a blind alley. After all, is this how it was all meant to turn out? Corporately speaking—that's to say when it comes to our churches—are we more or less where God wants us to be? Or do we find ourselves where we are right now because, relatively speaking, a few *Type A* personalities, starting two thousand years ago and continuing up to the present day, brought us to this place? Has the character of the church been shaped by the character of a handful of people or by the Holy Spirit? Perhaps more importantly, is 'church' itself—in the sense that most people understand the term—inspired by God or by man? I believe if one looks at today's church as a whole, there are some serious questions that need to be addressed.

John the Baptist had a question of his own, one personally addressed to Jesus. In Luke 7:20 we read:

'Are you the one who is to come, or should we expect someone else?'

Jesus reassured John that he was indeed 'the one', with unequivocal proof of His divinity: in verse 22 we read:

'The blind receive sight, the lame walk, those who have leprosy are cleansed, the deaf hear, the dead are raised, and the good news is proclaimed to the poor.'

Alfred Loisy observed, 'Jesus came proclaiming the Kingdom, and what arrived was the Church.' But, to borrow from John:

'Is the Church what we were supposed to expect, or should we expect something else?'

This is an important question, since we shall find that biblical support for the institution of the church is not nearly as compelling as the evidence which Jesus provided in support of his own claim to be the Messiah.

Is it possible, I wonder, that in pursuing the idea of *church* we are boldly marching in the wrong direction altogether? Has the enemy, rather like a fifth column operating behind our lines, pulled off a coup of truly staggering proportions?

It will be abundantly clear by now that I'm convinced that not only is this indeed the case, but—and of even greater concern—the problem appears not to have been recognized. As a direct result of enemy action, I would suggest that the Bride is not in fact marching after all—rather, she seems to be limping. As we've seen, increasing numbers of 'Christian soldiers' are going AWOL, in some cases being accused of desertion and a dereliction of duty; in the meantime, many of their comrades who remain in their respective churches are simply combat-ineffective.

As church management, church needs, and church initiatives have slowly but surely obscured our view of the risen Christ, so the passion and sense of purpose of large numbers of Christians has ebbed away; such people find themselves in a spiritual wasteland, wondering how on earth they came to be in such a place. These are real issues, and symptoms of church gone wrong. Large numbers of Christians have forgotten their God-given vision, their sense of calling and direction; like the church itself, they've lost their way.

Somehow the road signs got switched.
Somewhere along the way we took a wrong turning.

Despite this, the church marches on, although it's often not clear what direction it's taking. Psychologist Rollo May summed up the situation perfectly:

'It is an ironic habit of human beings to run faster when we have lost our way.'

In order to maintain silence in the ranks—and thereby discourage any potentially awkward or uncomfortable questions for the leadership concerning what's happening or where things are heading—one of the central qualities encouraged in congregations the world over is that of *submission*... not submission to God, however, but to those in authority. Romans 8:29 tells us that God wants us to 'be conformed to the image of his son'; but the goal of many church leaders appears to be that they simply want their members to conform, period.

One of the ways to achieve compliance on the part of the flock is through the use of slogans such as 'the need for unity'. The problem with this kind of thinking is that it fails to recognize that unity is not the same as uniformity: as someone else has said, unity is not about everyone doing the same thing, but about everyone following the same Person. The one-size-fits-all approach adopted by so many leaders simply serves to reinforce the growing sense of insignificance and anonymity and which is part of the reason why so many are leaving the church in the first place.

The X-Factor

In every Church, in every institution, there is something which sooner or later works against the very purpose for which it came into existence.

C.S. Lewis

If we make the mistake of assuming, unconsciously or otherwise, that the Bride of Christ is a thing outside of ourselves — an object or entity that exists apart from the people who constitute it — then ironically, the *institution* of church can become more important than the actual 'church' itself. Indeed, this is precisely where we find ourselves today: the *idea* of church has taken pre-eminence over the people who in reality *are* the church. Even worse, in some instances *church* has assumed greater importance than God Himself.

In a best-selling book on church growth, the reader is asked to place the following in order of priority:

- God
- Family
- Church
- Work

And what's given as the correct order?

- Church
- Family
- Work [4]

44

What's Number One? *Church.*

What's missing from this picture? *God.*

In an effort to reassure the reader as to why God is absent from the second list, the author adds this rider: 'God is not a separate priority. He is in all we do. He is in His Son, and the church is Christ's body.' Although initially this may sound perfectly reasonable, upon further reflection it quickly becomes evident that the author is guilty of employing some highly questionable logic. After all, if God truly is in all we do, then there's no need for a list such as this in the first place... we'd already be fulfilling its requirements. The fact is Jesus himself *explicitly* told people to make God, not church, their number one priority, to put His Name at the top of the list. The First Commandment reads:

> 'Love the Lord your God with all your heart and with all your soul and with all your mind and with all your strength.'
>
> *Mark 12:30*

The truth is, by subtly removing God and placing Church in His stead, the latter is promoted above God, regardless of any qualifying statements which anyone might add.

Of course, the author in this particular case is only one in a long line of people who have replaced God with church. In *The Divine Conspiracy*, Dallas Willard echoed C.S. Lewis' words to which I made reference earlier:

> 'Truthfully, it seems to be a general law of social/historical development that institutions tend to distort and destroy the central function that brought them into existence.' [5]

Many seem to have lost sight of one essential fact:

Church is not God.

John Calvin said, 'Faith consists in the knowledge of God and Christ, not in reverence for the Church'. It would appear, however, that many sincere believers are serving *church* rather than God, without really concerning themselves with the distinction. They're busy serving the man-made structures and programmes, along with all the other fleshly by-products that spring forth from *church-as-a-thing-in-itself*, deriving their security and sense of purpose from their involvement in various church activities rather than from a vibrant relationship with God. They have failed to recognize that being excited about church is not the same as being excited about Jesus.

Unintentional as it may be, we find that church rather than God is in pole position in many of today's fellowships. Just as Christ has been removed from 'Christmas' and substituted with an X to make 'Xmas', God has been unseated from His place of pre-eminence.

If we pursue the theme for a moment, most of the traditions which play such a central role in helping to produce the 'perfect' Christmas are pagan in origin, an uncomfortable reality which mirrors so much of what *church-as-a-thing-in-itself* is about. One might compare the latter to a plastic Christmas tree (or perhaps I should say, Xmas tree): it is man-made, with its roots in human tradition; it is also devoid of life, with only the simulation of it, but since we have decorated it with baubles of our own making we have failed to recognize the difference. Instead, we gaze upon adornments such as bishops, elders and deacons; buildings, finances, sermons and conferences; meetings and worship teams, rituals and traditions, offices and resources—and in so doing we can easily forget what God offers us:

> Eternal life in the form of a real man
> hanging on a real tree.

Focus

I lift my eyes to you, to you whose throne is in heaven.

Psalm 123:1

The experience of those involved in *The Weekend of Joy* is constantly replicated in churches the world over; whether one's contribution is coerced or voluntary, many believers feel as if they're on a kind of 'holy treadmill' as they engage in a plethora of church activities such that, rather than growing through their endeavours, many end up either physically or spiritually exhausted (or both). All of this is reminiscent of the difference in attitudes between Martha and Mary depicted in the following scene from Luke 10:38-42:

'As Jesus and his disciples were on their way, he came to a village where a woman named Martha opened her home to him. She had a sister called Mary, who sat at the Lord's feet listening to what he said. But Martha was distracted by all the preparations that had to be made. She came to him and asked, "Lord, don't you care that my sister has left me to do the work by myself? Tell her to help me!" "Martha, Martha," the Lord answered, "You are worried and upset about many things, but only one thing is needed. Mary has chosen what is better, and it will not be taken away from her."'

Martha and Mary offer a picture that contrasts the church situation we have today with the Bride as she's meant to be. Martha can be seen as a picture of *church-as-a-thing-in-itself*; caught in the activity trap and trying to 'make it happen' by her own efforts, the result is only too obvious—she ends up stressed and facing possible meltdown: busyness is not the same as fruitfulness. Mary, on the other hand, is sitting at the Lord's feet which is the posture of a disciple; as a woman within that culture this would have had added significance—and as Jesus put it, 'Mary has chosen what is better.'

I can't help thinking of Psalm 46:10 when I picture Mary in this scene: *'Be still and know that I am God.'* Martha is preoccupied by all the things that she believes ought to be done in order to receive Jesus while Mary, on the other hand, has:

'...fix[ed her] eyes upon Jesus, the author and perfecter of our faith, who for the joy set before him endured the cross, scorning its shame, and sat down at the right hand of the throne of God.'

Hebrews 12:2

Like Mary, the more we are *transfixed* by Jesus the more we will be *transformed* into his image. Someone once said that the greatest compliment a person can pay God is a changed life; we might go further and agree that one of *the* most important goals in every Christian's life should be this transformation.

But whilst I'm convinced that we're meant to follow Mary's example, I can't help thinking that, unfortunately, a 'Martha Mentality' has taken over and dominated the church at large; instead of being still and listening to Jesus, there are some who mistake motion for action — that's to say, there are people who fail to recognize that hustle and bustle doesn't necessarily get anything of value accomplished. There's a very real danger that trying to make church 'work' replaces Jesus' original intention for his body. This intention surely has more to do with the idea of a called-out community experiencing both individual and corporate spiritual transformation than it has with the idea that organising and attending meetings represent the high-water mark of Christian experience.

One major consequence of our wrong focus is that rather than offering the world a picture of Jesus, we ultimately present a picture of ourselves instead — a people whose lives are preoccupied with rushing to the next church event; rather like the priest and the Levite in the parable of the Good Samaritan, many are often too busy to stop and reach out to the very people with whom we are meant to engage. It's hardly surprising, then, that the world sees Christians as people who have cut themselves off from everyone else, a people who live and move and have their being in a kind of religious ghetto; a people who, in neglecting Jesus' transforming power are at risk of trying to make things happen largely through their own endeavours.

It's also no surprise that the effort of trying to sustain such a mammoth project often enervates rather than strengthens the body of Christ, creating more heat than light. The very structures we develop, supposedly to help people become disciples of Christ, ironically block their view of Jesus and thereby debilitate them. We have allowed church to compete with God for our affections: church fills our vision when God should. As Francis Frangipane said:

> 'There is only one thing that keeps most churches from prospering spiritually. They have yet to find God.' [6]

Church should be a group of people focused on Jesus, but more often than not Church ends up being a group of people focused on Church instead.

When Peter took his eyes off Jesus and looked at the waves, he began to sink. When we take our eyes off the Lord and look to the church for our direction and security, we likewise begin to go under. Surely it is better to follow David's example:

> 'But my eyes are fixed on you, O Sovereign LORD: in you I take refuge.'
>
> *Psalm 141:8*

We do not need to fix the church; rather, we need to fix our eyes upon Jesus, the author and perfecter of our faith. We need to focus on the Head rather than the body—only then will we begin to see his body manifest itself as a matter of course.

Mere Churchianity

The institutions of Churchianity are not Christianity. An institution is a good thing if it is second; immediately an institution recognizes itself it becomes the dominating factor.

Oswald Chambers

If it's true that God's people have, for the longest time, been building on the wrong foundation, it would certainly help to explain a lot of things: it would explain why there are considerable numbers of Christians who continue to be worn out and generally lacking in zeal for God—and of critical importance is the fact that unless this is recognized, it will continue to hinder the progress of God's kingdom on earth.

In the meantime, many Christians are encouraged to engage in constantly revised 'new and improved' programmes, often proposed as the remedy for the ills that beset the church, the world or both. For example, one leader I talked to felt that the antidote for the lack of 'religious enthusiasm' amongst the people in his own house group was to send them out door-knocking. But people can't give to others what they don't have themselves, and the more important consideration might have been to try and identify *why* so many of them were so dry in the first place.

Despite all that's on offer, often the end result is that many churches find themselves slowly but surely sucked into a whirlpool, circling the drain. Rather like a body struggling to get free of quicksand only to sink deeper, church leaders invent courses and design activities in order to combat dryness which, ironically, results in even more dryness. Beneath all the hype, the latest church growth methodologies and the pumped-up worship, often what's left is a body constituted of significant numbers of Christians with scant Biblical knowledge and little true experience of those things the programmes are trying desperately to generate. Whilst the ministries, the meetings and the music might look and sound impressive, people's lives continue more or less unchanged year in year out.

Many in leadership acknowledge that spiritual lethargy is a common condition, but like the pastor involved in *The Weekend of Joy*, they fail to understand that, in many cases, this passivity may well be *because of* rather than despite people's participation in church; it would appear that the efforts of those in leadership to 'fire people up' have instead encouraged a growing flood of refugees out from the church, weakening rather than strengthening it.

Not only are these self-inflicted wounds causing many of those on the inside to leave, they are also reinforcing the desire of those looking on from the outside to remain exactly where they are. I believe that a fundamental misunderstanding on the part of God's own people concerning what Jesus meant when he talked about his *ekklesia*, has, in turn, led to an even more muddled understanding of the *gospel itself* in the minds of unbelievers: most non-Christians with whom I talk equate Christianity with church attendance and with being a good person, over and above the notion that it might have anything to do with a personal relationship with God. Indeed, I'm convinced that the mixed message which the church sends out concerning the gospel of Jesus Christ—offering Churchianity rather than Christianity—is one of the reasons many remain in their unbelief. This is no light matter when we remember that what's at stake is the spiritual destiny of those presently outside the kingdom, for whom Jesus came bearing Good News and for which he made us his ambassadors.

The fact is, continually redesigning the church will never be the answer: people don't need yet more ideas about how to 'do church' differently—after all, there are more than enough of those around. Until we realise that the way we perceive the *ekklesia* is essentially different from the way the apostle Paul and the first Christians understood it—and more importantly, from the way God wants us to understand it today—then we are doomed to plod forever, constantly seeking new ways to organize the joy of the Lord.

The challenge facing us today is *not* how to continually invent a surfeit of activities in which those who attend church might engage, but rather to discern exactly how and why so many of God's people find themselves in the rut they are in. In Jeremiah 2:13 we read:

> '"My people have committed two sins:
> They have forsaken me,
> the spring of living water,
> and have dug their own cisterns,
> broken cisterns that cannot hold water."'

For broken cisterns we could just as well read broken systems: our failed programmes, strategies, techniques and methodologies. Instead of relying on the Holy Spirit we rely on our own efforts and abilities:

> 'Increasingly it seems we attempt to use the power of man's trained and directed intellect to take the place of divine inspiration...' [7]

Church-as-a-thing-in-itself is a man-made institution and it's time we understood that when we try to 'do church better' by designing our own structures and attempting to organize God's people within these same structures—when we forsake God's direction and dig our own cisterns—we are doomed to failure; it is impossible for mere men to build or create anything that can hold the fresh, living water of God. Broken cisterns allow fresh water to leak away whilst that which remains will become stagnant and eventually dry up altogether.

It's time to return to the source, the spring of living water, and enjoy the kind of body life God intends—and always intended—for us. The first step in this process will be for people to realise just how far we have strayed from the path laid out in Scripture.

It is not the answer that enlightens, but the question.

Eugène Ionesco

3

INTRODUCING THE QUESTION OF THE THREE R's:

Which Rock?
Whose Responsibility?
Why the Replacement?

Chinese Whispers

'What did he say?'
'Purple monkey dishwasher.'

The Simpsons

There's a well-known (and highly improbable) story set in World War I which involves a group of soldiers standing in a trench. The officer, who is at one end of the line, gives a message to the man next to him which he wants to be passed on down the line to the dispatch rider, who is standing at the other end. The message is: 'Send reinforcements, we are going to advance.' Accordingly, the message is passed down the line but by the time it reaches the dispatch rider it has metamorphosed into, 'Send three-and-fourpence, we are going to a dance.' Not *quite* the same thing...

In this story the first soldier in line was given a message which became increasingly distorted as it was passed on, and I can't help feeling that something similar has happened to our ecclesiology. I believe that while the first Christians started out with a correct understanding of the *ekklesia*, over time, that understanding has become distorted to such a degree that the *ekklesia* itself bears little resemblance to its originally intended form.

Unfortunately, when it comes to the Christian message, the human tendency to get it wrong has been present from the very beginning: one only has to read the New Testament epistles to see that right from the outset, people like Paul, Peter and others had to wrestle with and refute false teaching, incorrect ideas, heresies—you name it. However, I believe the threat we are to combat now is far more subtle by virtue of the fact that it has gone unnoticed for far longer, and is therefore much more dangerous than anything else Christ's people have had to deal with in the past. This is not a threat from 'out there'; it's been lurking behind our own lines for most of the church's lifespan and, although one cannot prove a negative, I believe this has significantly limited the impact of God's people on this world.

In an attempt to identify this threat, it would be good to begin with the following passage:

'"Who do you say I am?" Simon Peter answered, "You are the Christ, the Son of the living God." Jesus replied, "Blessed are you, Simon son of Jonah, for this was not revealed to you by man, but by my Father in heaven. And I tell you that you are Peter, and on this rock I will build my church, and the gates of Hades will not overcome it."'

Matthew 16:15-18

In particular, I would like to examine the phrase, '*on this rock I will build my church*'. These eight words contain three distinct elements, specifically:

On this rock

I will build

My church

To which rock was Jesus referring? What did Jesus mean when he talked about the church? Indeed, where does the word 'church' come from? And why, if Jesus said *he* would build it, are people trying to build it on his behalf?

Each of these issues will be examined in varying detail due to the fact that they have a direct bearing on the central argument proposed in this book: in each of the three cases, we will find that an insidious change in their meaning has taken place, to the detriment of the *ekklesia*. But to begin with I'd like to examine the following:

What did Jesus mean when he talked about

The Church?

It is probably impossible to think without words, but if we permit ourselves to think with the wrong words, we shall soon be entertaining erroneous thoughts; for words, which are given us for the expression of thought, have a habit of going beyond their proper bounds and determining the content of thought.

A.W. Tozer
The Knowledge of the Holy

4

BODY LANGUAGE

A Weighty Matter

Words, like eyeglasses, blur everything that they do not make more clear.

Joseph Joubert

As many people will know from their High School Physics class, technically speaking, telling someone how many stones, pounds or kilos you weigh isn't actually your weight, it's your mass. However, while many people are aware of this distinction, we all have a tacit understanding that giving one's weight in stones, pounds or kilos is, in everyday life at least, perfectly OK.

In the same way, the Greek word 'ekklesia' — translated as 'church' in our Bibles — actually refers to something quite different to how it is commonly understood: it refers to a people, not a place. It means, variously: assembly, congregation, a summoning or calling out. Originally, for the people at large, *ekklesia* meant a public gathering of citizens; it was used, for example, when people were 'called out' of the city to vote.

Whilst the majority of Christians with whom I talk claim to know and fully understand the distinction between *ekklesia* and *church*, they exhibit the same lack of concern as those who disregard the mass/weight issue; the attitude seems to be that as long as one is simply *aware* of the difference, this in itself will automatically prevent us from falling into any serious error. At the same time, there are those who would argue that it's just an issue of semantics and nothing more.

In reply to this, and as someone else has remarked, to talk of 'mere words' is much like talking of 'mere dynamite'; whilst using mass as weight hasn't caused any real problems in our day-to-day life, unfortunately the same can't be said regarding the difference between *church* and *ekklesia*: a failure to appreciate the distinction between these terms has played a significant role in helping to dismember the true body of Christ. Somewhat like the *butterfly effect*, an apparently negligible shift in meaning has led to a dramatic shift in thinking which, as far as God's people are concerned, has had disastrous consequences reaching as far as the present day.

After centuries of wrong emphasis, the common usage of the word 'church'—even amongst believers who claim to understand the proper meaning of *ekklesia*—is almost exclusively related to it being a place, a building, or a structure. People talk about 'going to church', or 'singing in church', for example. Sometimes one hears 'the church' referred to in a different sense, one which implies 'the people that run it' (as in, 'the church has decided…'). This implies a decision-making body which is separate from the majority who ironically *are* the church. Either way, the language we use when we talk about *the church* indicates a drift in our own understanding of the body, away from the originally intended meaning of *ekklesia*—the meaning that Jesus had in mind when he talked about it.

Assembling the Facts

To fail to study the Old Testament qahal is to fail to understand the important New Testament word, ekklesia.

E. W. Goodrick

When it comes to the subject of *church*, we have inherited a distinctly unhelpful mindset and one which is particularly difficult to shake off. I'm convinced that the vast majority of people are unable to read any scriptural reference to 'church' without seeing it through the lens of their own version of it, rather than reading what is simply there. Consequently, they do not recognize any contradictions between the Scriptures and their own church experience. The end result is that what the Bible actually says on the subject of the *ekklesia* is, in effect, hidden in plain sight.

Bear this in mind as we now return to the scene depicted in Matthew 16:18: Jesus proclaims to the disciples, 'I will build my church, and the gates of Hades will not overcome it.' Scripture doesn't record the reaction of those present, but imagine for one moment the disciples looking at each other, scratching their heads in bewilderment. Imagine further, if you will, after some prompting from the others, Peter asking Jesus, 'Umm... what's a *church*?'

I say this for the simple reason that Jesus could *not* have used the word 'church', not least because:

The church did not exist at that point in time.

Most people do not seem to consider the significance of the fact that Matthew 16:18 is the first occasion on which the word 'church' appears in our Bibles. (Two chapters later, in Matthew 18:15-17, we find *church* appearing for the second — and last — time in the whole of the gospel narratives.) There is no prior discussion anywhere in Scripture on the subject of church *per se*: rather, the word appears out of the blue, as it were, and the disciples would have had no context or frame of reference with which they could have made sense of what Jesus was saying — if he had used the word 'church' in the sense we understand it — and in which case neither Peter nor anyone else would have had the faintest idea what Jesus was talking about. His words would have been about as comprehensible as *purple monkey dishwasher* to those listening to him. But this in itself makes no sense: Jesus had to be saying *something* which was intelligible to everyone present. The question is, if Jesus didn't say 'church' then what *did* he say?

Since he was a Jew, it is far more likely that Jesus would have been speaking Aramaic or Hebrew to the disciples and thus wouldn't have used the Greek word *ekklesia*, let alone *church*. If we try to identify the word he actually used, we have a potential source of help in the form of the *Septuagint* (often abbreviated to LXX): begun in the third century before Christ and completed around 130 BC, this Greek translation of the Old Testament was so-called because it was the work of seventy or so scholars. Regarding this, New Testament Greek scholar Edward W. Goodrick wrote the following:

The Christian writers of the New Testament were converts from Judaism. When they became Christians, they had no idea of abandoning their Jewish faith. They brought with them a theological vocabulary with Greek terms from the Hebrew Bible via the LXX [Septuagint]. And with little or no change, they used these terms in the New Testament they were writing.' [1]

Of particular importance is the fact that the Septuagint frequently translates the Hebrew word for 'assembly' or 'congregation' — *qâhâl* — as *ekklesia*. In *The Spreading Flame*, F.F. Bruce wrote:

> '...ekklesia was used in the LXX to render the Hebrew word qahal, the congregation of Israel, the nation in its theocratic character, organized as a religious community.' [2]

Qâhâl is a word with which those present would almost certainly have been familiar, appearing 120 times in their own scriptures. To give just one example, in the NIV, Psalm 22:22 reads:

> 'I will declare your name to my people;
> in the *assembly* I will praise you.'

The word used here for assembly is *qâhâl* in the Hebrew Old Testament and *ekklesia* in the Greek Septuagint. This verse reappears in the New Testament where it is quoted in Hebrews 2:12; it's interesting to note that the King James Version renders it as follows:

> '...I will declare thy name unto my brethren, in the midst of the *church* will I sing praise unto thee.'

In the light of this, it seems more than reasonable to assume that *qâhâl* was the word Jesus used and one which would have held particular significance for a Jewish listener: Jesus' declaration would have highlighted the fact that there was to be a continuity between the assembly of God's people under the existing Mosaic Covenant and the assembly of His people under the New; in this sense Jesus' words would have implied 'business as usual'. While some Christians regard the New Covenant as drawing a line under Old Testament Judaism, with Christianity representing a complete break from it, there was, in fact, an unbroken progression—at least in this vital regard—from one to the other. This is supported by the commonly accepted view that the first Christians were simply faithful and committed Jews who, as Goodrick pointed out, didn't even consider the idea that they were joining a new religion.

These 'enlightened Jews' nevertheless differed from their contemporaries in one very important respect: they believed that Jesus of Nazareth was the long-awaited Messiah. But whilst these Hebrew Christians readily accepted Jesus' claim that he was indeed 'the Christ the Son of the living God' (Matthew 16:16) we can also establish that none of them had grasped the full import of the words which followed: '...on this rock I will build my assembly...'

Embedded within this statement was a message, not just for the Jews, but for the whole world, the implications of which would only become clear with hindsight and as events within the nascent Christian community unfolded. The heart of this message was intimately involved with the *ekklesia* and in order to understand the latter more fully, we need now to turn to 'the birth of the church' as recorded in the New Testament.

Two Tribes, One Tree

For we were all baptised by one Spirit so as to form one body—whether Jews or Gentiles, slave or free—and we were all given the one Spirit to drink.

1 Corinthians 12:12-13

In Acts 2 we read of the events at Pentecost, with around three thousand Jews being added to the original company of believers; as unprecedented as this was, one of the more unusual aspects of the whole scene was large numbers of people 'speaking in tongues'. This was something which would assume particular significance in a subsequent manifestation of the same phenomenon, in what some have described as the 'Gentile Pentecost'.

In Acts 10 we read of the salvation of Cornelius, a Roman centurion, along with his household:

concerning the *ekklesia/qâhâl* were meant, not just for Jews...
but for *everybody*.

As far as Paul was concerned, his training as a Pharisee
meant that he would have been more familiar than most with
the idea and meaning of the qâhâl and he clearly grasped what
was happening quicker than many others; but even then, it
was only through revelation that he could fully comprehend
what Christ's work on the cross meant in regard to the qâhâl,
reconciling both Jew and Gentile. Addressing the Gentile
believers at Ephesus, Paul writes of 'the mystery made known
to me by revelation' (Ephesians 3:3) going on to add:

> 'This mystery is that through the gospel the Gentiles are
> heirs together with Israel, members together of one
> body, and sharers together in the promise in Christ
> Jesus' (verse 6).

It would appear, however, that this unity came under pressure
due to an assumption on the part of the Gentile Christians that
they had replaced the Jews in God's affections, thereby
creating in them a disdainful, arrogant attitude towards the
latter. This was something Paul clearly sought to redress:

> 'If some of the branches have been broken off, and you,
> though a wild olive shoot, have been grafted in among
> the others and now share in the nourishing sap from the
> olive root, do not consider yourself to be superior to
> those other branches. If you do, consider this: You do
> not support the root, but the root supports you.'
>
> *Romans 11:17-18*

Both Jews and Gentiles were now part of one assembly, one
body, one olive tree — the *qâhâl*. But while the 'dividing wall of
hostility' between both Jewish and Gentile Christians had been
removed (Ephesians 2:14), a newer, much more subtle and far
more dangerous challenge began to develop.

It presented a threat which is still with us today.

This problem had nothing to do with the separation between
Jew and Gentile; rather, it was (and continues to be) concerned
with the separation of God from His people due to the growth
of something called *The Church* which sprang up between the
two.

One Tribe, Two Trees

Eisegesis: the interpretation of a text (as of the Bible) by reading into it one's own ideas.

Merriam Webster online dictionary

If one pauses for a moment and asks 'Where's *church* in all this?' we realise that *it isn't there. It doesn't feature anywhere in this historical process.* Neither Peter, nor Paul—indeed *no-one*— appears to be thinking in terms of 'church' in any way, shape or form. They're certainly thinking about the *body* but within the context of the *qâhâl*; their primary concern was how to resolve one of the main dilemmas confronting this same body. As we've just seen, this concerned the relationship between Jewish and Gentile believers and the growing recognition that God's plan was always that the latter were to be assimilated into the *qâhâl*, allowing them to take their seat in the assembly alongside those of their Jewish brethren who had been elected by God.

The reason we unthinkingly assume the church *is* present in these accounts is because *church* has been substituted for *ekklesia* in our Bibles. This represents a highly dangerous anachronism, the word itself only entering common usage centuries after the events described: the whole mistaken concept of a new and separate entity called *The Church* would only arise later on. In effect, the word *church* was and continues to be retrofitted into Scripture, its inclusion projecting meaning back into the text which isn't in the original.

The significance of this is that, on every occasion where our Bibles record Paul (or anyone else) addressing individual churches, or where he's writing about the church in general— he's not in fact talking about *church* or *churches* at all—indeed, he couldn't have been: he's actually talking about the *assembly of God*, the *qâhâl*, in all its manifestations. New Testament scholar James D.G. Dunn writes:

'Paul was able to speak of "the assemblies (plural) of God," whereas LXX usage is almost always singular. Paul evidently had no problem with conceiving "the assembly of God" as manifested in many different places at the same time – the churches (of God) in Judea, in Galatia, in Asia, or in Macedonia. Each gathering of those baptised in the name of the Lord Jesus was the assembly of God in that place. This is all the more striking when we recall that Paul also speaks of "the church in (someone's) house" – the church in the house of Priscilla and Aquila, of Nympha, and of Philemon. The point is that wherever believers met for fellowship and worship they were in direct continuity with the assembly of Israel, they were the assembly of God.' [3]

The New Covenant represented a quantum change, *not* because it inaugurated a brand-new religion which would be represented by a brand-new thing called The Church – but because it inaugurated a new way of being accepted by God into His *assembly...* by faith in Christ rather than observing the Law... and not only that: this assembly was no longer restricted to the Jews but open to *all* those who believed in Jesus as the Messiah, the Son of God – both Jew and Gentile alike.

The man-made invention of *church* has managed to interpose itself between the *qâhâl* of the Old Testament and the *ekklesia* of the New, thereby breaking the link between the two and to devastating effect. The result is that it's easy to make the mistake of thinking that Jesus' declaration in Matthew 16:18 suggests a kind of 'Year Zero', representing a clean break between Christianity and Judaism and thereby disguising the continuous nature of the situation – which in turn, clouds the understanding of the *ekklesia*.

When we stand back and attempt to survey the situation through the eyes of the first Christians, it becomes increasingly evident that the institution of the church is *not* an outgrowth from the olive tree Paul describes in Romans 11 – which is a picture of the true *ekklesia*, the *qâhâl*; rather, the church *is a separate, second tree* planted by men rather than God. It is *not* supported by the root and nourished by the sap to which Paul refers in the same passage, but rather, it is rooted in man's ideas and fed by the flesh. One represents the Tree of Life; the other is more like a *bonsai*, its growth constrained by those who wish to control it. The problem has been that for centuries, large numbers of people have been leaning out of the first, stretching across to the other in order to attend to it.

It is, as many of them have discovered, back-breaking work.

Language is the source of misunderstandings.

Antoine de Saint-Exupery

5

UPON THIS MISTRANSLATION
WE WILL BUILD OUR CHURCH

Church – For want of a better Word
Curious and Curiouser

The writers of the New Testament understood that the Greek word *ekklesia* translated their Hebrew word *qâhâl* and meant the community or congregation of God.[1] But that being the case, it raises a crucial question: if *qâhâl/ekklesia* refers to some sort of gathering or assembly—something which the disciples would have had no problem understanding—then why don't our English translations simply say 'gathering' or 'assembly'? Why is *ekklesia* rendered as 'church' in our Bibles?

This in turn raises another, more fundamental question, namely:

Where does the actual word 'church' come from?

Circular Reasoning
The Accidental Church

In Easton's Bible Dictionary, we find the following entry under *Church*:

'Derived probably from the Greek *kuriakon* (i.e., "the Lord's house"), which was used by ancient authors for the place of worship. In the New Testament it is the translation of the Greek word *ecclesia*, which is synonymous with the Hebrew *kahal* of the Old Testament, both words meaning simply an assembly, the character of which can only be known from the connection in which the word is found. There is no clear instance of its being used for a place of meeting or of worship, although in post-apostolic times it early received this meaning.' [2]

Alan Knox expands upon the metamorphosis of *kuriakon* into *church*, suggesting that:

'Eventually, the place where believers met together came to be called "the Lord's house" using the term κυριακόν (*kuriakon*), which is the neuter version (literally, "the Lord's thing"). This word made its way into both German ("Kirche"), Anglo-Saxon ("circe"), and Middle English ("chirche"). [3]

Whilst *kuriakon-to-church* is commonly proposed, this etymology is by no means universally accepted; for example, we find the following entry in Smith's Bible Dictionary:

'The word [church] is generally said to be derived from the Greek *kyriakos*, meaning the lord's house. But the derivation has been too hastily assumed...(in fact) the derivation of the word 'church' is uncertain.' [4]

This hesitancy is justified since the foregoing explanations fail to address the question as to why or how *kirk/church* came to be assimilated into some European languages but not others: whilst Anglophones, for example, use the word *church*, the French continue to use *eglise*, the Spanish *iglesia* and the Latin Vulgate *ecclesiam*, all of which are clearly derived from the original *ekklesia*. As Smith's Bible Dictionary observes:

'[*Church*, or the equivalent] is found in the Teutonic and Slavonic languages and answers to the derivatives of *ekklesia*, which are usually found in the romance languages and by foreign importation elsewhere.' [5]

If the *kuriakon* theory is correct, then we would expect *everyone* to talk of *church* (or something similar) yet clearly, they don't. But if 'church' did *not* originate with *kuriakon*, then where did it come from? In E. Cobham Brewer's *Dictionary of Phrase and Fable*, we read:

'The etymology of this word is generally assumed to be from the Greek, *Kuriou oikos* (house of God); but this is most improbable, as the word existed in all the Celtic dialects long before the introduction of Greek. No doubt the word means "a circle." The places of worship among the German and Celtic nations were always circular (Welsh, *cyrch*; French, *cirque*; Scotch, *kirk*; Greek, *kirk-os*, etc.) Compare Anglo-Saxon *circe*, a church, with *circol*, a circle.' [6]

History certainly lends support to the 'circle' origin of 'church': for instance, when Pope Gregory sent instructions to missionaries in Britain, he advised them to Christianize pagan places of worship rather than remove them:

'The idol temples of that race [the English] should by no means be destroyed, but only the idols in them. Take holy water and sprinkle it in these shrines, build altars and place relics in them. For if the shrines are well built, it is essential that they should be changed from the worship of devils to the service of the true God. When the people see that their shrines are not destroyed they will be able to banish error from their hearts and be more ready to come to the places they are familiar with, but now recognizing and worshipping the true God.' [7]

There is certainly evidence of Christian meeting places being built at the site of earlier pagan structures. It is highly probable that early Christian gatherings would have taken place in the old 'circles', and following on from this, it is equally plausible that these gatherings would have retained their original designation, being referred to as a *circe* or *kirk*. For my part, I find this explanation for the origin of the word 'church' the most compelling. It is interesting to consider the very real possibility that 'church' is derived from the name for a pagan shrine or meeting place!

Regardless of the precise truth of the matter, one thing is certain: neither *chirche*, nor its derivative, *church*, are direct translations of the Greek word *ekklesia*. Indeed, Martin Luther described the word 'church' as an obscure, ambiguous term, and as Alan Knox points out:

'It is interesting that when Luther translated the New Testament into vernacular German, he did not use the word "Kirche" to translate ἐκκλησία (ekklesia), he used the German word "Gemeinde", which means something similar to the English word "community". However, many Germans still refer to the "church" as the "Kirche"'. [8]

Despite Luther's efforts, Reformation theology nevertheless retained the word *church* within its lexicon; presumably it was simply too difficult—even for Luther—to undo fifteen hundred years of tradition in this particular case and thereby dispel a collective and mistaken mind-set, one which accepted the term and all that it implied.

Smoke and Mirrors

If thought corrupts language, language can also corrupt thought.

George Orwell, 1984

We are faced, then, with a rather strange situation: somewhat like the shell game, through sleight of hand one word was somehow replaced with another, without anyone seeming to spot the switch. Rather than being directly translated as 'gathering', 'assembly' or the equivalent, *ekklesia* was instead replaced with the word *church*, the latter either a modified transliteration of another, entirely different Greek word, *kuriakon* —'belonging to the Lord' —or alternatively, a derivation of the Celtic word for 'circle'. This was an error of the greatest possible magnitude and it raises the question as to how on earth it could have taken place.

We can begin to answer this when we realise that, whether obtaining from *kuriakon* or *circle*, a particular word was already in use within the Christian community well before the various Bible translations were created. Initially used to describe the place where believers met, over time 'church' had become synonymous with the body itself. It appears to be the case that the word was inserted into Scripture as new Bible versions were developed, the translators substituting it for *ekklesia*.

A good example of this is the first significant English translation of the New Testament, produced under the auspices of John Wycliffe in 1382; it was not derived from the original Greek but from the Latin Vulgate Bible, and in Wycliffe's version we find that the Latin word *ecclesiam* is translated as *chirche*. It's not clear why Wycliffe (or those he'd commissioned) chose to write 'chirche' rather than 'congregation' or something similar, but one thought is that Wycliffe wasn't aware of the original Greek meaning; this, however, is extremely hard to imagine. Others have suggested that it is more likely that he simply selected the word that was already—and unfortunately—commonly used at that time. Either way, through Wycliffe the error was perpetuated.

The next major English translation was by William Tyndale, who, having been inspired by Luther's German translation of the New Testament, was determined to provide the equivalent for his own countrymen. Available from around 1526, his was the first English translation to be derived directly from Hebrew and Greek texts. Significantly, with one exception, *the word church does not appear anywhere in its pages;* instead the word *ekklesia* is translated as *congregation*. The exception occurs in Acts 19:37 which Tyndale translated as:

'For ye have brought hither these men, which are neither robbers of churches, nor yet blasphemers of your goddess.'

Interestingly, the Greek word he translated as 'churches' refers to pagan temples! (Referring to the preceding section, one can't help wondering if Tyndale was aware of a connection between the two.) It's probably not surprising then that Tyndale was vilified by the church establishment: Sir Thomas More, for example, condemned his translation as heretical, attacking—amongst a host of other things—Tyndale's decision to translate *ekklesia* as congregation rather than church. In defending his choice of word, Tyndale replied:

'In as much as the clergy...had appropriat[ed] unto themselves the term [Church] that of right is common unto all the whole congregation of them that believe in Christ...therefore in the translation of the New Testament where I found this word *Ecclesia*, I interpreted it by this word *congregation*.' [9]

Unfortunately, Tyndale's counterarguments did nothing to improve the situation but, if anything, served only to inflame it; not only did the Church publicly burn as many copies of his translation as it could lay its hands on, it also burnt Tyndale himself at the stake, but not before strangling him first. One might speculate that the punishment was made to fit the supposed crime inasmuch as the church was clearly desperate to prevent Tyndale's voice from being heard.

Despite his death, however, the Church found it was not that easy to extinguish the fire Tyndale had started; several other English translations followed which also translated *ekklesia* as *congregation*, notably the Coverdale, Matthew and Great Bibles. But this was to change once again with the advent of the Geneva Bible and the Bishops' Bible, along with the Catholic Douai-Reims translation, wherein the word 'church' was reinstated.

The truth is, by the time the first English Bibles were published, the damage had been done long, long before. *Church-as-a-thing-in-itself* had been around for one-and-a-half thousand years before Tyndale's Bible appeared with its translation of *ekklesia* as *congregation*; Tyndale was sawing against the grain of church history, and any gains he might have made were dealt a serious blow seventy-five years after his death with the publication of the most widely known English translation of all.

The King James Bible

Driving the nail home

Regarding the King James Bible (also known as the Authorized Version) Robert L. Thomas writes:

> 'The need to which the King James Version responded is interesting. The famous Hampton Court conference in 1604 had as its purpose *to determine what was wrong with the church*. The only significant action of the conference was the following resolution: "That a translation be made of the whole Bible, as consonant as can be to the original Hebrew and Greek; and this to be set out and printed, without any marginal notes, and only to be

used in all Churches of England in time of divine service."' [10] (Emphasis mine)

Despite the stated intention of being 'as consonant as can be to the original Hebrew and Greek', the Greek word *ekklesia*, which appears 115 times in the New Testament of the KJV, is consistently translated as *church*—except in Acts 19, verses 32, 39 and 41 where it is more accurately translated as *assembly*. The passage containing these verses concerns a riot in the city of Ephesus, and *ekklesia* is used to describe the mob which had gathered in the theatre there.

So—why is *ekklesia* translated in two different ways?

The KJV drew heavily from Tyndale's work—some estimates suggest as much as 83% of the King James Bible was derived from Tyndale's translation—and yet it differs in one crucial aspect: King James issued fifteen edicts concerning the translation process, the third of which stated that, 'The old ecclesiastical words to be kept, viz.: as the word 'church' not to be translated 'congregation' etc.' [11]

The motivation for this seems to be primarily political: since James was Head of the Church of England, it was essential that the translation contained the word *church* because he wished to emphasize his authority over it. Whilst the idea of the state manipulating the Word of God might come as an unwelcome surprise to some, the truth is, there is a long history of Bible translation committees nuancing Scripture to varying degrees in order to either emphasize or de-emphasize particular points of doctrine. Later, we will see that this fact is particularly important with regard to church leadership.

Paradoxically, the Authorized Version introduced (or at the very least, reinforced) a number of unauthorized ecclesiastical concepts. Considering that the Hampton Court conference 'had as its purpose to determine what was wrong with the church', it is hugely ironic that the failure to be faithful to the original Greek word *ekklesia* ensured that the roots of the very problem they were trying to remedy would, in fact, be driven deeper and continue to wreak havoc within the body of Christ.

Lost in Translation

The lie passed into history and became truth.   George Orwell, 1984

If, due to the substitution of the word 'church' in place of a more accurate translation of *ekklesia* — in Matthew 16:18 and elsewhere — we are indeed reading something more into Jesus' words than he could possibly have intended, then I suggest that this is no small error. I also hope to demonstrate in the following chapters that this particular distortion of Scripture is not an isolated case, although I consider it to be the most serious. I believe that, after centuries of tradition — which has so often been both influenced by and reflected in mistranslations — a lot of things are read into Scripture that were never anticipated by the writers of the New Testament, particularly in regard to those Scriptures dealing with the *ekklesia*.

It's interesting to note that Christians talk about the inerrancy of Scripture, in the sense that every word in the Bible is exactly how God intended; and yet 'church' — a word which exercises the minds of so many people — is found within its pages when it ought not to exist at all!

Like a cuckoo in the nest, the word 'church' has managed to shove aside 'congregation' or 'assembly' in our Bibles, obscuring the true meaning and purpose of the *ekklesia* — which is about a *people* — and instead, it has redirected attention towards a *place or institution* that is separate, or at a distance from the people themselves. The only reason we think in terms of 'church' *at all* is because the word itself has been shoehorned into Scripture, a square peg hammered into a round hole. Allowing this error to occur has both contributed to and helped perpetuate a model of body life that bears little resemblance to the way God envisioned it.

Some do recognize the problem presented by translating *ekklesia* as *church*; they believe that if the latter was replaced with a more accurate word in our Bibles, then that alone would cause the body to function properly. But I wonder if that's true? Consider, for example, the fact that — as we noted earlier — whilst 'church' is found in the English-speaking world, *eglise*, *iglesia* and *ecclesiam* are found in other parts of Europe, all of these words clearly derived from the original, yet each people group has nevertheless overseen the evolution of its respective *ekklesia-as-a-thing-in-itself*. Of course, one could argue that rather than transliterating the word *ekklesia*, if each of these groups had simply translated the word into its own vernacular (as 'congregation' or 'assembly', for example) then the problem of *church-as-a-thing-in-itself* would never have arisen. But as we have already seen, despite German Bibles continuing in the tradition of Luther and using the word 'Gemeinde' (community) to translate *ekklesia*, German believers nevertheless still flock to their *Kirchen* every Sunday. All of this suggests that merely changing the translation will not cause the *ekklesia* to function as it ought.

Even if it was agreed that in all future editions of the Bible, the word 'church' would be replaced by another more accurate word — again, using 'congregation' or the equivalent — would there be books in a hundred years' time discussing the problem of *congregation-as-a-thing-in-itself* or the equivalent? My personal feeling is that this would, indeed, be the case: for example, and as we shall see, documents from around 100AD suggest that the body of Christ had already come to be regarded as a *thing-in-itself* well before the substitution of *church* for *ekklesia* began to occur. Clearly, the misunderstanding concerning Christ's *ekklesia* had already taken place long before there were Bible (mis)translations and I would contend that rather than being the cause of this misunderstanding, translation errors simply contributed to the confusion by both reflecting and reinforcing a pre-existing condition.

Thus, whilst exchanging the word 'church' for something closer in meaning to the original *ekklesia* would definitely be a step in the right direction, I'm of the opinion that this alone would not solve the problem of *church-as-thing-in-itself*. The mishandling of the word *ekklesia*, as serious as it is, is not the root issue when it comes to a discussion concerning our misunderstanding of Christ's intention for his body. It would seem there is a deeper, more fundamental problem at work.

It's time, therefore, to look beyond the presenting symptoms of inaccuracies in translation, deliberate or otherwise, and to consider the underlying disease.

The natural man is a born enemy of Christianity...He strives against the freedom of the Gospel, and he longs with all his strength for a religion of law and statute...He longs for a legally appointed Church, for a kingdom of Christ which may be seen with the eyes of the natural man, for a temple of God, built with earthly gold and precious stones, that shall take the heart captive through outward sanctities, traditional ceremonies, gorgeous vestments, and a ritual that tunes the soul to the right pitch of devotion...He desires, as the keystone of the whole, a fixed body of doctrine that shall give certain intelligence concerning all divine mysteries, presented to him in a literal form, giving an answer to every possible question...He desires a rock which his eyes can see — the visible Church, the visible Word of God. Everything must be made visible, so that he may grasp it.

Rudolph Sohm
Outlines of Church History

Perhaps necessary to fight politically for ekklesia?

6

WORSHIPPING WHAT OUR
HANDS HAVE MADE

Space – The Final Frontier
To boldly go where no religion has gone before

Buildings, priests and rituals: these three elements were not unique to Judaism, but were and continue to be common to the vast majority of religions. However, whilst these remain as permanent features of other faiths, God never intended that the model of the Old Testament would continue forever. Hebrews 10:1 says,

> 'The law is only a shadow of the good things that are coming — not the realities themselves.'

One of the central purposes of the Old Covenant was to act as a 'holding pattern':

> 'So the law was our guardian until Christ came that we might be justified by faith. Now that this faith has come, we are no longer under a guardian.'
>
> *Galatians 3:24, 25*

With its temple, priests and ceremonial laws, the Old Covenant acted as a visible introduction to the invisible realm, a foreshadowing of an impending and deeper reality, a reality which would arrive in the form of a carpenter's son and made accessible through his being nailed to a piece of wood. The veil hanging in front of the Holy of Holies and through which only the High Priest could pass had been torn in two as the result of a man hanging on a cross, thereby allowing all men passage into the presence of God.

In a radically new development, God did away with the whole temple complex and all that went with it; one could almost imagine the *space* in the Holy of Holies had been preserved while everything surrounding it was torn down to leave even more space. Instead of the former show of religion with its rituals and performances, all of which placed God at a distance, all God's people were filled by the outpouring of His Spirit; the Holy of Holies was now to be found in the heart of each and every believer. The necessity and practice of going to a building 'where God lived' therefore ceased, and man himself became the dwelling place of God. As a result of Jesus' work on the cross, the gulf that already existed between Judaism and all other religions suddenly took on a totally different dimension.

Jesus' death and resurrection not only removed the need for an edifice of stone and wood, but it also abolished the need for both the priesthood and the ceremonial laws that were intimately connected to the temple and part and parcel of the whole Jewish religion. But this being the case, just how, then, did we find ourselves once more being herded inside designated buildings, once again filling these so-called 'sacred spaces' with priests along with their cultic performances and their religious paraphernalia? Somehow we have managed to rehang the veil between God and men, because the truth is—whether by accident or design—our current structures and practices are strikingly reminiscent of those found in the Old Testament: it would appear that, like the Phoenix rising from the ashes, the temple, and all that goes with it, has been reborn. In what follows, I shall try to establish just how it was that the Christian community allowed such a monumental mistake to take place.

A Golden Calf: Unholy Cow

A lot of organized religion seems like a man who was told that the only thing he could give God was to be found in a mirror. So he went off and made God a hugely elaborate ornamental mirror.

Milton Jones

Roman general Pompey is said to have emerged from the Holy of Holies within the temple in Jerusalem convinced that the Jews were secretly atheists. The reason? He found no idols there. It was inconceivable to Pompey that anyone could worship a god without statues, images or icons of that same god. Their absence was one of the most significant distinguishing features of Judaism; such practices were a massive departure from those of all other religions and something which was revolutionary from a human point of view. It was a line in the sand (though not the only one) which set the Jews apart from the surrounding pagan cultures. Psalm 135:15-18 tells us:

> 'The idols of the nations are silver and gold,
> made by human hands.
> They have mouths, but cannot speak,
> eyes, but cannot see.
> They have ears, but cannot hear,
> nor is there breath in their mouths.
> Those who make them will be like them,
> and so will all who trust in them.'

Pompey might have found a very different temple, however, if certain Jews had had their way earlier on in Israel's history:

The book of Exodus recounts the story of Israel's deliverance from bondage in Egypt where God's people had been enslaved in order to build pyramids in honour of the Pharaohs and their gods. We read how, not long after their escape, God begins to shape the Hebrew community, providing them with laws and commandments in preparation for life in the Promised Land, a place where He would dwell amongst them. Beginning in Chapter 20, God delivers the terms of His covenant verbally to His people, a contract which the Jews agree to in Chapter 24. Within the covenant, we find explicit commandments from God concerning His 'pride of place' in the lives of His children: the first commandment states,

> 'I am the LORD your God... you shall have no other gods before me.'

The second says:

> 'You shall not make for yourself an idol in the form of anything in heaven above or on the earth beneath or in the waters below. You shall not bow down to them or worship them.'

Exodus 20: 3-5

> 'While Peter was still speaking these words, the Holy Spirit came on all who heard the message. The circumcised believers who had come with Peter were astonished that the gift of the Holy Spirit had been poured out even on Gentiles. For they heard them speaking in tongues and praising God' (vv. 44-46).

The spectacle of Gentiles speaking in tongues blind-sided everyone, causing an inquest to be held as a result. Upon his return to Jerusalem, Peter has to endure a classic demonstration of how to miss the point:

> '...the circumcised believers criticised him and said, "You went into the house of uncircumcised men and ate with them."'

> *Acts 11:2-3*

Peter eventually gets the opportunity to defend his actions by providing those assembled with some of the context surrounding events at Caesarea:

> '"As I began to speak, the Holy Spirit came on them as he had come on us at the beginning...So if God gave them the same gift he gave us who believed in the Lord Jesus Christ, who was I to think that I could stand in God's way?"'

> *Acts 11:15, 17*

As much of a paradigm shift as these events represented, it was nevertheless accepted by those gathered as recorded in verse 18:

> 'When they heard this, they had no further objections and praised God, saying, "So then, even to Gentiles God has granted repentance that leads to life."'

The events described in Acts 10 represented a landmark in the history of 'the church'; it was a transforming event, allowing Christ's body to break free from the constraints of its Jewish heritage and extend its reach to the whole world. That salvation was available to the Gentiles as well as the Jews was a radically new and unexpected development. For Peter (as for anyone else who cared to reflect on these matters) there would have been the dawning realisation that Jesus' words to him

Later, in verse 23, God reaffirms the second commandment with the following:

> 'Do not make any gods to be alongside me; do not make for yourselves gods of silver or gods of gold.'

Unfortunately, however, it didn't take very long after their flight from Egypt for the Jews to cast off restraint and completely ignore God's prohibition regarding the fabrication and worship of idols, thereby forsaking the one true God who had delivered them from the tyranny of the Pharaoh. Shortly after delivering His commandments, God called Moses to meet with Him on Mount Sinai to confirm the covenant in stone. However, because Moses was gone for so long, the people of Israel grew impatient; regrettably, they decided to take things into their own hands (something which occurs with disturbing regularity within our churches today) and they approached Aaron with the following proposition:

> 'Come, make us gods who will go before us. As for this fellow Moses who brought us up out of Egypt, we don't know what has happened to him.'

> *Exodus 32:1*

As the account unfolds, we find how the Jews persuade Aaron to forge a calf from gold which they then bow before and worship, despite God's commandments. They don't want to wait for 'this fellow', Moses, to come back down the mountain and recount his dialogue with God; instead,

> *They decide to manufacture something themselves.*

Despite the fact that, upon his return, Moses' response is to deal with the Jews 'ever so severely' (to borrow an Old Testament phrase), accounts of other events many hundreds of years later reveal that the Israelites never really learned from their mistake: in Jeremiah, for example, we find God chastising his 'stiff-necked' people for exactly the same offence:

> 'I will pronounce judgments on my people because of their wickedness in forsaking me, in burning incense to other gods and in worshipping what their hands have made.'

> *Jeremiah 1:16*

And again, in Hosea 8:4b-6 we read:

> 'With their silver and gold
> they make idols for themselves
> to their own destruction.
> Samaria, throw out your calf-idol!
> My anger burns against them.
> How long will they be incapable of purity?
> They are from Israel!
> This calf—a metalworker has made it;
> it is not God.
> It will be broken in pieces,
> that calf of Samaria.'

Fourteen hundred years after God had delivered His people from physical bondage and slavery in Egypt into a new life in the Promised Land, Jesus called out his people—his *ekklesia*—from the world, setting them free from spiritual bondage, from the law of sin and death.

In Galatians 5:1 Paul tells us that:

> 'It is for freedom that Christ has set us free. Stand firm, then, and do not let yourselves be burdened again by a yoke of slavery.'

And yet, just like their predecessors, it didn't take long for God's people to start making something that would replace Him; this weakness would eventually result in the monument we have decided to call *church*... a monument, not to the Lord, but to ourselves. Jesus said he would build his *ekklesia*; we have subverted this by saying we will build, not an *ekklesia*—since this is impossible for mere humans—but *church* instead. Then, like the golden calf, we have bowed down and worshipped it.

And so we have come full circle: from slavery to liberation only to return to a voluntary burden, taken on at the behest of those who have called us to build—not pyramids this time—but churches. The result of all this effort is that many of God's children are worn down, devoid of passion and lacking joy.

Why have we allowed ourselves to be enslaved again for the past two thousand years when Christ died once and for all in order to set us free?

The Man Who Fell to Earth

Mission Control: Eden—we have a problem

The roots of the predicament in which we find ourselves entangled today are to be found in the Garden of Eden and in man's failure to trust God, even in the middle of Paradise. *Church-as-a-thing-in-itself,* in a sense, represents one of the fruits plucked from the Tree of Knowledge—

It is the fruit of man's fallen nature and Satan's exploitation of it.

The Fall was, in effect, the result of Adam's desire— encouraged by the devil—to become independent of God. At the bottom of the Fall lay Adam and Eve's efforts to seek their own security apart from that which God Himself provided; in the same way, the attempt to exercise control over our circumstances is one of the ways in which the descendants of Adam and Eve—you and I—try to gain our security. Not only do we try to control other people but, to some extent, we attempt to do the same with God Himself:

> 'Left to ourselves we tend immediately to reduce God to manageable terms. We want to get Him where we can use Him, or at least know where He is when we need Him. We want a God we can in some measure control.' [1]

The underlying motivation beneath the Israelites' decision to forge a golden calf was their need to make visible the invisible; their attempt to represent the ineffable in solid, measurable terms was in order to foster a religion that could be managed. Unfortunately, this bovine—a creature of our own making and whose DNA both originated and was bound up in our fall from grace—was never put to death. The golden calf is a symbol of organized, man-made religion, the mindset behind it the same as the one which helped to create church as we know it and which continues to sustain it. The simple fact of the matter is, like the golden calf,

Church-as-a-thing-in-itself is the product of our own fleshly desire for control.

The attraction of the church—with its structures and ceremonies, its liturgies and its reassuring ministrants—is the security of the 'known' and the certainties which all these outward symbols offer. Like the golden calf, *church-as-a-thing-in-itself* is something we can fabricate, built from stone and wood and paid for with gold and silver; it is something which has shape and form and thus something which we can see and understand. And, like the golden calf, it is equally lifeless.

It goes without saying that having this man-inspired forgery called *church* masquerading as Christ's *ekklesia* is far-removed from God's original intention for his people, both past, present and future. John Wimber said, 'Perhaps God wants His church back', but whilst Wimber certainly touches upon an important point, I very much doubt that God would want to take back the 'church' at all—nor the baggage that comes with it. God doesn't want our Mission Statements; He is not interested in the minutes of the last council meeting; He does not require the paper qualifications we have deemed necessary to qualify someone for ministry. Instead, He wants a relationship with us... and yet the *Good News* appears to have got lost in our filing cabinets, filed somewhere between *F* for *Finances* and *H* for *Human Resources*.

God doesn't want his church back: He wants His children to come home:

To sit at His feet,

Be still,

And know that He is God.

I Will Build *My* Church

Unless the Lord builds the house, its builders labour in vain

Psalm 127:1

In Ephesians 5:27, concerning Jesus we read,

'...that *He* might present to *Himself* the church in all her glory...' [NASB]

This verse serves as a very clear reminder as to who has taken on the responsibility to build the *ekklesia* ('the church'). The truth of this statement has nevertheless been ignored by God's people for many centuries, right up to the present, where we find the vast majority of leaders endeavouring to present *their* church to Jesus as a result of *their* own efforts. Using the very methods and practices that have already led many a congregation to a dead end, they try to lift the whole body, including themselves, by the bootstraps, and not surprisingly the effort required to lift such a dead weight often results in a spiritually exhausted, lethargic and disheartened body as well as the burnout of the leaders themselves. If Paul was with us today, I can imagine him delivering the same warning as he delivered to a group of believers two thousand years ago:

> 'Are you so foolish? After beginning with the Spirit, are you now trying to attain your goal by human effort?'
>
> *Galatians 3:31*

In the light of these verses and others, the *ekklesia* is clearly not something that any human can build; unfortunately, it has not prevented thousands from trying. Tozer points out that those who insist on attempting to build the body of Christ apart from him do so at their own peril:

> 'All religious leaders should remember that they will either let the Holy Spirit work through them or their work will be in vain. Every proud religious edifice erected by the zeal and labour of the flesh will perish in the hot fires of judgment. In the eyes of humanity such labours may be praiseworthy, but before God the results will be wood, hay and stubble.' [2]

It seems strange how many of the same people who claim to put their faith in Jesus don't appear to trust him when he says *he* will build *his* church: despite Tozer's warning and those of many others, people have chosen to ignore them such that more often than not, we find mere men rather than Jesus doing the building and — unsurprisingly — doing it rather badly.

> *Rather than an expression of devotion to God, the church is the outcome of our lack of faith in Him.*

❖   ❖   ❖

Objection Overruled

You cannot solve problems by using the same kind of thinking that created them in the first place.

Albert Einstein

Many years ago, Liz and I were part of a large Charismatic church. During one midweek house group meeting, the person leading it had lamented the lack of direction and depth that seemed to exist within our small group; he recognized, as we all did, that the meetings were stale and lifeless, and he was wrestling with the question of what could be done to resolve the problem. Liz, trying to be both tactful and helpful, suggested we pray and seek the direction of the Holy Spirit. Raising his eyebrows somewhat quizzically, the leader replied, 'I think that's a bit too *mystical.'*

A similar situation occurred a few months later when another leader was having coffee with us: he couldn't quite put his finger on the problem, but he was concerned that there was 'something missing' in the lives of large numbers of people within the church. Like the pastor who would organize The Weekend of Joy several years later, he sat there mulling over what could be done about the situation. I wondered aloud if, perhaps, the real problem to be tackled was a lack of true love for God. The response, just like that of the house group leader, was swift and in this case, one of frustration — a reaction which, as it would turn out, was a foretaste of reactions that would come in the future:

'It's easy for *you* to say we need to love God more — but *practically speaking* — just how do we get people to *do* that?'

As a good friend pointed out to me later when I recounted the story to him, this person might just as well have asked how — practically speaking — can we be made to love our spouses?

All these leaders were struggling with the same dilemma: what could they do differently with 'their' churches in order to fire up 'their' people? They seemed unable to appreciate that this very line of thinking was part of the problem in the first place, and that their attempts to find a solution only served to make matters worse. My conviction is the same now as it was then, and connected to something I suggested earlier, which is:

We are not called to fix the church but rather
to fix our eyes upon Jesus.

If we concentrate on the Head rather than on the body — however mystical this might seem — then God will take care of the rest as far as *His* body is concerned. This, I would suggest, is the God-ordained, 'practical' solution.

I'm equally convinced that all the leaders I have mentioned would maintain that this mindset is over-spiritualized and simply too naïve, and that nothing of lasting value would be created should one adopt this approach; that, whatever else might happen, the fruit of such seemingly undirected thinking would certainly not be *real* church. If past experience is anything to draw on, their arguments would almost certainly be framed with phrases such as, 'the need for structure', or 'authority and submission', and include words like covering, accountability, commitment and many more besides — all these being supposed features of 'real churches'. But the problem is that such arguments in support of the types of leadership and structures which are automatically assumed to be biblical *don't actually stand up to biblical scrutiny*. These issues, however, will be addressed at a later stage.

In the meantime, I believe that while it's obvious that a healthy degree of planning and organisation *is* often necessary as a response to those things that *God* initiates, those who struggle most with the suggestion that we allow God to direct affairs appear to be people who plan and organize *in the absence of any clear leading from Him*. Indeed, it seems that frequently the planning and organising is a direct substitute for the presence of the Holy Spirit. Rather than following the 'pillar of cloud by day and the pillar of fire by night' for guidance, there are many people today who are walking in the 'light of their own fires' (Isaiah 50:10). Unfortunately, such fires offer cold comfort to those who gather round them: rather than imbuing everyone present with life-giving warmth and causing them, in turn, to glow with spiritual vitality, these same individuals flicker with barely ignited life themselves. In some cases, their flame dies out altogether.

The fact is, those who insist most strongly that church will not 'happen' unless someone rolls up their sleeves and starts organising things, are most often the ones who are responsible for helping to perpetuate the destructive myth that Christ's body is some kind of thing-in-itself. I also happen to believe that, whilst they may have a motivational effect in the short term, ironically it's these same people—with their 'can-do' rather than 'can-be' attitude—who often play a large role in the eventual discouragement of their fellow Christians (and possibly themselves in the process).

By unconsciously persuading others that Christian 'success' is based on our efforts, they reduce Christianity to some sort of formulaic process, to a gospel of works rather than grace. Inevitably, a spiritual decline follows amongst not only those in leadership, but also in those unfortunate enough to have been placed under their authority; rather than building a strong and healthy body of believers, those in charge contribute to its decline. As Wayne Jacobsen observed:

> '[Problems can] result from a system that puts more credibility in its own efforts than on the power of God, and its toll is taken in personal lives.' [3]

We cannot make church happen by trying to make church happen, nor should we try to in the first place. God never intended us to obsess about this thing we've labelled 'church'. On the contrary, *He,* rather than church, is the main event.

The Church-driven Church

It's an organisation practically designed to perpetuate its own weaknesses.

Peter Sissons

Whilst his comments were directed towards the British Broadcasting Corporation, television journalist Peter Sissons could equally well have been describing another BBC— *Building the Body of Christ.* Our efforts in this area have evolved into an institution more man-made than God-inspired, a project perpetually doomed to failure until we let go of the whole process.

Proverbs 3:5 warns, 'lean not on your own understanding': someone once said if you want to make God laugh, tell him your plans and if you *really* want to make Him laugh, tell Him what you know. I imagine that once He'd composed Himself, God's response to *our* plans for *His* body might sound similar to His Words in Isaiah 55:8-9:

> '"For my thoughts are not your thoughts, neither are your ways my ways," declares the LORD. "As the heavens are higher than the earth, so are my ways higher than your ways and my thoughts than your thoughts."'

God is reminding us that He 'works in mysterious ways, His wonders to perform'; even then, it seems mortal men simply cannot refrain from interfering with God's intentions for His people. It is part of human nature to want to organize, to put things into boxes and people into categories. It's in our DNA to compose lists, make charts and have diagrams for just about everything. Of course, our ability to both visualize and simplify things is not all bad; after all, where would we be without maps, for example? But there are dangers involved when adopting this same mindset within a church or ministry environment, where God requires us to walk by faith rather than sight. A failure to do just this has resulted in the institutional church, the manifestation of man's organisational spirit.

We must learn to resist the temptation to elevate our 'intelligent thoughts', our way of doing things, above the Lord's and thereby attempting to take over from Him; instead we need to stand aside and let God be God. This includes allowing Jesus to do what he promised *he* would do — which is to build *his* ekklesia — and trusting that he has better ways of doing this than anything we can ever come up with.

I do not believe that one can capture the precise shape or form of Christ's body, any more than one can capture the shape or form of God Himself. But more importantly, I don't think we're supposed to try. Indeed, it has been our preoccupation with how the *ekklesia* ought to look rather than with Christ himself which has birthed the aberration of *church-as-a-thing-in-itself*. If we *were* to give God a free hand in shaping his people, then I suspect that not only would the body look like nothing we *might* imagine... it would possibly look different to anything we *can* imagine.

In the meantime, within the pages that follow, I intend to demonstrate from the Word that *church-as-a-thing-in-itself* is an error of biblical proportions and one which must be confronted. For this to happen, we must take a long, hard look at the body in the mirror of Scripture. My fervent hope is that if we look long enough and honestly enough, the scales will fall away from our eyes... and it will be at this point that God's people will finally see that the image reflected there looks more like a golden calf than it does the Bride of Christ.

PART 2

BUILDING ON SAND

There is no church unless it is obedient to the word of God and is guided by it.

John Calvin

7

A TRAGEDY OF ERRORS

Crumbs from the Master's table

I am the bread of life. Whoever comes to me will never go hungry, and whoever believes in me will never be thirsty.

John 6:35

If the church is something other than or extra to that which God intended, then there ought to be evidence — or at least clues — which point to this fact. In this regard, I believe that the evidence can be found through a simple comparison of the practices of God's people in the New Testament with church practices as we typically experience them today. I hope to demonstrate that there are significant discrepancies which suggest that *church* is something we, rather than God, have created.

One relatively simple illustration of this may be found in 1 Corinthians 11:20-22 where we read the following concerning the Lord's Supper:

> 'When you come together, it is not the Lord's Supper you eat, for as you eat, each of you goes ahead without waiting for anybody else. One remains hungry, another gets drunk. Don't you have homes to eat and drink in? Or do you despise the church of God and humiliate those who have nothing? What shall I say to you? Shall I praise you for this? Certainly not!'

It seems clear from this passage that when the early church practiced communion, there was certainly enough food to satisfy an appetite and wine on which to get drunk (let me stress, however, that I'm not endorsing gluttony and drunkenness as a biblical practice!) The point here is simply that one gets the sense that the Lord's Supper was just that — a supper—a full, proper meal. This hardly squares with the current practice of a portion of bread and one beaker of wine or blackcurrant juice being passed along the pews; or, if you're Anglican or Catholic for example, of standing silently in line for a wafer and the same shared wine or blackcurrant juice, served to each person in turn by the minister. We've taken a God-inspired practice—a communal, and most likely noisy, celebratory meal—and desiccated it to such an extent that it has changed into holy ritual—silent, and like one of those wafers, flat and anaemic, drained of vitality by virtue of the fact that it contains the bare minimum of the original practice.

For those prepared to open their eyes and honestly reflect, it's possible to find numerous discrepancies between scriptural precedent and current practice; this one comparison involving the Lord's Supper merely represents in microcosm what *church-as-a-thing-in-itself* has done with so much of what God intended for His people—it has dried it out and reduced it to its bare bones. Christ's body has been denied its proper food and as a consequence it is, spiritually speaking, starving. Jesus multiplied loaves of bread and we've reduced them to wafers and crumbs. Jesus changed water into wine; we've taken the wine and changed it into blackcurrant juice.

All this leads us to a fundamental question: if, indeed, we can admit that we've 'got communion wrong', then we need to consider what other practices we might have taken from Scripture and distorted—and again, to the detriment of the body.

Custom-Made Church

You nullify the word of God for the sake of your tradition.

Mark 16:6b

The preceding description of the way in which communion is practiced, demonstrates that the church is not in fact innocent of ignoring Scripture, and, as we shall see, this is not an isolated example. However, any suggestion that the church has strayed from Scripture to any significant degree is usually met with incredulity, if not outright hostility. It's been my experience that the vast majority of Christians are so utterly convinced that the way we 'do church' is more or less entirely biblical, that they dismiss out of hand any suggestion that many of our existing practices might, in fact, have little or no foundation in the Word of God. Many within the church are completely closed to any suggestion that we might have deviated from God's original plans and replaced them with what, in many instances, are no more than man-made customs that have developed into tradition.

There's a joke which goes:

How many churchgoers does it take to change a light bulb?

'*Change*? You can't *change* it! My grandmother donated that light bulb!'

As *The Fellowship of the Broken Light Bulb*, the church has been content to sit in the dark for far too long, going through the motions of community based merely on rote and ritual. And if someone tries to light a match in order to see more clearly, often it's those around him who blow it out again.

The joke is meant to illustrate that the problem with any kind of tradition is that it is hard to break, especially when it's encrusted with age; we become comfortable with the well-tried manner of doing things, and for many of us, traditions are synonymous with security. As a result, people will fight long and hard to remain within their comfort zone rather than be open to what the Bible might really say on the subject of the church.

Paul found himself having to confront a similar mindset when introducing the New Covenant to a people steeped in tradition; even amongst those Jews who responded to the gospel of grace, there were those who felt themselves being pulled back to the old, familiar ways. A number of passages in the New Testament—for example in the book of Hebrews and in Paul's letter to the Galatians—show that a call was made by groups of converted Jews for all Christians to revert to some features of the Old Covenant, with its emphasis on works rather than faith and which involved (amongst other things) a return to outward ceremony such as circumcision. Ritual and form were in danger of assuming greater importance than the freedom and inner transformation offered by the New Covenant.

It seems that this threat was never fully disposed of, but instead actually managed to secure a permanent stranglehold on the body of Christ. Two thousand years after Paul's efforts to resist the Judaizing of the Christian faith, Arthur Wallis wrote:

> 'When we leave the picture of the churches as Scripture presents them, and plunge into the history of the succeeding centuries, we are immediately aware that a profound change has taken place. How come the development of a priestly caste wearing special vestments and adopting special titles? How is it that churches are now worshipping in 'consecrated buildings', with fixed forms of service, with rites and ceremonies, and numerous other ecclesiastical innovations? It is certain that none of this came from the New Testament. Little of it was inspired by the synagogue. The source of inspiration was the temple worship of the Old Testament. Only here do we find a priestly caste, priestly vestments, priestly rites and ceremonies, and the use of sacred buildings.' [1]

Despite the fact that the central features of Judaistic worship were wound up under the New Covenant, they have gradually been reinstated, but this begs the question — just how and why did the people of God consent to all this?

Things Fall Apart

'Church Not Biblical — Read all about it!'

If our foundational understanding of what we mean by *church* is indeed wrong — if the church is not founded upon Jesus but founded on *itself*... if it is regarded as a *thing-in-itself*, then there will inevitably follow a knock-on or domino effect of sorts. Indeed, when one looks at the history of the church, the following order of events can be observed:

> God is replaced by *Church*; instead of Jesus being the foundation and the focus, church becomes both.

A *clergy* caste of believers emerges, relegating everyone else to the category of *laity*.

The clergy administer the sacraments of Baptism and the Eucharist; as mediators between man and God they control the *meetings* including the *teaching*; in other words, *they control the laity*.

If and when numbers increase, instead of splitting off into more houses, at some point the decision is made to put all the eggs into one basket, so to speak—and a *building* is acquired. All this increases the clergy's ability to maintain control of the laity.

Sooner or later, both the clergy and the buildings require *financing*; as a result, *tithing* is encouraged alongside voluntary giving.

Of course, these aren't the only features which people normally associate with 'church'; however, they do represent some of the more significant, the majority of which are common to most denominations. In this part of the book I'd like to examine those Scriptures that—so we are told—support and therefore justify the existence of such practices. In particular, I want to discuss the scriptural foundations for:

- Church Leadership
- Meeting on the Sabbath
- Conduct of Meetings
- Sermons
- Church Buildings
- Church Finances and Tithing
- Church Structure

The aim of the following sections is to demonstrate that many (if not most) of our current practices are based on tradition and custom rather than Scripture; that what many assume to be biblical is actually just habit. As far as any Scriptures which do, in fact, appear to relate to some features of church as we know it, we are about to see that our application and outworking of them are very far removed from their original form or intention.

This, of course, ought to be hardly surprising: if the very concept of 'church' lacks a biblical foundation then we should expect to find that the church's associated structures, hierarchies and practices suffer from the same lack of biblical support. Or, to put it the other way round, a lack of biblical support for much of what the church does is surely evidence that our concept of church *itself* is erroneous.

Like a broken leg which wasn't set properly in the first place, *church-as-a-thing-in-itself* has been allowed to develop and grow over the centuries into the crooked and consequently dysfunctional shape we find today, and as I said earlier, this is the reason why the Bride is limping. There *is* a way forward, but it requires great courage, since:

The only cure for a broken leg which has been wrongly set is to break and reset it.

SECTION 1: CHURCH LEADERSHIP

The Priesthood of Some Believers

The totally unscriptural distinction between clergy and laity is now openly acknowledged, even from within the establishment. The doctrine of 'the priesthood of all believers' has long been a tenet of the faith, at least among evangelicals...Despite all this the divide between clergy and laity is still there and still clogging the chariot wheels. The full potential of the body of Christ will never be fully released until this wretched distinction is wholly removed. This is not likely to happen so long as those who avow it to be wrong perpetuate it by retaining their clerical office, using their clerical title and wearing their clerical garb. A man may assert that 'the divide' is unbiblical, but no one is likely to take him seriously until he breaks free from an establishment that could not exist without it. It is certainly costly to be a radical.

Arthur Wallis
The Radical Christian

8

SHEPHERDS AND HIRED HANDS:
Those Who Lead for Free and Those Who Lead for a Fee

Divided We Stand

All ministries are the creation of the Church. None can be traced back to Jesus, not even that of the bishop, and least of all that of the priest.

Herbert Haag

The shift in focus from Christ to the Church — from the head to the body — came about as a result of regarding the *ekklesia* as *a-thing-in-itself* and calling it *church*, which in turn set off a kind of slow-moving chain reaction. Historically speaking, one of the first major errors to creep into the church as a result of this change in emphasis was the creation of the clergy-laity system. Despite the fact that it had been abrogated under the New Covenant, the Old Testament priesthood was reintroduced into the *ekklesia* — rebranded, in some quarters, as the clergy — and has remained with us ever since.

Of all the mistakes which flowed from *church-as-a-thing-in-itself*, allowing a clergy caste to develop was probably the greatest, since it has, in turn, affected our meetings and our structures, encouraged an overemphasis on buildings and acted as a catalyst for the introduction of finances in order to prop up the whole edifice.

More importantly, the clergy-laity dichotomy has exerted a restraining effect on the spiritual lives of thousands if not millions of believers. Having shrugged off the shackles of the

Old Covenant by embracing the New, somehow — over time — God's people surrendered the freedom that Christ had bought them and placed themselves under the yoke of the former covenant once more; if anything has served to limit the potential of God's kingdom on earth it is this.

If we want to try and identify how, when or why our idea of leadership went awry, then perhaps a good place to begin would be to examine Jesus' words on the subject.

Authority in the Bible: Jesus' Model
The first shall be last and the last shall be first

Roman society was a highly structured, hierarchical and top-down affair: everyone had their place and everyone knew where that place was within the stratified system the Romans had developed:

> 'In Rome — and across the empire — status mattered. Who and what you were affected how you were treated and how you treated others. In the eyes of Roman law, people were not equal. The main legal distinctions were between those who were free, and those who were slaves. Of those who were classified as free inhabitants of the empire, these were categorized as either citizens or non-citizens. Citizens were further divided into the privileged and the non-privileged — with some Roman citizens being very clearly distinguished by their power and privilege. Legal status marked some fundamental boundaries in the life of a Roman man or woman.' [1]

This Roman-style system of authority is referred to by Jesus in Matthew 20:25-28 (also Mark 10:42–45) where he makes the following point:

> 'Jesus called them together and said, "You know that the rulers of the Gentiles lord it over them, and their high officials exercise authority over them. Not so with you. Instead, whoever wants to become great among you must be your servant, and whoever wants to be first must be your slave — just as the Son of Man did not come to be served, but to serve, and to give his life as a ransom for many."'

It seems very clear that just as Jesus reversed some commonly accepted ideas in his Sermon on the Mount ('You have heard it said... but *I* say...') here he is also taking the conventional idea of what constitutes authority and standing it on its head, denouncing the world's model of *top-down leadership* and introducing a kingdom model of *bottom-up servanthood*; Jesus talks about whoever wants to be first becoming last—that is, he talks about becoming servants and slaves, the absolute rock bottom of the pile as far as status is concerned.

A few chapters later, in Matthew 23:11-12, we find Jesus reaffirming his inverted model of authority and leadership, again with the emphasis on servanthood:

> 'The greatest among you will be your servant. For whoever exalts himself will be humbled, and whoever humbles himself will be exalted.'

True leadership, Jesus is saying, is found in servanthood which he illustrated in the washing of the disciples' feet, and one has to wonder how many people would be as anxious to attain some sort of church office if they knew they were going to be both referred to and treated as a *servant*.

It is noteworthy that when the subject of authority arises today, Jesus' words on the subject are rarely considered. Instead, selected passages from the Epistles are employed which are then used to reach conclusions which are diametrically opposite to those which Jesus presented. Rather than serving the body, the emphasis almost always becomes concerned with the body submitting to the authority of those in leadership.

Now clearly, none of the New Testament authors such as Paul, Peter, or the writer to the Hebrews were in a position to contradict Jesus' teaching on authority and nor would we expect them to. This being the case, if certain passages within the New Testament *appear* to be presenting a model seemingly at odds with Jesus' instructions, the logical conclusion is that they cannot *really* be saying what many have assumed they are saying. And indeed, they aren't; there is no conflict. The fact is Jesus' ideal for leadership is *not* contradicted by Paul or Peter, or anyone else, as we shall see in this chapter.

One has to wonder, then, how on earth we arrived at the situation we have inherited regarding church leadership, with its clergy-laity form of governance and the authority-submission hierarchy that comes with it. The commonly accepted idea of leadership in many churches is that, rather than servanthood and example, spiritual authority is based on the idea of rank (and so we find books with titles such as *God's Generals*, for example). Despite Jesus' exhortation to guard against it, the kind of power structures employed by 'the rulers of the Gentiles' are precisely what we find installed in almost all our churches, and nobody seems to think twice about what is clearly a paradoxical state of affairs.

The Clergy and the Laity – Mind the Gap

We all can't be heroes because somebody has to sit on the curb and clap as they go by.

Will Rogers

In his book, *Priest and Bishop*, Catholic Bible scholar Raymond E. Brown states that the three main functions of the priesthood in the Old Testament were:

- Discerning the will of God through use of the *Urim* and *Thummin*, 'sacred lots that were cast in order to discover God's answer to a problem that had been posed.'
- Teaching
- Performing sacrifices and cultic offerings. [2]

As Brown notes, discerning God's Will increasingly passed over to the prophets, whilst by the time of the New Testament, responsibility for teaching had been assumed by the scribes. The only significant role left to the priests at this time was the sacrifice; but even this function had been rendered obsolete by Jesus and his sacrifice on the cross; as Hebrews 10:12-14 tells us:

'Day after day every priest stands and performs his religious duties; again and again he offers the same sacrifices, which can never take away sins. But when this priest had offered for all time one sacrifice for sins, he sat down at the right hand of God, and since that time he waits for his enemies to be made his footstool.

For by one sacrifice he has made perfect forever those who are being made holy.'

Hans Kung observed in his book, *The Church,* 'the significance of these ideas for the New Testament is that all human priesthood has been fulfilled and finished...'[3] Even Brown, an advocate for the continuing existence of the priesthood, is forced to concede that,

> 'When we move from the OT to the NT, it is striking that while there are pagan priests and Jewish priests on the scene, no individual Christian is ever specifically identified as a priest.' [4]

Clearly a new order had been ushered in, with one of the changes being that the priesthood was no longer restricted to a relative few, but rather that *all* God's people were members of '...a holy priesthood...a royal priesthood' (1 Peter 2:5,9). Jesus has 'made us to be a kingdom and priests to serve his God and Father — to him be glory and power for ever and ever! Amen' (Revelation 1:6).

And yet, whilst Scripture clearly indicates that the New Covenant had abolished the need for a formal, priestly order, one only has to make a brief survey of the history of the church to discover that a separate class of Christians — one which bore a striking resemblance to the Old Testament priesthood — became a feature of the *ekklesia* surprisingly early on. In *The Radical Christian,* Arthur Wallis said the following:

> '[No developments were] more detrimental in the long term than the return to the priestly caste of the Old Testament. It brought a great divide between priests and people. It divided the flock of God into clergy and laity. It shackled the bulk of every congregation in ignorance, passivity and non-involvement. All priestly functions were now left to 'the professionals'. "Weren't they paid to do the job?"' [5]

But if, as Wallis implied, all this was contrary to the will of God, then how were such deleterious developments allowed to take place within the body of Christ? How did the priesthood of all believers that we see inaugurated in the New Testament mutate into the clergy-laity model, complete with bishops, elders and deacons such as we find in the church today?

Authority in the Bible: The New Testament Model

You don't have to hold a position in order to be a leader

Anthony J D'Angelo

I hope to demonstrate in what follows that whilst Scripture clearly identifies the fact that people have functions, ministries, gifts or roles—call them what you will—they are not to be mistaken as offices or positions, and neither should they be titles by which we label other people. This is most neatly illustrated in 1 Peter 5:1-3:

> 'To the *elders* among you, I appeal as a fellow *elder*...Be *shepherds* of God's flock that is under your care, serving as *overseers*—not because you must, but because you are willing, as God wants you to be; not greedy for money, but *eager to serve; not lording it over those entrusted to you, but being examples to the flock.*'

Peter is addressing the elders within his own fellowship and exhorting them to be shepherds, overseers, servants and examples to the flock; each elder was to embody, as far as possible, all of these qualities. However, over time, these characteristics—these roles—were divided piecemeal, formalized into ecclesiastical offices and parcelled out. This process is perhaps best illustrated by the following joke:

Scotland Yard is trying to track down a criminal whom it believes has fled to a remote part of Britain. It sends three mugshots of the fugitive to a rural police station—a front view along with left and right profiles—and then it waits for results. A few weeks later and with no news from their colleagues, someone at the Yard decides to call up the station in order to get a progress report:

'Hello, it's Scotland Yard here. Just wondered if you'd got anywhere with the case we sent down to you?'

The local bobby at the other end of the phone answers enthusiastically:

'We're doing really well. We've caught two of them and are close to arresting the third.'

This is not unlike the situation we find when it comes to the subject of church leadership. What 1 Peter 5:1-3 and other passages of Scripture are meant to illustrate is that an elder not only oversaw but he also shepherded and served. However, over time, *church-as-a-thing-in-itself* has managed to take the characteristics of this one individual and — like the mugshots — divided them into at least *four distinct leadership offices*: Elder; Pastor (from the Latin word for *shepherd*); Bishop (derived from *piscop* in *episcopoi*, the Greek word translated as *overseer*); and finally, Deacon (from *diakonos*, the Greek for *servant*). Unfortunately, unlike the joke about Scotland Yard, it's no laughing matter. Gradually, these office-bearers assumed a status which was the polar opposite of a servant; it separated them from everyone else, so that rather than *being among* the flock, as we read in 1 Peter 5:1, they found themselves *ruling over* it in a way which usurped the headship of Christ.

Returning to Peter's letter, he goes on to address the young men in the fellowship: 'be submissive to those who are older' (verse 5a). The Greek word for *older — presbuteros —* is the same as the one used for *elder* also in this passage, reinforcing the idea that the word 'elder' does not represent an ecclesiastical office but simply the social status afforded by advancing years; the young deferring to the old is something found in many cultures and has nothing to do with ecclesiastical offices or titles. Thus, we find Peter encouraging younger men to be submissive to the elders *because they are older* and — hopefully — wiser believers to whom they could turn as examples. Peter goes on to say:

> 'All of you, clothe yourselves with humility toward one another, because, "God opposes the proud but gives grace to the humble"' (verse 5b).

Both young and old alike are encouraged to be humble in their dealings with one another. This is hardly support for an autocratic system of church government, especially when we look back at Peter's words to the elders in verse 3 and which reflect Jesus' words in Matthew 20:25-28 regarding servanthood: '...*eager to serve; not lording it over those entrusted to you, but being examples to the flock.*'

A final point regarding the New Testament's teaching on leadership comes from Galatians 2:2. Here Paul describes his visit to the church in Jerusalem and he refers to '...those who *seemed* to be leaders...' A few verses later, he says, 'As for those who seemed to be important—whatever they were makes no difference to me; God does not judge by external appearance...' (Galatians 2:6). It strikes me as very telling that Paul did not state that he had talked to the Bishops, Elders or Pastors in Jerusalem, but to people whom, as far as he could tell, 'seemed' to be the leaders. This agrees with Jesus' teaching in Matthew 23:10:

> 'Do not be called leaders; for One is your Leader, *that is,* Christ.' [NASB] [6]

It is evident that despite what seem to be clear biblical guidelines regarding leadership, we have arrived at the exact *opposite* of Jesus' instructions. Almost all churches, regardless of denomination, have a clearly designated leadership with associated titles. We've already seen how these titles emerged due to roles gradually being reinvented as offices, helping to promote a bifurcation within the Christian community of the leaders and the led.

However, this fact alone does not fully explain how such a division came about—a division that enabled a mediating priestly order to re-emerge from the shadow of the Old Testament. What follows is an effort to provide at least some of the known details concerning the whole process. It is, of necessity, a very broad-brushed summary of how our clergy-laity model came into existence and has managed to remain with us, despite the absence of any biblical support.

The Death and Resurrection of the Priesthood
The Old has gone, the Old has come...

The first reference we have to the existence of the laity is found in Clement of Rome's *First Epistle to the Corinthians*, which was penned in 96 AD or thereabouts, and which also draws parallels between the Old Testament priesthood and the clergy. Writing around 110 AD, Ignatius, the Bishop of Antioch, makes reference in his letters not only to bishops like himself, but also to the supporting offices of elders and deacons.[7] Centuries later, Church historians would describe this clergy caste of bishops-elders-deacons as the *threefold ministry*. Whilst, at least initially, these office-bearers had greater authority than everyone else within their own local church, they were at this time still accountable to the main body of that same church. That said, the seeds had been planted for a gradual role reversal insofar as *the body was beginning to serve the leadership.*

A series of events stretching over several centuries would enable the clergy — now firmly established as a feature of the church — to enlarge its remit, thereby increasing its power over the body of Christ. The initial accountability of the clergy gradually diminished and was replaced by an increasing autocracy as the authority of the bishops grew in response to several factors, some of which will now be considered.

Combating Heresy

While the episcopate defended the creed of the Church against Gnosticism, and altered it in defending, it won possession of the Church herself as the reward of its chivalry.

Rudolph Sohm

God's people continually had to guard against various heresies and instances of false teaching: the refutation of *Gnosticism* (a belief system which, amongst other things, denied that Jesus had a real, physical body and which had serious implications concerning his birth, death and resurrection) and opposition to the Judaizing of gentile converts, to take two just examples, are the subjects of several New Testament books such as Galatians and Colossians. Some heresies were particularly vigorous, especially those of *Marcion* and *Montanus,* both of whom arrived independently on the scene sometime after the events described in the New Testament. However, whilst the validity of their teaching was rightly contested by the church, the attempts to dispose of the threat they presented led to unforeseen consequences which, in turn, would further corrupt the body of Christ.

Marcion

Marcion made his presence felt around the middle of the second century: the challenge he presented to the Christian community was rooted in the fact that he could not reconcile the God of the Old Testament with the God of the New. Essentially, he rejected the Old Testament as it stood, believing its teachings to be incompatible with the teachings of Jesus, whilst at the same time—and to make matters worse—he also endorsed ideas similar to those found in Gnosticism. However, despite holding clearly unbiblical views, Marcion nevertheless attracted a large following which spread widely throughout Christendom and persisted for several centuries.

Various heresies had, of course, always existed, but with Christians divided amongst themselves to a degree perhaps not seen before, it became clear that in order to combat false teaching there was a 'need for an agreed creed':

> 'Christianity now implied more than a life lived in the presence of God and Christ; it meant a doctrine to be protected by a creed or a form...The succession of office-bearers in the churches was the guarantee for the correctness of the tradition suggested by Irenaeus, urged by Tertullian...' [8]

The suppression of Marcionism thus acted as a catalyst for the development of the New Testament canon which would act as a benchmark against which all teaching could be measured; it led to the establishment of a centralized church law, and it also instigated a new look at how the church was structured. One direct outcome of all this was that, since it was the office-bearers who formulated that which would be regarded as orthodoxy, and who subsequently acted as defenders and guarantors of this same orthodoxy, it was this same group of people who now found themselves in a position of greater influence and authority than before. Within this developing context one might imagine the clergy as representing 'The Thin Red Line' between order and anarchy; but the problem was that the very act of protecting true doctrine via an intermediary priesthood reinforced the position of a clerical order which, in itself, stood outside scriptural precedent.

Montanus

In Ephesians 4:11, we read:

> 'So Christ himself gave the apostles, the prophets, the evangelists, the pastors and teachers, to equip his people for works of service, so that the body of Christ may be built up until we all reach unity in the faith and in the knowledge of the Son of God and become mature, attaining to the whole measure of the fullness of Christ.'

Up to the time of Montanus' arrival in the mid-to-late second century, ministries could, broadly speaking, be classified into two distinct groups. Firstly, there were *apostles*, *prophets* and *teachers* who had a roving commission and who brought the word of God to the churches they visited;[9] secondly, there were the local ministries — which would later be designated as *bishop*, *elder* and *deacon* — and which emerged from fellowships which had been established by the former group.

Whilst Paul clearly expected leaders to be present within every body of believers, his writings do not suggest that he anticipated the formation of anything like the bishop-elder-deacon hierarchy. This raises the question as to how the so-called *threefold ministry* (something not identified in Scripture) became established while the apostles and prophets (who *are* present in Scripture) all but disappeared from the pages of history.[10] Why, out of all the various ministries listed in Ephesians 4:11, did the *pastor* come to be regarded as having a more important 'office' than that of apostle, prophet, evangelist or teacher? Just how, exactly, did the pastor end up as 'the last man standing' in terms of ultimate authority within many of our churches today?

In the early church, those with an itinerant ministry were undoubtedly given authority over the local leadership, especially in matters of discipline. However, the authority of these wandering groups of believers increasingly became a source of contention as the role and influence of the local, bishop-led clergies increased, particularly after their victory over Marcion. This would all come to a head with Montanus' arrival on the scene; he brought with him a teaching which became known as the New Prophecy, and if Marcion had delivered a right hook to the body, Montanus was about to follow up with a left.

Montanus and his followers laid particular emphasis on prophecy, but both the manner in which they delivered their prophecies along with some of the content of their prophetic utterances caused concern within the Christian community. It's difficult today to know to what degree Montanism was indeed heretical; it's interesting to note that Tertullian, described as 'the father of Latin Christianity' and thought to be the person who coined the word *Trinity*, was one of its chief proponents, and the movement attracted a large following which — like Marcionism — continued to exist for several centuries before finally disappearing.

The Montanists maintained — as had all prophets before them — that the ministry of prophecy superseded that of the bishops. However, this time round, the bishops were more inclined to flex the muscles they had developed grappling with and prevailing over the Marcionites not so many years before; quite apart from the issue of whether Montanus was indeed heretical or otherwise, far from accepting that those with a prophetic gift ought to have the final say on matters affecting the local churches (as they might have done in earlier times) the clergy now insisted that any true prophet would submit to *their* authority instead.

The upshot of this power struggle was, to put it simply, that the Montanists lost. Part of the fallout from these events was that, whilst the church continued to acknowledge the validity of prophecy, the status of the prophet and the apostle were nevertheless greatly diminished. Their function as the mouthpiece of God became appropriated to an increased degree by the local leadership, leaving the way open for the latter to gain ascendency over those with an itinerant ministry.

One of the main outcomes of these internecine disputes, then, was a cementing of the control of the clergy and in particular, that of the bishop:

'The tendency was to think that the churches were summed up in their bishops, and these officials thus acquired a new position with reference to the whole church.' [11]

'By the beginning of the 3rd century it was everywhere accepted. When we seek to trace the causes why the college of elders received a president, who became the centre of all the ecclesiastical life in the local church and the one potent office-bearer, we are reduced to conjecture.' [12]

Whilst the Christian community was certainly correct in combating Marcion's and Montanus' teaching, the church's victory over them was pyrrhic. Ironically, in resisting false doctrine, the church simply reinforced a more subtle and possibly equally debilitating one—namely, the necessity of a separate, priestly order which would act as an intermediary between God and the rest of the *ekklesia*.

Writing around the end of the second century, Tertullian made his own contribution to the establishment of *church-as-a-thing-in-itself*. He is the first person on record to apply the term 'priest' to the bishops and other clerics,[13] arguing that they alone were responsible for the ministry of 'word and sacrament', conducting baptisms, offering the Eucharist and delivering teaching within the church. The most obvious corollary of this was that it stripped from the body the biblically supported notion of the priesthood of all believers.

We also find that Tertullian had borrowed the nomenclature used by the Romans to divide their own society into two groups—*ordo* referring to people of rank (from which we obtain the word 'ordination') and *pleb*, referring to the common people—and applied it to the church. Needless to say, *ordo* referred to the clergy, while the laity were referred to as *plebs*:

'Such language proved very significant. In Roman thinking, people of any importance belonged to one *ordo* (class or rank) or another, the nobodies who had no order were the *plebs*. As the church adopted this sort of language, it fostered the idea that lay Christians were *plebs*—nobodies. The Christians of significance were the clergy, designated as such by their solemn ordinations.' [14]

Tertullian would hand down his ecclesiology like a family heirloom, to be taken up and developed by possibly his most well-known successor whose own legacy we shall now examine.

The Perfect Storm

Where the Bishop is, there is the Church.   Cyprian

In the middle of the third century there occurred a confluence of circumstances which would not only confer even greater authority upon the clergy, but which would expand the role of the bishops further still to include something of greater concern than that of mere power over the people of God.

Beginning in 250 AD, persecution of Christians was renewed under the Roman emperor Decius; rather like the Nazi pogrom against the Jews many centuries later, Decius' efforts were much more thorough and systematic than that of his predecessors, reaching into every corner and village of the empire. The persecution was particularly severe in Carthage, Hannibal's old stamping ground and the home of Tertullian who had died there twenty-five years previously; but it was also where Cyprian — destined to become one of the most influential people in church history — presided as bishop.

A lawyer and teacher of rhetoric who became a Christian in middle age, Cyprian was elevated to the position of bishop a mere two years after his baptism, and it was during his tenure that the clergy both in Carthage and further afield took on a disturbingly new character. Roman persecution provided Cyprian with extra impetus in the formulation and introduction of practices new to the church — practices that would prove to be highly damaging.

Cyprian, possibly more than any of his predecessors, was obsessed with the authority of the bishop, demanding obedience to the office or suffer the pain of excommunication. Consider, for instance, the following pronouncements:

'God speaks through the bishop as He formerly spoke through His apostles, and the Church is founded on the bishops, and every act of the Church is controlled by these same rulers.' [15]

'It is a fundamental and inviolable principle that the Church is nothing other than the people united around their Bishop and the flock bound to their shepherd. The Bishop is in the Church and the Church in the Bishop, and if anyone is not with the Bishop, he is not in the Church.' [16]

Cyprian's own conception of the local bishop having complete control of his church would inevitably lead others, in turn, to conclude that the establishment of a 'bishop of bishops' was the only logical outcome for ruling the church universal. Thus would Cyprian's ecclesiology lend support to those who followed him for the creation of a super-bishop — the pope — whose position would be justified and sustained by inventing the unbiblical doctrines of apostolic succession and papal supremacy.

More disturbingly, if that's possible, under Cyprian's supervision the role of the clergy gradually expanded from one of simple autocracy (which was bad enough) to include the role of *mediation,* thereby strengthening their grip further still. As with Tertullian, as far as Cyprian was concerned, priest and bishop were synonymous terms, and in his eyes, the ministry of the bishop was as a mediating priest who offered Christ's sacrifice — in the form of the Eucharist — on behalf of the people, and it was through the administration of the sacraments of Baptism and the Eucharist that church leaders began to assume a role reminiscent of the sacrificing priesthood of the Old Testament:

'[Cyprian] conceived that the bishops were a special priesthood and had a special sacrifice to offer...The whole conception of Christian thought began to change, and the change dates from Cyprian and his influence.' [17]

This 'sacrificing priesthood' further secured its foothold on the top rung of a ladder it had itself constructed, and in so doing — and by the greatest of ironies — it *sacrificed the priesthood of all believers.* In the words of Church historian Allen Brent, Cyprian's legacy failed 'abysmally' and 'spectacularly'[18], crippling the body for centuries to come.

But it wasn't only Cyprian's innovations which had such a damaging effect on Christ's people. There were other polluted streams which began to pool within the church. Whilst most people are aware of the more well-known clerical offices such as bishop, elder, deacon and so on (which Cyprian did his utmost to develop, reinforce and protect, particularly that of the bishop) what's not so well known is the fact that the clergy of the third century also had the following offices: subdeacons, exorcists, readers, acolytes, door-keepers and even grave-diggers! One might wonder from where these ministries derived — they certainly don't appear in any lists Paul wrote in his letters: some of them were in fact directly transplanted from the surrounding pagan religions, and whilst most of these offices have long-since disappeared, the very fact that they were adopted at all provides a useful insight into the mindset of the church during this period.

As we come to the close of the third century, we find that the distance between the clergy and the laity had become even wider than before: the majority of Christians had become increasingly side-lined within the body, their main function being merely to attend church services, their primary contribution one of simple obedience — something which has continued right up to the present. *Church*, as an organisation to be protected by the clergy, had become more important than the spiritual growth of the ordinary men and women who looked to them for guidance. And the whole process of decay to which the body was subject didn't stop there.

It was set to become worse still.

Further Down the Slippery Slope

The conquering Christian Church took its hierarchic weapons from the arsenal of the enemy.

Theodor Mommsen

Periodic persecution by various Roman emperors during the first three centuries of the church's existence helped to ensure that the clergy remained relatively limited in number. Unfortunately, this would all change during the reign of Constantine in the 4th century: the Edict of Milan in 313 AD officially granted Christians freedom of religious expression, and not only was the threat of persecution lifted, but in addition a number of highly attractive 'perks' came with the office of bishop. Here are just a few examples:

- Clergy, along with their wives, children, and servants, did not have to pay any taxes, and they enjoyed tax-exempt status if they started their own business.

- Clergy were exempt from all compulsory public services and municipal duties. Their sons were expected to continue in the clergy and were therefore able to enjoy the same privileges unless obligated by service in the Senate.

- Bishops were allowed to retain property.

- Bishops were afforded a rank equal to senators. [19]

As a direct result of Constantine's reforms, things changed dramatically and most definitely not for the better. Suddenly there was a huge increase in the number of those who 'felt called' into ministry, resulting in the exponential growth of a professional clergy. A mere seven years after the Edict of Milan, Constantine found himself having to draw up laws to prevent wealthy individuals from avoiding taxes by becoming clerics.[20] Further to this, and again, in direct contradiction to Jesus' instructions on the subject of leadership, some of the ideas for the governance of God's people began to be patterned on that of the 'rulers of the gentiles': the church began to develop an increasingly hierarchical and centralized structure with the clerics overseeing a growing number of churches and not just their own. This in turn created a need for a more efficient administrative model... and it just so happened that the Romans already had one which fit the bill.

Just as Roman governors were representatives of the emperor, so the bishops saw themselves as God's representatives, supposedly set there by His authority and responsible to Him alone, enjoying a form of divine right. These 'ambassadors of God' established themselves and their supporting structures throughout the empire, using as a template not only the administrative and organisational but also the ceremonial model of the imperial, pagan state religion. By the end of the fourth century,

> 'The chasuble, dalmatic, stole, and maniple (items of episcopal garb) were borrowed directly from the Roman magistracy, and in every municipality where there had been a *flamen* (a priest of a particular deity) to supervise the worship of the emperor, there was now a bishop who inherited his privileges. These included an imperial salary, a seat on the city council, the right of direct access to the emperor, and rank second only to the provincial governor. Bishops were now becoming persons of great influence and office, accompanied by a retinue of servants bearing their insignia of office in processions, which instead of the Roman eagle was now the cross.' [21]

Over time, other offices were added to the existing clerical hierarchy, based not on Scripture but once again on Roman geopolitical divisions. For example, the bishops of the five major cities of the Christianized empire (Rome, Constantinople, Alexandria, Antioch and Jerusalem) were afforded the office of *Patriarch* and were inferior in rank only to the pope himself; below them were the *Metropolitans*, these being bishops of the churches in the provincial capitals and in turn, superior to other bishops in the province. This Roman-inspired administrative model ran through Christian organisation from top to bottom, and so we find, for example, that Christian councils would often have the same number of members as found in pagan assemblies.

> 'The spirit of compromise with paganism, which this imitation even of the externals of pagan religious administration could scarcely fail to produce, [led] to much corruption both in the beliefs and in the life of the Christian Church.' [22]

Many of the features associated with *church-as-a-thing-in-itself* flourished on Constantine's watch: as we shall see in Chapter 12, he ordered that large numbers of church buildings be erected, and within those buildings we find that fixed forms of worship were observed which had no basis in Scripture but rather, were incorporated and adapted from paganism. It is from this source rather than the Bible that we derived ceremonies involving one-person orations, candles and incense, liturgies and choirs, to list just a few.

Tragically, while the Roman Empire has long since passed, many of the extra-biblical practices which originated either before or during that time—including the clergy-laity system—continue to fetter Christ's people nearly two thousand years later.

Building on the Wrong Rock
Rock and Role

When Jesus said to Peter, 'On this rock I will build my church', to which rock was he referring? In *How to Choose a Bible Version,* Robert L. Thomas writes:

> 'Roman Catholic translations of Matthew 16:18 often have some type of note to support the view that Peter is the 'rock' on which Christ built the church. That is the case because of that organisation's belief that Peter was the first pope of the Roman Catholic Church.' [23]

'This rock' was assumed to be concerned with matters of authority, rather than—as we shall see in a moment—a matter of faith. Unfortunately, the misinterpretation of Jesus' words by people of influence within the early church increasingly burdened the *ekklesia* with a form of church governance which, as we've already seen, is difficult if not impossible to locate within the New Testament. Eventually it furnished us with the 'Vicar of Christ' — the pope.

Of course, outside of the Catholic Church, the traditional 'take' on Matthew 16:18 is that the rock is Peter's confession rather than Peter himself; that Jesus is simply stating that he will build his *ekklesia* upon a foundation which is constituted by those who declare, by faith, that Jesus is 'the Christ, the Son of the living God.' But since this interpretation didn't gain widespread currency until well over a thousand years after the fact, it meant that whilst the Reformers denounced the *papacy* as unscriptural, the legacy of a hierarchical church government remained. Many of the other offices within the Catholic Church carried over into the majority of Protestant denominations—for example, the Catholic *priest* was simply replaced with the *pastor*. However, as we've just seen, not only is the priestly office invalid, but by implication, the office of *pastor*—along with all the other offices found within both branches of Christianity—is as insupportable from Scripture as that of the pope.

Human beings seem to have a perpetual tendency to have somebody else talk to God for them. We are content to have the message second-hand. One of Israel's fatal mistakes was their insistence upon having a human king rather than resting in the theocratic rule of God over them. We can detect a note of sadness in the word of the Lord, "They have rejected me from being king over them" (1 Samuel 8.7). The history of religion is the story of an almost desperate scramble to have a king, a mediator, a priest, a pastor, a go-between. In this way we do not need to go to God ourselves...We do not need to observe Western culture very closely to realise that it is captivated by the religion of the mediator.

Richard Foster
Celebration of Discipline

9

BROUGHT TO BOOK

Invasion of the Body Snatchers

No Bishop, no King   *James I*

As time progressed, the separation of the clergy and the laity became an increasingly accepted and entrenched feature of the church throughout Christendom. However, this didn't mean there weren't dissenters: church history is replete with the names of individuals and movements who fought for a return to a more biblical model of pastoral oversight, but whose efforts would come to nothing, crushed by the weight of the church hierarchy.

One obvious, powerful tool for reform would have been (and still remains) the production of a Bible unsullied by translators with a particular agenda in mind. Of course, both Wycliffe and Tyndale, amongst others, *did* attempt just such a thing, but, as we saw earlier, their efforts were undone by the King James translation.

Whilst we recall that the commissioning of the King James Bible was the most significant outcome of the Hampton Court conference, we also need to remember that the latter was convened by James initially in order to discuss the problems which existed between the Anglicans and Puritans, with the hope of 'reformation of some things amiss in ecclesiastical matters.' The Puritans were concerned about some of the practices and structures within the Anglican Church, which they saw as being very similar to those of Roman Catholicism and they were pressing for change. Amongst other things, the Puritans *wanted to be exempt from certain ceremonies and rituals which they claimed were not found in the written Word and to reform the hierarchies which put the bishops firmly at the top.* This point was underscored by the fact that whilst the bishops arrived at the conference in full regalia, the Puritans — as was their practice — turned up in normal attire.

The idea for a new Bible translation was that of John Rainolds, the leader of the Puritan delegation, whose intent was 'the removal of the High Church terminology used in the Bishop's Bible.'[1] However, since James ruled the Church through his bishops who in turn supported his supremacy as head of state, the fifty or so scholars who were given responsibility for the translation were directed *not* to depart from the offending 'High Church terminology' but rather to reinforce it:

> 'King James gave the translators instructions, which were...to guarantee that the new version would conform to the ecclesiology of the Church of England...He wanted the episcopal structure of the Established Church, and traditional beliefs about an ordained clergy to be reflected in the new translation.' [2]

In, *Bible: The Story of The King James Version,* Gordon Campbell writes:

> 'The decision to retain 'bishop' (instead of 'elder' or 'senior') reflects a decision to favour episcopacy rather than presbyterianism as a model of church government; as disagreement about the form of government was a gaping fault line between the church hierarchy and the Puritan minority, this decision was critically important: the KJV was not intended to be a puritan Bible.' [3]

As a result of James' instructions, the version of the Bible which bears his name is littered with words like bishop, ordain, appoint, obey, submit, and so on — words which *aren't* in the original Greek. The introduction of these terms reinforced the idea of a hierarchical authority structure and supported the notion of a clergy as distinct from everyone else — which, of course, was the whole point.

Spin Doctors

He who controls the language controls the masses.

Saul Alinsky, Rules for Radicals

A case by case review of each and every instance of questionable translation is beyond the scope of this book; however, it's worth giving one or two examples of a distinctly unhelpful choice of word. For instance, in Romans 12:4, *praxis* was translated as 'office' instead of 'function', so that the KJV reads:

> '...we have many members in one body, and all members have not the same office:'

Other translations such as the NIV render the same verse more accurately as:

> 'For just as each of us has one body with many members, and these members do not all have the same function...'

Another example — one which is often cited as support for authoritarian leadership within the church — is found in Hebrews 13:17. In the KJV, it reads:

> 'Obey them that have the rule over you, and submit yourselves:'

This is a striking example of a piece of text being translated, once again, with a particular agenda in mind. The three words, *obey, rule* and *submit* reinforce one another to drive home the sense of a two-tier authority structure — the rulers and the ruled.

Concerning this, Frank Viola notes that the Greek word translated as 'obey' is '*peitho*', which connotes the idea of being *persuaded by someone's example;* [4] as for the word translated as *rule* – *hēgeomai* — this can also be written as *lead* or even *guide*. Finally, the Greek word translated as 'submit' — *hupeikete* — can also be understood to mean to *yield* or *defer*. Thus, an alternative rendition of Hebrews 13:17 might well read, 'Be persuaded by those who guide you, and defer to them.' This offers quite a different sense of what the passage is saying compared to the doctored version which has been used by some to enforce compliance, and it certainly seems to be far more consistent with Jesus' words regarding authority.

Over the centuries, older, more reliable Greek and Hebrew manuscripts have been discovered and made available for Bible translators: this, combined with less state interference means that later Bible versions have rectified some of these translation errors; however, problematic passages still exist even in these newer versions, and as a result mis-understandings concerning the New Testament's message regarding authority remain with us today. A case in point is the following:

Dis-appointing Elders
By their fruit you will recognize them. *Matthew 7:16*

In the KJV and some other versions, Acts 14:23 reads:

'Paul and Barnabas *ordained* elders for them in each church and, with prayer and fasting, committed them to the Lord, in whom they had put their trust.'

In Titus 1:5 (also KJV) we read:

'The reason I left you in Crete was that you might put in order what was left unfinished and *ordain* elders in every town, as I directed you.'

With its implication of ecclesiastical office, the use of the word *ordain* is yet another example of the KJV's efforts to reinforce the clergy model: the word derives from *ordo*, which as we saw earlier, was imported into the church from Roman society and signified a person of rank. Ordination was (and remains) a religious practice instituted by the church *after* the period of the New Testament and when the *ekklesia* had already begun to lose its way; as such it would not have meant anything to the first Christians, and to offer a translation in this way is simply—and one could argue, deliberately—misleading. The term 'ordain' was a word superimposed onto biblical texts, more transplanted than translated.

Whilst other versions such as the NIV use the word 'appoint' rather than 'ordain', most people maintain that this does not detract in any way from the argument that both Acts 14 and Titus 1 provide biblical support for church offices. But is this really the case?

The Greek word translated as 'appoint/ordain' in Titus is *kathistēmi*, whilst in Acts the word *cheirotoneō* is also translated as 'appoint' or 'ordain'. Both *kathistēmi* and *cheirotoneō*,

> '...carry the idea of acknowledging those whom others have already endorsed. This is how these words are used outside the NT in first-century literature...Biblical recognition is merely the outward confirmation by the church of those who have already been charged by the Spirit to a specific task.' [5]

The only other time *cheirotoneō* appears in the New Testament is in 2 Corinthians 8:19, where mention is made of the fact that Titus (coincidentally) has been chosen (*cheirotoneō*) to help collect money from the Corinthian church. Whilst there is clearly no problem in saying that Titus had been appointed for the task, he certainly wouldn't have needed to be *ordained* — or anything similar — in order to fulfil it; he was simply selected since he exhibited the kind of trustworthy character which Paul would later instruct Titus himself to look for in those elders who desired to serve as overseers of the Christian community in Crete (Titus 1:6-8).

History tells us that elders would have already existed in each and every Jewish community which Paul visited with the purpose of proclaiming the gospel: this is confirmed by the Old Testament which is replete with references to elders of villages, towns and cities; they were the 'go-to' people when communal decisions needed to be made or local disputes needed to be resolved. Some of these existing elders would have responded to the gospel message, and — because they were already elders in the wider community — they would have had a great deal of influence within the newly formed Christian body. However, judging from Paul's letter to Titus it would appear that, despite having made a profession of faith, the lives of some of the newly converted elders in Crete did not exhibit 'fruit in keeping with repentance' (Matthew 3:8): 'They claim to know God, but by their actions they deny him' (Titus 1:16). Paul's instruction to Titus was therefore to 'appoint' — in other words, to recognize and endorse — only those elders who modelled 'the fruits of the Spirit'.

When verse 5 is understood in this way, I would suggest that the true meaning of Paul's words becomes evident. It becomes clear that Paul is *not*, as some read it, instructing Titus to use some kind of template for church governance in order to create an authority structure out of thin air; rather, he is trying to ensure that sound, Christian leadership-by-example emerges from the problematic context within which Titus had found himself.

❖   ❖   ❖

Before closing this section, I'd like to turn to one final example of how language can be misapplied in order to redirect the meaning of a passage of Scripture. In 1 Timothy 3:10 the NIV reads:

> 'They must first be tested; and then if there is nothing against them, let them *serve as deacons*.'

This translation is extremely misleading and does grave injustice to the original: 'serving as deacons' would mean 'serving as servants' and is clearly tautological; more importantly, it suggests or implies the existence of the office of deacon. In fact, the word *diakonos* appears just once in the text, and the Lexham English Bible (a recent and relatively literal translation) renders the verse thus:

> '...and these also must be tested first; then let them serve if they are above reproach.'

It is little wonder that so many people are convinced that the kind of government found in the vast majority of churches is entirely biblical. The fact that it manifestly *is not*, has served neither the body nor the kingdom well.

Losing Ground by Forging a Head

The real leader has no need to lead—he is content to point the way.
Henry Miller

We saw earlier how the mistranslation of the individual word *ekklesia* was and continues to be an important contributing factor in perpetuating *church-as-a-thing-in-itself...* but as we've also just seen, the mishandling of the Word didn't stop there.

The Bible's message concerning pastoral care was subtly distorted by those who stood to gain from such endeavours; by manipulating Scripture—either directly by tinkering with the translation, or indirectly by employing very selective teaching—a model of church governance was introduced which, coincidentally, put those who promoted it in charge. The church became, as Brunner put it, 'a hierarchical, sacerdotal community in which the grace of God is controlled by a spiritual elite.' [6]

Compounding the whole problem of authority is the fact that an autocratic leadership model is the one that many see presently outworked in their fellowships, with the result that the vast majority of people today simply accept such authority structures as a given. Most people—whether clergy or laity—read passages relating to leadership and authority in the light of their current experience, and as a result it doesn't occur to them to investigate the validity of a hierarchy which, by its very existence, relegates the majority to a second-class status not found in the Bible. An understanding regarding authority and submission has thus been inherited which has its origins in a flawed concept of leadership dating back almost two millennia.

There are too many in positions of authority who appear only too happy to cherry-pick from those Scriptures that, on the surface, appear to suggest a hierarchical form of church leadership; they manipulate the texts and then extrapolate from them in order to both justify and preserve their role within it. At the same time, such individuals conveniently ignore those passages which tell us that true leadership is characterized by servanthood—those verses which state that kingdom authority is the antithesis of that found in the world.

The truth of the matter is that there exists in some *a need to lead*—and by lead, I mean in the worldly rather than the biblical sense. For example, in 3 John 1:9 we find the following:

'I wrote to the church, but Diotrephes, who loves to be first, will have nothing to do with us.'

It's a sad fact that, judging from church history, Diotrephes' attitude was far from unique. His example illustrates a problem which has plagued the Christian community to this day. In *Excellence in Leadership: The pattern of Nehemiah,* John White wrote:

> 'Since the world began, there have been two ideas about being a leader. One is that to be a leader you must show who is the boss. The other idea — to serve. The first idea is by far the more common.' [7]

One of man's greatest weaknesses — namely, the desire to lord it over others as opposed to serving them — has been exploited by Satan who has thereby succeeded in substantially incapacitating the whole body. As with the example of Diotrephes, 'who loved to be first', it is often a character defect rather than a positive character trait which enables some to become established in positions of authority:

> 'The free man has never been a religious tyrant, nor has he sought to lord it over God's heritage. It is fear and lack of self-assurance that has led some men to try to bring others under their feet. They have had some interest to protect, some position to secure, so they have demanded subjection from their followers as a guarantee of their own safety...(they) will grow smaller and smaller trying to get big...and their whole relationship toward other Christians will be one of suspicion and mistrust.' [8]

Not all the blame can be laid at the door of those who are cut from the same cloth as Diotrephes, however: on the other side of the coin, we must allow for the fact that there is a deep-seated proclivity in many human beings to have someone else take charge — *a need to be led* — and God's people appear to be as vulnerable to this as anyone else. For instance, in 1 Samuel 8:19-20 we read how, despite God's intentions to the contrary, the Israelites wanted a human figurehead to lead them rather than to rely on the invisible God:

> '"We want a king over us. Then we will be like all the other nations, with a king to lead us and to go out before us and fight our battles."'

Jeremiah 5:31 reveals the same weakness resurfacing many years later and God lamenting the fact that,

'...the priests rule by their own authority, and my people love it this way.'

This verse suggests a kind of dysfunctional co-dependency amongst God's people—and yet despite God's clear disapproval, this unhealthy state of affairs continues to be encouraged by those who, through the use of carefully selected passages, attempt to provide a thin veneer of scriptural support for an authority structure which, in point of fact, does not in itself have a shred of genuine biblical authority.

In George Orwell's *Animal Farm*, the slogan, *All animals are equal, but some are more equal than others* is used to create and reinforce a two-tier authority system within the community; much the same happens in our churches today. Like the sheep in George Orwell's *Animal Farm*, many are only too eager to accept the pronouncements of their leaders on the subject of authority, dutifully obeying their directives, with far-reaching and disastrous results.

The symbiotic relationship between those few who need to lead and the vast majority of the remainder who need to be led represents a purely fleshly exercise in human relationships— and it has absolutely no place in the kingdom of God.

The place which ought to be occupied by God has been taken up by mere men, a major consequence of which has been the shifting of the centre of gravity of the whole body—away from God and towards a minority who stand at the front of the meeting, causing an imbalance within the overwhelming majority of Christian fellowships. It manifests itself in an unbiblical polarisation of the body, into what some have described as 'the core' and 'the congregation'.

With this in mind, now would be an appropriate moment to examine the person who, regardless of denomination, is more often than not the ultimate authority figure in any church. At the apex of the authority-accountability pyramid and afforded the greatest honour and influence is, ironically, the holder of the least defensible office within the clergy-laity model.

The Pastor

E Pluribus Unum: Out of Many, One.

Jesus' speech in Matthew 20 and Mark 10 concerning the 'rulers of the gentiles' and his condemnation of their approach to leadership, was in response to John and James' request to be afforded a higher status than the other disciples, something which, unsurprisingly, didn't go down well with the latter. Why, then—especially when we recognize that Jesus was unimpressed with the brothers' petition to be elevated above the others—do we endorse the whole idea of *the single pastor* who presides over the church and who holds ultimate power and authority within it?

In addition to Matthew 20 and Mark 10, we also need to remember Peter's words: 'To the elders among you, I *appeal* as a *fellow elder...*' He didn't refer to himself or to anyone else as a pastor but as a fellow elder; he didn't *order* them to do anything from a position of authority higher than the others but rather he *appealed* to them. Not only is this is a far cry from the *obey-rule-submit* formula advocated by some and which we considered earlier, but it is also important to recognize that if Peter couldn't claim seniority, then who could? [9]

Whatever else one might think about leadership, it is plural: there is certainly no case for *primus inter pares...* 'first among equals'... indeed, if Jesus' words on the subject of leadership and authority are anything to go by, then if anything, it ought to be a case of 'last among equals.' Regrettably, however, Christian leadership has found itself outworked in a way very much removed from both Jesus' and Peter's description of it, and one question that it forces us to ask is: just where did the office of 'pastor' come from?

From a historical perspective, we find instances where the terms pastor and bishop appear to have been regarded as synonymous: within some ancient documents, we observe that pastor and bishop are used interchangeably. One example is the *Original Sources of the Apostolic Canons*, dated somewhere between 140 and 180 AD; other examples include Cyprian's *Epistles* and Eusebius' *Ecclesiastical History*.

As far as Scripture is concerned, it's very interesting to note that—depending on the translation—the term 'pastor' is either used just *once or not at all* in the whole of the New Testament, Ephesians 4:11 being the single occasion where it occurs:

> 'It was he who gave some to be apostles, some to be prophets, some to be evangelists, and some to be pastors and teachers...'

The original Greek word translated here as 'pastor' is *poimen* which means *shepherd*, but the reason we find 'pastor' and not 'shepherd' in our Bibles is because *pastor* is the Latin word for shepherd. This verse, then, should speak of apostles, prophets, evangelists, *shepherds* and teachers and this is, in fact, how it is rendered in the Wycliffe, Tyndale, Coverdale, Matthew and Great Bibles. Technically, then, like *church*, the word *pastor* ought not to appear *at all* within the New Testament.

The word *poimen* appears eighteen times in the New Testament and is translated as *shepherd* or *shepherds* on every occasion—apart from here in Ephesians 4:11. Quite why this solitary exception exists is difficult to establish, but once again we find a particularly unhelpful choice of word clouding or even directly creating an unwanted state of affairs, this time regarding authority within the church.

Considering the fact that the term *elder*, for example, appears approximately thirty times in regard to New Testament church leadership, it's strange then that the term *shepherd* should be singled out and changed in this one instance out of eighteen to *pastor*, and this title subsequently employed to signify a preeminent role or office within the church. Of course, had the role of elder not been artificially subdivided into separate offices in the first place, none of this would have been possible.

We come to see then, that with effectively no biblical support for *any* kind of titular position within the body of Christ, there is even less justification (if that were possible) for the 'office' of Pastor. Of course, there can be no disputing the fact that those who shepherd should be present within any Christian community, but this is not to say that the *office* of shepherd (or pastor) ought to exist.

With these facts in mind, it is therefore more than a little surprising that an individual with the title of Pastor is almost universally present in churches the world over and that he or she holds the most influential position within them. Today, whole churches find themselves being directed by one person — something which the Scriptures do not support, and with good reason. As many people know from bitter experience, the existence of a solitary individual who holds ultimate authority over a group of believers can lead to serious abuse — especially when this person has few, if any, checks and balances. A single individual permitted to set the tone for the whole church can stall the spiritual growth of many, as indeed happens far too often.

This being the case, if the generally accepted model is wrong, particularly the top-down hierarchy headed by the pastor or his equivalent — then what alternative exists for pastoral care and spiritual growth, if any? As it happens, one has been present all the time — the one God intended in the first place.

The one found in Scripture.

Equal in the Eyes of God

Once the clergy/laity distinction is removed the concept of ministry changes. It ceases to be the proprietary right of the few and becomes the privilege of all.

Arthur Wallis

If we are to fully examine the argument for and against the kind of authority structures found in most churches today, at some point we need to read what the apostle Paul had to say on the subject. At the beginning of this book I referred to the physicist Wolfgang Pauli, in whose honour there is something called *Pauli's Exclusion Principle*; I'd like to borrow this and discuss something which we might call *Paul's Inclusion Principle*.

Several people have pointed out that when one reads the introduction to all Paul's letters to the various churches, it is evident that they are *not* addressed to 'the pastor' but are open letters addressed to the whole church; indeed, as Church historian Thomas M. Lindsay observed, Paul makes scant allusion to office-bearers of any kind. In his book, *The Church and Ministry in the Early Centuries*, Lindsay wrote:

'The apostle sends greetings to persons of different sexes and positions in life, but never to office-bearers as such. Nor among his many exhortations does he allude to the need of organisation under hierarchical authority, still less does he prescribe a form of organisation which was to be uniform throughout the whole Church of Christ.' [10]

It's not just Paul who addresses local congregations in this fashion. As we saw earlier in 1 Peter 5:1-3, Peter writes, 'To the elders *among you...*' and he goes on to exhort the elders — in the presence of the whole body, since his letter was open to all — to serve those with whom they are fellowshipping. This certainly puts a new perspective on the meaning of accountability!

Returning to Paul, not only do we find him talking to the whole Christian community in each of his letters, but in 1 Corinthians for example, we find Paul openly addressing issues which — in today's churches — would only be discussed behind closed doors by those in leadership. All kinds of sin were in evidence: someone was sleeping with his stepmother; there was the threat of division; people were suing each other; gluttony was taking place during communion — all these things were happening and no doubt more besides. But the part that is often overlooked is that not only does Paul address his letter to *everybody*, but he tells the *whole* church to resolve these issues.

Within Christendom, there are those who are gifted as shepherds; they are recognized as people who reflect God's character and wisdom in their own lives. They might not have an official title (in fact, according to Jesus, they shouldn't) but they are clearly identifiable as leaders by virtue of their words and their actions. However, although they have a vital role to play in the nurturing of the body, it's not all down to them. Whilst the rest of the flock will instinctively turn to such individuals for input and guidance where necessary, it's clear from the letter to the Corinthians, as well as from the open letters to other New Testament churches, that pastoral responsibility (including the handling of sin and other issues) falls to the whole congregation.

Despite such a clear description in Scripture of how pastoral care ought to be outworked, slowly but surely *Paul's Inclusion Principle* of involving everyone as much as possible has gradually been allowed to dwindle, with more and more responsibility being taken over by fewer and fewer people—in many cases with a single person steering the whole ship—not necessarily because the latter has a great desire to take the burden off everyone else, but rather so that he or she can strengthen their grip on the helm:

> *Rather than of a band of brothers, most churches have ended up with a one-man band instead.*

It is somewhat ironic that we have come to unquestioningly embrace the idea that Paul's open letters to whole churches—including his teaching on whole body participation—need to be analysed for a week behind closed doors by one person who is paid to teach on them to the rest of the body as it sits silently in the pews on a Sunday morning.

The harmful effects of all this cannot be overstated. If denied the opportunity for 'one-anothering' on anything but a superficial level, Christians will not experience the kind of spiritual growth which passages such as Ephesians 4:15-16 describes... rather the exact opposite is much more likely to occur, and indeed we see this outworked in many lives today. And the damage doesn't stop there. Not only are the rank and file disabled, but cries of stress and even burnout are a common refrain from pastors and others in leadership, with whole books written on the subject. But the fact is one cannot have it both ways... it's no good leaders refusing to delegate because they would rather keep hold of the reins, or micro-managing in order to maintain control, yet at the same time complain of overwork and of a body that fails to thrive. The meagre fruit in the lives of many—in both leaders and led—speaks for itself, and it seems patently obvious that none of this can be God's will. It is significant that, ultimately, no-one is prepared to acknowledge the simple truth of the matter:

> *That it is the system itself which inevitably produces such poor results.*

Leading is not Lording
Appointed but not Anointed

Offices such as pastor, priest, vicar and the like exist because, so we are told, they can be found in the Word: words such as covering, accountability and authority are commonly used to describe and justify those leadership structures which are present within the vast majority of churches, regardless of denomination because these too – again, so we are told – are biblical principles.

However, a careful examination of Scripture reveals that all these notions are, in fact, bereft of any biblical support. The truth of the matter is, since *church-as-a-thing-in-itself* is an abstraction with a 'reality' that is far removed from the people who genuinely *are* the church (or more accurately, the *ekklesia*) then it's hardly surprising that roles within this man-made institution have become correspondingly abstracted into offices, positions or titles with a reality apart from the function they are supposed to represent.

We are taught that these structures and offices exist in order to keep God's people from error and excess – that leaders will always be required to 'reign over in order to rein in' – and yet, ironically, the clergy-laity form of leadership is, in and of itself, an error of the greatest possible magnitude. Every so often, church leaders warn of the dangers of denominationalism and of division, yet these same people seem oblivious to the fact that they owe their very position to an unwarranted division within Christ's body, one which represents possibly the greatest schism in the history of the church.

An unbiblical human hierarchy invested with un-warranted power and authority has been allowed to develop and for centuries has been used to dominate God's people. Whether or not it is acknowledged by the majority, the uncomfortable truth of the matter is:

The Goal is Control.

Let us be clear: leaders should be found among the flock and not over it. They are part of the body and not the head, despite the assertions of some of those who claim to have been anointed for leadership. In fact, those who make such claims have too often usurped the place of the anointer Himself. Jesus is the one and only head of the *ekklesia*, and according to him the role of the leadership is to support and serve the individuals who—along with themselves—make up the body. In other words:

Leaders exist in order to serve the rest of the body:
The body does not exist in order to serve the leadership.

SECTION 2: CHURCH PRACTICE

We Can't go on Meeting like This

It is easier to move a mountain than it is to move a person entrenched in the 'traditions of men which make the word of God of no effect. (Matt. 15:6-9)'

Gary Amirault

10

THE SABBATH

Everybody's Living for the Weekend

Going to church doesn't make you a Christian any more than standing in a garage makes you a car.

Laurence J. Peter

Virtually all Christians (as well as non-Christians) accept without reservation that going to church on the Sabbath is an automatic requirement of the Christian faith. Very few believers question the idea of large (or not so large) numbers of people going to a particular building every Sunday and engaging in those activities which we normally associate with 'going to church'. A failure to attend church on the Sabbath is regarded almost as an act of apostasy in the eyes of many and often elicits the charge that one is being disobedient to Scripture. It's said that the practice of attending a meeting in a building, on a Sunday, can be found in clear, unambiguous terms in any Bible one cares to look at—but is this really the case?

The Old Testament

A shadow of the things that were to come.

Colossians 2:16-17

Have you ever wondered what Jews did on the Sabbath during the Old Testament era? *They rested.* The Jewish word 'Shabbat' from which we derive *Sabbath* comes from the root *Shin-Beit-Tav*, meaning to cease, to end, or to rest[1], usually interpreted to refer to a cessation of labour. Exodus 20:8-11 states:

'Remember the Sabbath day by keeping it holy. Six days you shall labour and do all your work, but the seventh day is a Sabbath to the LORD your God. On it you shall not do any work, neither you, nor your son or daughter, nor your manservant or maidservant, nor your animals, nor the alien within your gates. For in six days the LORD made the heavens and the earth, the sea, and all that is in them, but he rested on the seventh day. Therefore the LORD blessed the Sabbath day and made it holy.'

God told the Hebrews to set aside one day each week as a holy day, a day on which they were to do no work in remembrance of God's act of creation. But there was a second reason for the Jews to observe the Sabbath:

'Remember that you were slaves in Egypt and that the LORD your God brought you out of there with a mighty hand and an outstretched arm. Therefore the LORD your God has commanded you to observe the Sabbath day.'

Deuteronomy 5:15

The observance of the Sabbath then, was twofold: both as a commemoration of creation and of delivery from slavery in Egypt. However, the ultimate purpose of the Sabbath was not so much concerned with physical rest as an end in itself, as it was with the fact that this gave people an opportunity for spiritual refreshment—a point which, many centuries later, would be lost on the Pharisees who majored on the letter rather than the spirit of the law. However, whilst it's clear that there was a spiritual dimension to the observance of the Sabbath, notice that no reference is made in the passages above concerning the attendance of meetings or participation in worship.

Amongst the many restrictions which developed in order to enforce Sabbath observance, the following verses from Exodus 16:29-30 were taken by the Jewish people to mean that travel on the Sabbath was forbidden:

'"Everyone is to stay where they are on the seventh day; no one is to go out." So the people rested on the seventh day.'

Nevertheless, rabbinical Judaism would subsequently find ways to interpret and apply other passages of Scripture to the one above such that people could 'legally' be allowed to walk a distance of up to 2000 cubits (less than half a mile). Called a *Sabbath Day's Journey*, the only biblical reference to it is found in Acts 1:12:

'Then they returned to Jerusalem from the hill called the Mount of Olives, a Sabbath day's walk from the city.'

The significance of these facts is that if, as some maintain today, observing the Sabbath involves going to a meeting (despite the absence of any such instruction in the passages above) then an obvious question arises: during the temple period, unless you lived in Jerusalem (and less than half a mile from the temple) *where would you have gone*? One must remember that the *synagogue* did not come into existence until centuries later, which is something we will look at in a moment.

It seems clear that the instructions given for the Sabbath were intended to keep people at home, and thus one thing we can say about the activities of Old Testament Jews on the Sabbath is this: the majority did *not* go to a meeting in a building. Observing the Sabbath was not connected to the idea of collective worship; any spiritual focus would presumably have been more or less private or at most a household affair.

Thus far, we can conclude that as far as the Old Testament is concerned, there is no support for the idea that Christians should meet together on the Sabbath for worship.

The New Testament

The Sabbath was made for man, not man for the Sabbath.

Mark 2:22

Moving forward to the time of Jesus, one of the first things we notice is that many Jews *were* now meeting, in synagogues, gathering together in a set place at set times in a way which is absent from the Old Testament. But, unlike our modern church practices, synagogue meetings were (and continue to be) held daily and not just on the Sabbath; Hebrews 3:13 seems to echo this practice when it talks about gathering together daily and is something we'll return to later.

These designated buildings came into being as a direct result of the Babylonian exile, where the institution of the synagogue and the practices held therein had emerged in an effort to maintain religious and racial cohesion whilst the Jews languished in a foreign land far from home. However, despite the fact that the latter part of the Old Testament consists of post-exilic writings, the synagogue is first referred to in the New Testament, specifically Matthew 4:23. Importantly in terms of this discussion, the synagogue and the meetings held in them developed due to pragmatic reasons, and it needs to be made clear that, whilst they may have been a good idea, *there is no mandate from God anywhere in Scripture calling for or endorsing their institution.*

Whilst some Jews would indeed go to the synagogue on the Sabbath, for many others their observance of and practices on the Sabbath had not changed since Old Testament times. It's interesting to read passages such as the one following, where—just as in the Old Testament—there is no mention of meetings; rather we read of the continuing practice of refraining from all but the most essential activities:

> 'The women who had come with Jesus from Galilee followed Joseph and saw the tomb and how his body was laid in it. Then they went home and prepared spices and perfumes. *But they rested on the Sabbath in obedience to the commandment.'*
>
> *Luke 23:55-6*

As most people know, the Jewish Sabbath lasts from dusk on Friday to dusk the following day, Saturday. The question becomes, then, why did the early Christians decide to start meeting on a *Sunday*? As it turns out, the answer is directly related to the preceding passage: the reason Christians began to meet on Sunday is because Jesus was raised up on a Sunday, hence its designation as 'the Lord's Day' (Revelation 1:10 for example). Consequently, whilst Jews continued to observe the Sabbath, 'the Lord's Day' eventually superseded the Sabbath as a day of religious observance amongst the Christian community. However, there's no suggestion in the Bible that God had decreed this as a special day as such and, like the synagogue, it has no explicit biblical support. Arthur

Wallis wrote:

> 'We do not have any clear evidence that God Authorized the early church to change the sabbath day to the first day of the week, in commemoration of our Lord's resurrection. On the contrary, there is good evidence that God never intended any special day to replace the sabbath. *The age for special days was over*...Sabbaths, whether of 'the-seventh-day' or 'the-first-day-of-the-week' variety, are a thing of the past. They are, according to Paul, "a shadow of the things that were to come; the reality, however is found in Christ." The sabbath itself was to find fulfilment in an 'every-day-of-the-week' sabbath rest of the people of God...as the letter to the Hebrews teaches.' [2] (Emphasis mine)

The 'shadow of the things that were to come' to which Wallis refers is found in Colossians 2:16-17:

> 'Therefore do not let anyone judge you by what you eat or drink, or with regard to a religious festival, a New Moon celebration or a Sabbath day. These are a shadow of the things that were to come; the reality, however, is found in Christ.'

Galatians 4:9-11 reinforces this idea:

> 'But now that you know God — or rather are known by God — how is it that you are turning back to those weak and miserable principles? Do you wish to be enslaved by them all over again? You are observing special days and months and seasons and years! I fear for you, that somehow I have wasted my efforts on you.'

In fact, some verses seem to suggest that, whether we observe special days or not, we 'do so to the Lord'; in other words, ritual observance of a weekly Sabbath is not required, but rather such observance is optional according to the conscience of each individual Christian:

> 'One man considers one day more sacred than another; another man considers every day alike. Each one should be fully convinced in his or her own mind.'
>
> *Romans 14:5-6*

Put together, the preceding verses seem to suggest that the fourth commandment concerning the keeping of the Sabbath is no longer binding under the New Covenant. Certainly, historical figures such as Augustine and Justin Martyr subscribed to this view, along with both Martin Luther and John Calvin.

It does need to be recognized that whilst Luther and Calvin repudiated the seventh-day Sabbath, they nevertheless held first-day-of-the-week Sunday services. This, however, was for practical rather than for doctrinal reasons: Calvin, for instance, argued that it was necessary to set aside Sundays for meetings 'as a remedy needed to keep order in the church', and it would seem safe to say that neither Calvin nor Luther would argue that their practices in this regard were either biblical or binding upon anyone.

The Sabbath or the Lord's Day? Saturday or Sunday? Or neither?

You have let go of the commands of God and are holding on to the traditions of men.

Mark 7:8

The terms *Sabbath* and *The Lord's Day* have become more or less synonymous in the minds of many; however, the early Christians didn't see Sunday as a substitute or replacement for the Jewish Sabbath, but rather, as we've seen, the original designations of both days were as commemorations of two different events. While some have suggested that there is in fact a natural link between the two themes of creation and resurrection, with the Sabbath segueing into the Lord's Day as part of God's overall design, others, such as Arthur Wallis, argue that the New Testament indicates that 'the age for special days was over.'

The confusion surrounding the Sabbath was not helped by Constantine who, in 321 AD, managed to cloud the issue by decreeing that both Christians and non-Christians should be united in observing the 'venerable day of the sun'—a pagan rather than a Christian concept—not by gathering together for worship, but by observing the Old Testament practice of resting from one's labours. Constantine's misguided contribution would have cemented the idea of a Sunday Sabbath/Lord's Day within the traditions of the church, regardless of what the Bible might have to say on the subject.

Clearly, even today, the debate over the Sabbath continues. Some say it doesn't matter *what* day you call the Sabbath, as long as you observe it at some point in the week (although that theoretically puts paid to the idea of Sunday Church). Non-Sabbatarians would contest the idea of setting aside *any* day as a Sabbath, claiming that the Sabbath is a metaphor for the rest all Christians enter into '*Today*' (Hebrews 4) as a result of accepting Christ; their view is that we ought to both recognize and enjoy a *seven*-day rather than *seventh*-day Sabbath rest.

All of this suggests that the apparently simple issue of the Sabbath and what we do (or don't do) during it, is anything but simple.

One thing that *can* be stated with certainty is that those who refer to Sunday as the Sabbath are in error; the Sabbath is a day of rest observed by Jews on the seventh day and, according to Scripture, not binding on Christians. As far as *the Lord's Day* is concerned, we meet together on Sunday, not because we are given instructions in the Bible to do so — because no such instructions exist — but because this is the tradition which developed in the early church.

As James Gibbons, Archbishop of Baltimore, wrote:

'...you may read the Bible from Genesis to Revelation, and you will not find a single line authorising the sanctification of Sunday. The Scriptures enforce the religious observance of Saturday, a day which we never sanctify.' [3]

Going to church on what many incorrectly call the Sabbath is, as Stan Firth puts it, *based on custom rather than a command from God*. This being the case, it follows that non-participation in this particular activity is *not* an indisputable violation of Scripture. It's surprising, then, how many Bible-believing Christians seem to think that church attendance on a Sunday is non-negotiable. Despite the sentiment expressed in Colossians 2:16-17 — '*Therefore do not let anyone judge you...with regard to a...Sabbath day'* — judging people who do not attend church on Sunday is an all too common occurrence.

As Archbishop Gibbons said in so many words, one can search the Bible from cover to cover, and never in a month of Sundays find support for holding church on that particular day of the week. Even so, the custom of meeting on a Sunday is deeply ingrained within the general Christian culture, as we all know.

It's time to move on and examine just what it is that most Christians do in church on 'The Sabbath'; it's time to consider the subject of church meetings, both in Scripture and in practice.

The Church of faith extends far beyond the Church as a worshipping community; there are true members of the Church of faith who belong to no worshipping congregation, just as there are many members of the worshipping community who do not belong to the true Church.

Emil Brunner

11 ˙

MEETING EXPECTATIONS

Attendance: One of the Sacred Cows of *Church-as-a-thing-in-itself*
Close Encounters of the Herd Kind

How many of us have heard the rejoinder, 'How are you doing? I haven't seen you in church lately', which translates as, 'I haven't seen you in the *meetings* lately.' Many unconsciously equate other people's spiritual wellbeing with attendance at meetings: going to church in effect means going to meetings.

On one occasion, someone remarked that he hadn't seen me in church for a while. 'I've been in church all the time,' I replied, 'I just didn't make it to the meetings.' I wasn't trying to be clever, but rather, I was actually trying to make a serious point. (If I'd *really* wanted to be clever, I could have said, 'I'm sorry I didn't make it to the meetings, but I was too busy witnessing, bringing people to faith, raising the dead, and running a soup kitchen for the local homeless people. I hope my non-attendance won't get me kicked out of the church.')

Commitment to meetings is more or less regarded as synonymous with commitment to church — and by extension, commitment to God. Regular attendance at meetings, or otherwise, is often regarded as an indicator as to whether an individual is 'in or out of *church*' or even by some, as 'in or out' of the Christian faith altogether.

In the first instance, the word 'commitment' is used in order to encourage a preparedness in others to turn up on a Sunday, since, as far as *church-as-a-thing-in-itself* is concerned:

Attendance at meetings is both the primary obligation and minimum requirement of any Christian.

Beyond this, commitment is usually extended to imply 'serving' — which is to say, the degree to which any given individual is prepared to help out with any of the logistics which arise from running the meetings, such as chair-stacking or joining the welcoming committee.

Meetings are probably the most significant feature of any church: church 'happens' within a scheduled time slot once or maybe twice a week, and as a consequence, the form becomes all-important, with the perceived 'success' of the meetings (however one defines this) often regarded as the main barometer of a church's overall health; if the building is full and the meetings are lively (where and when appropriate, of course) then it's assumed that the body is doing well spiritually. This, unfortunately, is not always the case: the *church* might on the surface be doing well, but the genuine spiritual health of the Christians within it may not be equally vibrant.

By way of illustration, I'd like to relate the following personal experience: the day after a large church that we attended was featured in the TV series, *Songs of Praise*, the mother of one of the members called her daughter to say how wonderfully the church had come across through the programme. The mother remarked, 'I wish *I* went to a church like that!' to which her daughter replied, 'So do I!'

This anecdote highlights the fact that appearances can be deceiving, and for this reason it's important for us to take a closer look at the true value and effectiveness of church meetings in the sense that most people understand the term, and in the way that most people normally experience them. In this chapter, I'd like to examine various aspects of a typical church meeting and see how they compare to Scripture. Just how closely are our meetings aligned to Paul's recommend-ations as described in the New Testament? How many of the activities religiously carried out in our churches every Sunday square with the Word of God?

Doing things by The Book

You are in error because you do not know the Scriptures or the power of God.

Matthew 22:29

If we wish to try and identify what a typical New Testament meeting might have looked like then 1 Corinthians 14 is the most logical place from which to start, since it's here we find the most detailed description of a Christian gathering.

In verse 26 we read the following:

'What then shall we say, brothers? *When you come together, everyone has a hymn, or a word of instruction, a revelation, a tongue or an interpretation.'*

The word *everyone* does not mean that everyone present would necessarily take part but rather that, 'each comes prepared to contribute, yet is equally ready to remain silent as the need becomes evident.'[1] Nevertheless, it seems clear that there was an expectation on Paul's part that all those present in meetings would have at least the *opportunity* to participate in the proceedings.

Is Paul's description reminiscent of your Sunday meetings? Does this verse reflect the practices in your church? Do the majority arrive eager to share something—with a hymn, a word or a testimony for example? Other than collective participation in worship or the occasional reading, is there the opportunity for you to meaningfully contribute to the proceedings?

While the sort of participation Paul describes *does* happen to varying degrees in home groups associated with some churches, other than in minorities such as the Quakers (and whose meetings, more often than not, are characterized by silence rather than by active contribution) it certainly is not the case within the context of a traditional Sunday meeting.

While some concede that there is little similarity between a typical church meeting today and the picture painted in Corinthians, they contend that this is in fact a good thing since it is evident that the meetings at Corinth were somewhat chaotic, to say the least. Some people were babbling incoherently in tongues while others prophesied simultaneously, and above the din, the women were chatting away, holding a meeting of their own (or perhaps trying to find out if anyone knew what was happening!) The case made in support of our comparatively pedestrian meetings today is that without proper supervision and direction, this level of confusion would occur in *any* church meeting and that this is exactly why those in leadership organize and then control the meetings the way they do. It's suggested that if we *were* to allow for everyone to participate then anarchy would be the inevitable outcome.

So, is this a valid argument? With regard to the situation in Corinth, it's clear that *something* had to be done in an effort to bring order out of chaos; but the question is what?

It's interesting to notice that Paul's remedy was *not* the one which we find employed today: in other words, his solution *wasn't* to bring order to the meetings by appointing leaders who would then more or less prohibit the participation of the vast majority of the people assembled. *Rather, it involved the people learning to regulate their own behaviour* with the hoped-for result that things would be done, as Paul put it, 'in a fitting and orderly way'. Thomas Lindsay noted:

'What cannot fail to strike us in this picture is the untrammelled liberty of the worship... When we consider the rebukes that the apostle considered it necessary to administer, it is also somewhat surprising to find so few injunctions which take the form of definite rules for public worship, and to observe the confidence which the apostle had that if certain broad principles were laid down and observed, the community was of itself able to conduct all things with that attention to decency and order which ensured edification...' [2]

In the following example, we see how Paul offers guidance but expects the group to implement it themselves; it's also clear that he anticipates a number of people — if not everyone — to be involved. In Chapter 14, verses 27-33 we read:

'If anyone speaks in a tongue, two — or at the most three — should speak, one at a time, and someone must interpret. If there is no interpreter, the speaker should keep quiet in the church and speak to himself and to God.

Two or three prophets should speak, and the others should weigh carefully what is said. And if a revelation comes to someone who is sitting down, the first speaker should stop. For you can all prophesy in turn so that everyone may be instructed and encouraged. The spirits of prophets are subject to the control of prophets. For God is not a God of disorder but of peace — as in all the congregations of the Lord's people.'

It's obvious, then, that responsibility for the proceedings was a collective affair, with Paul keen to encourage wide, if not universal involvement. But was this simply out of a sense of 'fair play', or was he aiming at something deeper?

Christianity is not a Spectator Sport

We fell into Spectator Christianity, where loneliness doesn't end at church–it starts there.

Jim Rutz

Although the passages we've been looking at deal with the use of sign gifts, the validity of such gifts today is not the issue under consideration. Putting aside one's personal views on the charismata, I want to see if it's possible to uncover an underlying principle which can be inferred from Paul's instructions regarding our 'gathering together'.

In 1 Corinthians 14:26, a verse which we looked at earlier, in the second half we read:

'When you come together, everyone has a hymn, or a word of instruction, a revelation, a tongue or an interpretation. *All of these must be done for the strengthening of the church.'*

If one reads the whole of Chapter 14, it becomes evident that the people concerned had to be organized — not in order to make sure that there was sufficient participation during the meeting, but rather because people had *too much* to say! Since the goal was 'the strengthening' of those assembled, this meant that there had to be some sort of prioritisation; instead of deciding what to include in the meeting, *in some ways it was a case of having to decide what to leave out.* Those speaking in tongues, therefore, were asked to keep it to themselves, unless there was someone present who was able to offer an interpretation that would enlighten and thereby strengthen the congregation. Prophecy, on the other hand, was regarded by Paul as the more important gift:

> 'For anyone who speaks in a tongue does not speak to men but to God. Indeed, no one understands him; he utters mysteries with his spirit. *But everyone who prophesies speaks to men for their strengthening, encouragement and comfort. He who speaks in a tongue edifies himself, but he who prophesies edifies the church.* I would like every one of you to speak in tongues, but I would rather have you prophesy. He who prophesies is greater than one who speaks in tongues, unless he interprets, *so that the church may be edified.'*
>
> *1 Corinthians 14:2-5*

Further on Paul writes:

> 'For you can all prophesy in turn so that everyone may be instructed and encouraged.'
>
> *1 Corinthians 14:31*

The main thrust of Paul's comments was that in meeting together, the central aim was not concerned with exercising the gift of prophecy for its own sake, but one of *mutual encouragement and edification: '...*try to excel in gifts that *build up the church'* (1 Corinthians 14:12).

Judging from the type of problem which Paul was trying to rectify at Corinth, the sense one gets is that he was trying to move a set of self-centred and spiritually immature individuals—as evidenced by both their private lives and their conduct during meetings, including the Lord's Supper—towards the more altruistic idea of one-anothering (or mutual edification as Paul puts it) as part of their spiritual growth. I believe that Paul recognized that consideration of others in meetings was an important factor in this growth.

Perhaps there's an essential principle at work here regarding the conduct of Christian gatherings in general, and not just those with manifestly obvious problems like the meetings at Corinth. This principle might be expressed as follows:

> Each individual is a potential participant, with a view to edifying, strengthening or building up one's brothers and sisters in Christ.

I believe the purpose of our meeting together is the same for us today as it was for the *ekklesia* in Corinth two thousand years ago: to strengthen the elect through mutual edification, which in turn encourages every-member participation.

It is with this in mind that we need to consider the second argument presented by those who support the idea of meetings being controlled by a small minority. Some contend that whilst every-member participation might be possible when the number of people involved is small (evidence suggests that the church at Corinth numbered about fifty individuals), it would be a practical impossibility in congregations such as we find today where the number of those attending is in the hundreds or even thousands; there simply wouldn't be enough time for large numbers of people to contribute just because they felt moved to do so. But if strengthening the body is the priority, then room for every-member participation has to be a precondition, and since this is not possible in large meetings, such gatherings should therefore be the exception rather than the rule. It's interesting to note that in China, for instance, people meet not in large buildings at all but in houses, because the government has ruled that groups of more than twenty-five are illegal... and yet, far from limiting growth, it is here that we find one of the fastest growing Christian populations in the world, with over one hundred million believers. Perhaps there's a lesson for the Western church here, but at the very least, it raises the following question:

Why do we need church buildings at all?

The whole topic of buildings will be addressed in the next chapter. In the meantime, we need to consider the consequences of allowing a small group of people to take upon themselves the responsibility for controlling the majority, thereby relegating the latter to mere observers of, rather than participants in what is supposed to be a joint act of worship — all supposedly 'for the sake of order'.

Conducting Meetings
Orchestral Manoeuvres in the Dark

An orchestra, as we all know, is made up of a number of independent instruments which, rather like Christians within the body of Christ, together form another whole. One of the most prominent musicians in an orchestra is the *principal first violin*, also referred to as the *concertmaster* or *leader*. One of the concertmaster's duties is to co-ordinate the tuning of the entire orchestra prior to the appearance of the conductor; he or she ensures that every single musician is ready and able to fulfil his part. To an untrained ear, however, even though the tuning is coordinated, it still sounds like a cacophony; but once the conductor arrives and brings the different instruments together in one accord — out of the chaos, order appears: the music begins.

When Paul arrived at Corinth, the meetings must have felt and sounded to him rather like an orchestra tuning up — in other words, a din. Each individual appeared to be purely concerned with exercising his own gift, regardless of what anyone else was doing. In response, Paul took on the role of an orchestra leader, and in so doing he was instrumental in guiding the meetings such that instead of a jarring, discordant noise, he was able to establish some measure of peace and harmony. Crucially, though, and like the orchestra leader, Paul understood that his function was to prepare the body for the Conductor, and to give way to Him upon His arrival.

We have here a picture of how our meetings ought to be, except that — unlike any human conductor — not only did God design and make each and every instrument, but He composed the entire musical score as well. He desires to conduct our meeting together as we gather to worship Him and, if we allow Him to do so, the result will be a symphony of praise.

But now imagine this: you've taken your seat in the *Berlin Philharmonic* concert hall, the audience having applauded the arrival of the conductor — none other than Sir Simon Rattle himself—and you now eagerly await the opening movement. Suddenly the *Konzertmeister* mounts the dais, and promptly informs Sir Simon that he can take over, thank you, and seizing the baton, he proceeds to conduct the orchestra himself. Shocking as that would seem, in effect this is precisely what happens week in and week out in our church meetings, the orchestra ending up playing music with a heavy violin emphasis—which is hardly surprising since the *leader* has written it himself.

But what this also means is that there is no longer any part for the humble but essential triangle player and others like him, whose roles have now been reduced to that of functionaries rather than musicians; under the direction of the *leader*, they are given the job of not only setting out the chairs ready for the performance by the string section, but also of sitting on them in order to provide an audience. And although the music is orderly, it's also dull, repetitive and uninspiring. The magic has gone.

The orchestra *leader* has become a choke-point within the body, restricting the participation of both God and men. The outcome of all this is that the majority of the musicians lose heart and more or less cease to use their instruments at all, losing the level of skill they once had. More importantly, they also lose the joy they once knew.

For some, the situation appears so hopeless that they quit the orchestra altogether.

Jesus has left the building

Dear God, we had a good time at church today. Wish you could have been there.

In the preceding scenario, not only would the members of the orchestra become disenchanted if they lost the opportunity to participate, but so too would the conductor. I once read that during the apartheid regime in South Africa, people used to tell the following joke:

A black African is sitting disconsolately outside a 'Whites Only' church when Jesus walks up to him and asks, 'Why do you look so sad?' The man looks up at him and says, 'You see that church over there? They won't let me in', to which Jesus replies: 'I wouldn't worry about that—they haven't let me in for years!'

This is not unlike the story we find ourselves in today; just how do our current practices allow for *God's* participation? The fact that most of our meetings are so predictable, both in terms of the sequence of events and their overall length, seems to suggest that men, rather than God, are directing proceedings. Not only are the majority of those present denied the opportunity to participate to any substantial degree but it seems that there is little or no room in church for God *Himself*.

Jesus said, 'Where two or three are gathered in my name, there am I with them', and I've heard it suggested that he was here referring to the minimum numbers required for 'church'. What seems to concern these people the most, however, is how to define *church* when in fact Jesus' main point was that *he would be present,* regardless of whether there are two or two thousand people. And therein lies the rub; this attitude betrays where our concern ultimately lies—with church rather than with Jesus.

C.S. Lewis observed, 'It is in the process of being worshipped that God communicates His presence to men.' Unfortunately, rather than worshipping God, the emphasis has shifted to worshipping *church-as-a-thing-in-itself* instead, and as a direct consequence, whilst we have order, we no longer have the presence of God: the Holy Spirit has been quenched, the glory has departed.

Martyn Lloyd Jones said that he believed one of the greatest mistakes we'd made was to box *God* in…

But I wonder if we haven't boxed Him out instead.

Restricted Access
Behold, I stand at the door and knock.   *Revelation 3.20*

In his book, *Introducing Early Christianity*, Church historian Laurie Guy writes:

'Three things markedly influenced early Christian worship. One was its awareness of the presence and ongoing activity of the Holy Spirit, fostering dimensions of spontaneity and immediacy. The second was Christianity's Jewish roots, fostering continuity with the past and a richness of formal liturgy. The third was the home setting, fostering informality and congregational participation. It was the Jewish strand (or that part of human nature that desires order, continuity and repetition) that became predominant.' [3]

The Church's return to its Jewish roots manifested itself, amongst other ways, in the hijacking of Jesus' words, 'no-one comes to the Father except through me', appropriated by a mediating priesthood who stood in front of the altar and announced to God's people, 'No-one comes to the father except through us.' God's children no longer had direct access to their own Father but (so they were told) could only enter His presence via the ministrations of a priestly class. This situation represented a blatant return to practices found under the Old Covenant and yet it appears to have gone unrecognized, remaining with us right up to the present.

One has to wonder, then, what Paul would make of our meetings were he to walk into one of them; would he even recognize what was going on? More importantly, would he be impressed by the orderliness which typifies our meetings? In fact, I imagine he would be as much concerned by the restraint exercised by today's congregations as he was by the lack of it in the meetings at Corinth. For instance, with the possible exception of a shared time of worship — which in itself is usually directed from the front — how do meetings where the bulk of the congregation sit passively in rows, help to strengthen the whole body? It certainly doesn't seem to be the case that people have much of a chance for mutual edification in the way Paul envisaged, and it causes me to wonder: what advice, if any, would he give this time round? 1 Corinthians 11:17 comes to mind:

'I have no praise for you, for your meetings do more harm than good.'

Even if we *didn't* have Paul's instructions regarding the way we go about our meeting together, it seems self-evident that people will grow more if they are allowed to participate in the proceedings... after all, isn't this one of the ways we raise our children or teach them in school? Ultimately the real question is: is it more important to have large, 'orderly' meetings where people are relegated to the role of spectators and are spiritually stunted as a result, or smaller, 'messier' meetings where people grow through participation?

Meetings should allow for a high level of participation involving those present, with a view to the strengthening of the whole body; however, since such universal participation is difficult to control and therefore undesirable from a leadership point of view, the latter almost never make room for it. Yet by restricting individual involvement, the very purpose of gathering together has been undermined, making such meetings largely redundant. The main reason for our gathering together has been subverted from that of spiritual growth to — in effect — providing an audience for those who lead from the front in one form or another.

Reduced from the status of brothers and sisters at a family gathering to observers of a performance, personally, I think one thing is certain:

Most people want to be part of the action rather than part of the scenery.

A Captive Audience
Seen but not heard

When we compare our meetings today with Scripture, we find there is, in fact, no comparison. While this should cause us to question upon what we actually base our existing practices, to ask something that seems as fundamental and as obvious as this can be regarded as tantamount to heresy; people will defend the existing state of affairs without, it would seem, questioning the scriptural basis for what it is they do on any given Sunday.

I once asked a pastor why our church meetings didn't remotely resemble those described in the New Testament. His answer was that, as far as meetings were concerned, there really wasn't all that much to go on. My thought, both then and now, is that even if there *isn't* a huge amount of Scripture on this subject, surely we ought nevertheless to follow it where and when we can? The fact is, church leaders will often select particular verses which they then use in order to coerce people to attend meetings (Hebrews 10:25 is a commonly used and much abused example, as we shall see) whilst at the same time conveniently ignoring other verses which encourage every-member participation. Those who tell others that they ought to turn up to meetings — because the Bible says so — are the same people who turn a blind eye to what the Bible also has to say concerning what should happen once everyone is together.

Despite the fact that Romans 8:1 tells us, 'there is now no condemnation for those who are in Christ Jesus', guilt and condemnation are precisely the tools employed in an effort to manipulate people into going to meetings. And so phrases such as, 'I hope to see you in church next week', or the more ominous, 'You need to be more committed', are usually resorted to when 'lay' people, often with good reason, start to show signs of not wanting to turn up on a Sunday, or exhibit a reluctance to sign up to the various rotas. Slogans such as these are used as a stick with which to beat the sheep back to a barren pasture; the saints are not so much equipped by church as whipped into attending it.

All of this begs the question, *to what* or *to whom* ought any Christian be committed? It's one thing to be committed to *God*; it's another thing entirely to be committed to someone else's idea of a programme or activity, and especially so if the latter are perceived to be of doubtful value or have questionable scriptural backing.

As far as rotas and volunteering are concerned, I've frequently heard leaders lament the fact that things aren't working because people are not pulling their weight, treating the sheep as scapegoats. It's common nowadays to hear the '80/20' rule cited: that 80 per cent of the work (however one defines this) is done by only 20 per cent of the members. Apart from being concerned that this rule is borrowed from the business world, the fact of the matter is:

> The real reason why things aren't working is because the whole set-up is completely and utterly flawed at its very core.

Numb and Number

The things that can be counted don't count, and the things that count can't be counted.

Albert Einstein

If the Christian message represents the greatest story ever told, then it ought to be standing room only at every church in the land. It takes real skill, therefore, to beat the life out of the gospel to such an extent that we have to 'guilt' Christians — let alone the unsaved — into attending church, and it bears eloquent testimony to the fact that something seems to have gone horribly wrong with our understanding of the gospel. Not least, it sends the message that Christianity is, after all, about works rather than faith. The Good News of Jesus Christ has become the Bad News of *Church-as-a-thing-in-itself*.

People are pressurized into attending church, not necessarily because of a great desire on the part of those employing such methods of persuasion to see people grow in their *faith*, but from a desire to see a growth in *numbers*; however, whilst church growth is a matter of *addition*, the growth of Christ's body is a matter of *nutrition*, something made more or less impossible by denying the majority of Christians any meaningful contribution to the proceedings.

All of this suggests that the part of the body with which many leaders are mostly concerned is *bottoms on seats,* and whilst those who 'exercise their ministries' on a Sunday morning have the opportunity to experience some sort of affirmation and sense of purpose, often the primary experience of the rest of the body is a numb posterior; the only thing many are called upon to exercise is their ability to stay awake... perhaps we should talk of *Bored Again Christians*.

As we've seen, order has become more important than participation and, by implication, more important than the personal, spiritual growth of the vast majority of Christians. The outcome has been that instead of being strengthened, the *ekklesia* has been weakened, and by this — in today's context — I don't mean there aren't enough volunteers to put out the chairs, wash the coffee cups, switch off the lights and close the building afterwards; rather, I'm referring to the weakening of the *spiritual* condition of those who are gathered together. If we look around at the church today, I think many would agree that much of it is in an enfeebled state indeed.

One danger to any successful movement is that it becomes an institution and begins the slow process that leads to stagnation, one form of "loss of soul." Stagnation of a religious institution is like a box constructed around a quest in which the quest begins to define itself in terms of the box rather than the vision by which it was formed. When the trappings become more important than the message, the institution takes the path to stagnation. The process of stagnation begins, for example, when a congregation begins to think of its church as a building instead of the people and spirit.

James A. Ellison

12

HOUSE OF GOD OR HOUSE OF CARDS?

Stone Memorials of a Dead Religion?
Shutting up Shop

As a result of declining church membership and dwindling attendance on Sundays, more church buildings are closing down than are opening: every year more than 4000 churches in the US close their doors,[1] whilst in Britain the picture is much the same. Many churches are being converted into alternative venues such as discos, night clubs and bars—and even into mosques and Sikh Temples.

I need to make it clear that I, for one, do not lament the closure of these buildings as such, since, as we shall see, *the idea of designated church buildings has no foundation in Scripture.* But, whilst losing dead wood is no bad thing, it's troubling nevertheless because the loss is *not* due to the fact that something better and more biblically based is replacing these buildings. It's not the closure of the buildings themselves that should concern us but rather what their gradual disappearance represents—it suggests a loss of ground by God's people and is surely an admission that something is fundamentally wrong, at least within certain sections of the church.

One of the most common outcomes regarding *church-as-a-thing-in-itself* is what many have referred to as the 'edifice complex': the absolute necessity of owning, or at least renting a building is regarded more or less as a given by most churches, the need for them so embedded in our psyche that it's hard for many people to even imagine a church existing without one. Operating out of a building is a concept so hard-wired into the thinking of most Christians that to even ask where the idea comes from is viewed as almost nonsensical.

Regardless of what Scripture may or may not have to say on the subject, the need to meet in a building is presented as self-evident, their existence perceived as necessary from a purely practical point of view, if nothing else. As part of the argument for buildings, it's suggested that one only has to consider activities such as youth work, Alpha Courses and conferences—not to mention a thousand and one other possible uses—in order to recognize the value in having one's own premises. And of course, as important as these things are, they are not nearly as important as the main reason given for having access to buildings—namely, church meetings.

Many Christians regard the opportunity of moving into such premises as a sign of God's approval—but is it a snare instead? Wayne Jacobsen notes:

> 'Jesus and the early church both kept structures to a minimum, preferring the power of the Spirit and the relationships between believers to provide ministry...Money and buildings, though useful, are not essential. A ministry that demands them in order to be successful misunderstands the heart of ministry itself.' [2]

Could it be that the mindset which demands a building is, paradoxically, the reason behind the closure of so many of these so-called 'sacred spaces' in the first place?

Lamp on a Hill or a Black Hole?

Let me warn you of one thing: beware of Antichrist. What an evil this is, this love of building that possesses you.

Hilary of Poitiers

Several years ago, I talked on separate occasions with two different people, both of whom told me that their churches had acquired new, larger premises. In one case the new building occupied a prime spot in a southern English city. It cost the congregation (so I was told) one million pounds to buy and it needed, I believe, a further two million pounds to refurbish. Whilst the raising of the money was vaunted as a great testimony to the congregation's commitment to its church, it raises some important questions.

In both cases, one of the main reasons given for the move to new premises was that it was felt that the church needed to be more visible, and by obtaining a larger building it would (a bit like a *Hi Vis* neon yellow jacket) help provide a clear, physical presence in their respective localities.

The validity of such reasoning, however, is questionable: many of us, for instance, are aware of the existence of Jehovah's Witnesses in our own neighbourhoods, yet how many Kingdom Halls could we locate if asked? Any? None? In sharp contrast to the Witnesses, who don't appear to need high-profile or high-visibility buildings in order to make their presence known, it appears that we find it easier to let a pile of bricks speak for us rather than facing the daunting task of doing it ourselves.

The problem with owning a building is that instead of being a lamp on a hill, buildings can often become more like black holes, sucking in huge amounts of time, energy and money while at the same time allowing very little light to escape.

Far from giving us any indication that we should be investing in real estate, Scripture consistently points us towards the simplicity of the gospel which began in a manger in Bethlehem and continued in the humble dwellings of the believers themselves. In 1 Corinthians 16:19, for example, we read:

'Aquila and Priscilla greet you warmly in the Lord, and so does the church that meets at their house.'

Other examples can be found in Acts 5:42 and Acts 20:20, as well as Romans 16, verses 5 and 23; Colossians 4:15 and Philemon 1:1-2 also refer to churches meeting in people's houses.

That the first believers met in homes is not a matter for debate; however, some people contend that the New Testament also makes a case for church meetings to be held in purpose-built buildings. As we are about to see, the argument for this is specious at best.

Demolishing the Argument for Church Buildings
Tearing Down Strongholds

In 1 Corinthians 3:16-17, we read:

> 'Don't you know that you yourselves are God's temple and that God's Spirit dwells in your midst? If anyone destroys God's temple, God will destroy that person; for God's temple is sacred, and you together are that temple.'

Whilst it is universally agreed that with the sending of the Holy Spirit the temple served no further purpose, this in and of itself does not necessarily negate the possibility of using church buildings; nevertheless, as I hope to demonstrate in this chapter, there are plenty of sound reasons for not using them.

Of course, the perceived wisdom is that one of the ways in which a church demonstrates that 'it has arrived' is by acquiring its own premises. In an attempt to defend their use, a pastor once suggested to me that the following passage provides scriptural support for the existence of church buildings today:

> 'Paul entered the synagogue and spoke boldly there for three months, arguing persuasively about the kingdom of God. But some of them became obstinate; they refused to believe and publicly maligned the Way. So Paul left them. He took the disciples with him and had discussions daily in the lecture hall of Tyrannus. This went on for two years, so that all the Jews and Greeks who lived in the province of Asia heard the word of the Lord.'
>
> *Acts 19: 8-10*

However, in spite of the pastor's assertion, there are several reasons why one cannot extrapolate from this isolated incident in order to construct a general case for church buildings:

- Moving into the lecture hall was Plan B, not Plan A: Paul only used the hall because speaking in the synagogue had become more trouble than it was worth.

- This is the only case where we find Paul using a building as a forum for teaching in this way — we do not see him speaking in similar edifices in his other epistles, and we cannot establish a pattern based on one example.

- Paul's speeches were evangelistic in nature; he was not preaching to the converted, unlike the situation we find today.

- The passage says that Paul had 'discussions daily.' We notice two things here: firstly, Paul had *discussions*, which implies dialogue — nothing like the monologue we experience today in the form of the sermon; secondly, it also says that these discussions were held *daily*, not once a week on a Sunday.

- There's no evidence to suggest that the local Christians owned or rented the lecture hall.

- Using the hall in this way went on for two years after which, presumably it ended. Our church buildings today are usually intended for permanent or at least long-term use.

If one wants to insist — based on this passage — that the idea of meeting in buildings has a biblical foundation, then one has to be totally consistent and use buildings in the way the passage suggests; thus daily discussions involving unbelievers should be held in such buildings as can be procured rent free, but with the understanding that at some point these discussions might have to be relocated elsewhere. Is this how today's church buildings are utilized?

There's no comparison.

Perhaps it would be good to give God the last word on the importance *He* places on buildings:

> "'However, the Most High does not live in houses made by men. As the prophet says "'Heaven is my throne, and the earth is my footstool. What kind of house will you build for me? says the Lord. Or where will my

resting place be? Has not my hand made all these things?'"

Acts 7:48-50

Moving on from this particular debate, a pertinent question at this point might be: exactly *how* did the church make the transition from small, home-based gatherings to large meetings in church buildings?

Constantine: Architect of Disaster
The Ekklesia: Called Out or Boxed In?

In *Beyond Radical* Gene Edwards wrote the following:

'Until a Roman emperor named Constantine came along (about 300 years after Pentecost), the Christian faith was the only religion in history that met in homes. It was the only "lay" led movement in the history of religion. Christianity alone had no institutions, no set rituals, no temples. That was unprecedented in human history. It is what made Christianity unique. And virile. And elastic, flexible, and adaptable. It had low overheads! Costs were minimal. Constantine changed all that.' [3]

Under Constantine, the Christian community had finally found long-term relief after the terrible persecution visited upon it by some of his predecessors, particularly Diocletian. However, whilst Constantine professed the Christian faith, in reality he didn't limit himself exclusively to the Christian God: his beliefs were most certainly eclectic. For example, history records that, 'even when Constantine dedicated the new capital of Constantinople, which became the seat of Byzantine Christianity for a millennium, he did so wearing the Apollonian sun-rayed Diadem.'[4] Not only that, but Constantine chose to retain the title of *pontifex maximus* until his death, a title Roman emperors bore as heads of the pagan priesthood (and from which the honorific title *pontiff* is derived).

In spite of his affiliation to other religions as well as Christianity, it's generally believed that Constantine saw the Church in particular as a prospective unifying force with which he might bring stability to the empire. One of the most obvious signs that the Christian faith had acquired political approval and been provided with official status was the provision of church buildings to be used as places of Christian worship. Constantine ordered the construction of a number of buildings not only in Rome, but in other major cities within the empire, using the *basilica* as the template for their design:

'The Roman basilicas were a cross between a public place of assembly, a law court, a meeting place for business men, and a king's judgment hall... The Christian architects adopted the pagan plan, installing an altar near the large, rounded recess, or apse, at one end of the edifice, where the king or judge sat; the bishop was now to take the place of the pagan dignitary. The congregation itself crowded into the body of the basilica... This basic structure has remained ever since as one of the most common styles of church building.' [5]

By 380 AD, Christianity had travelled full circle; under Theodosius it became the official religion of the empire where previously it had been persecuted – or at best tolerated. That Constantine had laid the foundations for his successor by deliberately melding the Christian religion with the state itself can be seen from the following comment by Howard Wilson:

'I find it hard to imagine the extraordinary effect this building, and the others which followed it, must have had on the minds of contemporary Christians, in whose memory the persecutions were so recent and so vivid; and remain curious as to the effect it must have had on the liturgy, hitherto adapted to far smaller, humbler and less overwhelming locations. Possibly some idea of the demonstrative effect of Constantine's first buildings may be given by the adjacent Baptistery, which the neophyte entered between porphyry columns – an imperial prerogative. What clearer statement could there be that by becoming a Christian, one was entering the imperial domain?' [6]

Clearly, then, the idea of our modern day church buildings did not originate with believers nor with Scripture, but rather with a Roman emperor seemingly intent on advancing a socio-political agenda. Laurie Guy makes the following observation:

'The home setting fostered the relational dimension of the faith. Christians were "brothers" and "sisters" together... The home setting placed a brake on hierarchy and formality. Setting markedly influences worship. The shift from homes in the third century to impressive basilicas in the fourth allowed for a great flowering of formality, ritual and structuring.' [7]

Initially, the *ekklesia* was a family of brothers and sisters who met informally in homes; slowly but surely, however, it mutated into an organisation run by clerics who officiated at formal meetings in state-funded buildings. The result was that by the end of the fourth century, we find an illegitimate, mediating priesthood that is now conducting extra-biblical rituals within edifices whose existence had no foundation in the New Testament. In other words:

The relational had been replaced by the institutional.

God's heart for family had been replaced by man's desire to organize and control.

Christianity had been at its most potent when it was persecuted as an enemy of the state, but it became progressively weakened once Christians became a 'protected species'. The *ekklesia* had withstood the full-frontal assault of persecution; it now succumbed to a much more subtle approach: it had been embraced by the empire itself. Constantine — the first ostensibly Christian emperor — had managed to do more harm to the body of Christ in twenty years than all his predecessors had managed to do in the previous two hundred. It's little wonder, then, that many see Constantine's influence as having such an injurious effect on the body of Christ. Gene Edwards remarks:

'The damage that was done will never be redressed. Any hope of a true grasp of ecclesiology died not long after Constantine died in 337 A.D.

Following the introduction of the temple into our faith, there came the secret language, the remote priest, the silent followers, the rituals...The loss for all of us has been staggering. These things we acquired have been a curse for the simple faith Jesus the carpenter launched.' [8]

There's a line in the old hymn, *Rock of Ages*, which runs:

Nothing in my hand I bring, simply to the cross I cling.

The reality, however, gradually came to look quite different: rather than arriving at the foot of the cross empty-handed, a time came when God's people turned up armed with picks and shovels, mortar and stones, wooden pews and stained glass. Rather than looking to 'the old rugged cross', they decided to follow on from Constantine's lead and build grand cathedrals and imposing churches instead.

The erection of church buildings introduced a significant change to the Christian landscape, both physically and theologically: their presence reinforced the confusion which surrounded the meaning of the *ekklesia*, serving to cement the initial and more grievous error of believing that the *ekklesia* was *a thing-in-itself*. And so it was that God's people took another step towards accepting the idea of an entity which existed apart from themselves. Instead of being composed of living stones, the *ekklesia* increasingly came to refer to the lifeless stones of which church buildings were made. This process led to a gradual decline in spiritual vitality, draining the life from individual believers down the centuries; the result has been that church buildings have become, over time, little more than large boxes, rather like oversized coffins, within which the body of Christ is confined.

'Buildings are Essential'
Set in Stone or False Premises?

Those who regard the existence of church buildings as non-negotiable argue that accounts of the early church meeting in homes, such as those found in Acts and the Epistles, are simply not applicable today: they suggest that since the churches were young and therefore small, this meant that meeting in people's houses didn't present a logistical problem; but, they reason, the large size of many of today's congregations makes gathering in homes an unrealistic option for anything other than midweek group meetings. This is essentially the same argument as that presented in the previous chapter regarding meetings, which is hardly surprising since the subject of both meetings and buildings are inextricably linked.

I would argue that the obvious solution to the 'problem' of how to deal with increasing numbers of people is to simply meet in more houses; as we saw in the last chapter, Chinese Christians have done exactly this and growth has been far from limited as a result. As with any living organism, the body of Christ will grow naturally by cell division; thus, when one house or group becomes too small to contain the body, it splits into another house (or group), and on and on.

In *Gods' Smuggler*, Brother Andrew wrote the following description of his own experience:

> 'We believe our group has grown as big as it ought to. We have stopped short of being an organisation, we are an organism instead, a living and spontaneous association of individuals who know one another intimately, care for each other deeply, and feel the kind of respect for one another that makes rules and bye-laws unnecessary. A group is the right size, I would guess, when each member can pray every day, for every other member, individually and by name, interceding for his personal needs as well as for the success of a particular mission. But what is to prevent twenty, fifty, one hundred such groups from springing up wherever the call is heard — each obedient to its own particular genius, each working in its different way for the coming of the one Kingdom?' [9]

In this natural, almost familial setting, the possibility of every-member participation remains; this is in stark contrast to the limited opportunities that are available in today's large, platform-led meetings where the body is constrained and genuine spiritual growth is inevitably hindered as a result.

It is hugely ironic, then, that the main reason given for having buildings — namely, the necessity of accommodating large numbers of people—is precisely the reason for not having them! There is no use pointing to all the fantastic uses that a building offers *if it defeats the primary purpose for which it is purportedly intended*—namely that of encouraging spiritual growth. In terms of how or where Christians meet, the priority *has* to be that the setting encourages, supports and allows for the New Testament principles of participation and the associated mutual edification. This is far less likely to occur when individuals congregate *en masse* in 'sacred spaces' in the hope of encountering God, rather than recognising that God dwells within these same individuals... that each believer is, in a sense, a 'sacred space' in himself.

Who is my Neighbour?

Is Christ divided?   *1 Corinthians 1:13*

Over the course of time, God's people have come to accept the unbiblical idea of *church-as-a-thing-in-itself* and to make matters worse, denominationalism has proceeded to dismember an already marred body. In concrete terms, one of the most significant outcomes has been the erection of not one, but several church buildings in each and every town and city in which Christendom has established itself. The result has been to divert peoples' attention, time and energy towards their own particular pile of bricks and away from the rest of the town or city, draining the spiritual life and vitality from where it is most needed: where we live.   As Wayne Jacobsen observed:

> 'While claiming to be essential gatherings for believers, our Sunday morning events do more to fragment the body of Christ in any locality.' [10]

Liz and I have experienced the truth of this ourselves: we once lived in a suburb in which a good proportion of Christians also resided, but since we all belonged to different fellowships we had little or no interaction with one another. Sunday mornings would see everyone getting into their cars and driving to their respective churches, all of them located somewhere other than where we all actually lived: the result was that, apart from the occasional and almost completely ineffective door-to-door campaigns, our neighbourhood experienced little, if any, Christian impact. I think it's reasonable to assume that this picture would have been and continues to be duplicated, not just in that suburb and city, but throughout the country and the world as a whole. Far from aiding the kingdom, buildings are a contributing factor in the enemy's attempts to divide and rule.

The Monuments Men

Is it then the walls of a church that make a Christian?

Augustine, Confessions

In *Loving God*, Chuck Colson observes:

> 'Isn't it interesting that Jesus didn't set up an office in the temple and wait for people to come to him for counselling? Instead, *he* went to *them*... imagine what would happen if we gave as much attention to individual lives as we give to our buildings — how much healing would result, how much transformation?' [11]

Within the *ekklesia*, leaders *minister*: in *church-as-a-thing-in-itself*, leaders *administer* instead; rather than building people, they build... buildings. And yet, despite arguments which militate against their use, it is evident that surrendering our church buildings does not appeal to most modern Christians (particularly leaders) for whom a large congregation meeting in a large building is seen as a measure of success and something to which one ought to aspire. Perhaps meeting in houses isn't perceived to be as 'glamorous' or doesn't feel as powerful. More importantly, I believe some — and again, especially those in leadership — would be concerned about how to control a large number of separate meetings. Without a building with which to gather the people around themselves, those appointed as leaders would lose much of their influence over everyone else.

That buildings have helped to concentrate power in the hands of the priesthood — whatever the religion — has held true throughout the ages; indeed, one has to wonder whether this was a factor in Constantine's thinking when deciding to embark upon his church building programme. But today, over sixteen hundred years later, increasing numbers of Christians are being turned off by the centralized authority of *church-as-a-thing-in-itself* which Constantine helped to develop, and many are leaving the institution as a result. It's no wonder, then, that so many of our buildings are closing down and being sold off; as we saw earlier, a great number of them are currently owned by the world...

But then, in a way, they always have been.

Isn't it staggering when you think that one sermon on the day of Pentecost produced 3000 Christian people? And we had some cities yesterday where 3000 sermons were preached and nobody was saved. And it doesn't even faze us. The church used to be a lightning bolt, now it's a cruise ship. We are not marching to Zion — we are sailing there with ease. In the apostolic church it says they were all amazed — and now in our churches everybody wants to be amused. The church began in the upper room with a bunch of men agonising, and it's ending in the supper room with a bunch of people organising. We mistake rattle for revival, and commotion for creation, and action for unction.

You know brethren, you never have to advertise a fire. You don't have to advertise it in the newspaper, forget it. You let the glory of the Lord fill the temple; people will come from hundreds of miles. Because it's starvation everywhere.

Leonard Ravenhill
Weeping between the porch and the altar

13

TALKING HEADS

Download Unsuccessful

Always learning but never able to come to a knowledge of the truth.
2 Timothy 3:7

There are two major elements common to the majority of church services — the worship and the sermon, and of the two, the sermon is probably regarded as *the* central, defining feature of Sunday church. It's inclusion in the proceedings is simply non-negotiable. But just how effective are sermons as a vehicle for encouraging spiritual growth?

Søren Kierkegaard certainly seemed to think that sermonising, at least within the commonly accepted context of Sunday church, was largely ineffective as a means of spiritual transformation:

'If the pastor's activity in the church is merely a once-a-week attempt to tow the congregation's cargo ship a little closer to eternity, the whole thing comes to nothing, because a human life, unlike a cargo ship, cannot lie in the same place until the next Sunday.'[1]

In fact, evidence exists that despite the huge amount of time and effort that often goes into producing an individual sermon, generally speaking, the lasting effect on people's lives is minimal. For example, a few years ago I came across the following research on this topic which gave me pause for thought:

'Myers and Jeeves…cite studies that indicate a low level of comprehension, with only 10 percent recalling the sermon from the week before and 30 percent denying that they had even heard a sermon on that topic.' [2]

This caused me to question just how many sermons I could personally recall: I calculated that out of the hundreds that I must have heard, I could count on the fingers of one hand those I could recollect in any great detail; of those, there were only two or three which I considered to have had any sort of lasting effect. One thing did seem to be certain, however: judging not only from the statistics but also from numerous conversations with others, my apparent immunity to any of the supposed benefits available from listening to a sermon was far from unique.

Each and every Sunday without fail, thousands of sermons are delivered from pulpits all over the world, including many that are skilfully constructed and well-rehearsed. But the fact that the overwhelming majority are ineffective to such a high degree ought to cause us to wonder just how much of this particular activity is, indeed, initiated by God? With this in mind, I'm particularly interested by the following comments from the late Dallas Willard:

> 'A leading American pastor laments, "Why is today's church so weak... [having] less and less impact on our culture? Why are Christians indistinguishable from the world?"
>
> *Should we not at least consider the possibility that this poor result is not in spite of what we teach and how we teach, but precisely because of it?* Might that not lead to our discerning why the power of Jesus and his gospel has been cut off from ordinary human existence, leaving it adrift from the flow of his eternal kind of life?'[3] (Emphasis mine.)

If Willard's observation is correct — if there *is* something amiss with what and how we teach — then it makes sense to take a look at the whole subject.

A Closed Shop
Whose church is it anyway?

The generally accepted idea of church teaching is that more often than not, it is delivered by the same person — usually the pastor or at most the same few people — week in, week out, in the form of a sermon. One might be forgiven for thinking that if teaching is meant to equip the saints, then surely this would be evidenced by a steady flow of new teachers—as well as those with other gifting. But how often, if at all, do we see a church generate a plentiful and continual supply of people from its own congregation who are given the opportunity to take on the role of teaching? It is rare indeed.

Some of those who teach argue that Scripture itself makes clear that their own number is meant to be limited, citing the following from James 3:1:

> 'Not many of you should presume to be teachers, my brothers, because you know that we who teach will be judged more strictly.'

Consider the words, 'Not many of *you* should presume'; when one reads the context, James was talking to a particular group of people whose conduct he knew well, and he was warning them not to presume to be teachers *because many of them did not set an example by their everyday speech.* Support for this is found in verses 9-12, where we read:

> 'With the tongue we praise our Lord and Father, and with it we curse human beings, who have been made in God's likeness. Out of the same mouth come praise and cursing. My brothers and sisters, this should not be. Can both fresh water and salt water flow from the same spring? My brothers and sisters, can a fig tree bear olives, or a grapevine bear figs? Neither can a salt spring produce fresh water.'

James is telling his audience that the words emanating from their own mouths on a day-to-day basis disqualified most of them from the role of teacher. Speaking on spiritual truths in certain settings and yet speaking inappropriately on other occasions, would cause their teaching to lack any credibility in the eyes of everyone else and simply open them up to the charge of hypocrisy. Like James, the apostle Paul also reminded those who would teach of the need to not only 'talk the talk', but also of the necessity of 'walking the walk'. In 1 Corinthians 4:17, Paul writes:

'[Timothy] will remind you of *my way of life in Christ Jesus, which agrees with what I teach everywhere in every church.*'

Elsewhere, Paul instructs Timothy to:

'...train yourself to be godly...set an example for the believers in speech, in life, in love, in faith and in purity...Be diligent in these matters; give yourself wholly to them, so that everyone may see your progress. *Watch your life and doctrine closely.* Persevere in them, because if you do, you will save both yourself and your hearers.'

1 Timothy 4:7-8, 12-16

Returning to James, when he says that those who teach will be judged more strictly, he's not referring to any judgment regarding the quality of the message itself but rather the quality of the *messenger* — he's talking about what the teacher says when he's *not* teaching.

Now, whilst James' reservations were addressed to a specific community, it's safe to say that his advice applies to all of us — we *all* struggle with the tongue. But we also need to notice what James *didn't* say: he didn't say, 'Not many of you have the ability to teach'; he didn't say, 'Not many of you will ever become teachers': it's inconceivable that James would not want as many people as possible to be mature enough to be able to teach, especially if that was their gifting. What he said, *based upon their conduct at the time*, was, 'not many of you should *presume* to be teachers'.

I say this for the simple reason that we are about to see that Scripture indicates that teaching is, in fact, open to a much wider number of Christians than many of us have been led to believe. Ironically, the argument that it is a biblical principle to consciously allow for only a handful of teachers is, itself, an example of faulty teaching. It becomes evident that some have extrapolated from a single verse in order to dissuade others from joining them on the platform, and therein lies the real problem...because, in the beginning, there was no platform and — by implication — no separate, priestly minority which monopolized the teaching.

Let My People Grow!

*I start with the premise that the function of leadership is to produce
more leaders, not more followers.*

Ralph Nader

In Chapter 11, I suggested that as far as meetings were
concerned, Paul's goal was that everything should be done in
order to strengthen the *ekklesia,* and that one way to achieve
this was through every-member ministry. Unfortunately,
however, once an elite group of Christians had been
established, the foundation was laid for increasing control of
meetings by those in authority, whilst participation from the
rest of the body was correspondingly restricted. Less and less
room was available for people to exercise their gifts —
including that of teaching, the latter becoming almost
exclusively limited to the existing leaders.

However, contrary to current practice, Scripture suggests
that in principle, teaching is open to everyone in some
measure and it is not the preserve of a select few. For instance,
in Colossians 3:16 Paul writes:

'Let the word of Christ dwell in you richly *as you teach
and admonish one another* with all wisdom, and as you
sing psalms, hymns and spiritual songs with gratitude
in your hearts to God.'

Now, clearly, there are those who will be particularly gifted in
the area of teaching; for example, in 1 Corinthians 12:29, Paul
asks rhetorically, 'Are all teachers?' with the assumption being
in the negative. But this should not preclude many others from
contributing as well, which is quite unlike what happens
today.

Looking at another passage, this time from the book of
Hebrews, the author writes:

'We have much to say about this, but it is hard to make
it clear to you because you no longer try to understand.
In fact, *though by this time you ought to be teachers,* you
need someone to teach you the elementary truths of
God's word all over again. You need milk, not solid
food!'

Hebrews 5:11-12

The passage implies—yet again—that there should be a sizeable number of teachers and not just a handful. Whilst the text suggests a failure on the part of the Hebrews to apply what they had been taught, one thing we can assume with a great deal of confidence is that their lack of growth was *not* due to poor teaching. We cannot, however, conclude the same today.

While a lack of application will always be a potential cause of poor growth on the part of any individual, I think it's also fair to say that the blame isn't always the fault of the 'layman'. If a student or a disciple isn't learning, this can equally be the fault of the teacher: in fact, one could argue that it is at least partly because a lot of today's teaching is so inadequate that so many within the main body are ill-equipped to become teachers themselves—that the gifting of many of those who teach is so lacking that they inadvertently limit the number of those to whom God has also given the gift. In this way, the very people to whom the 'qualified' teachers should be passing on the baton are left running on the spot.

However, these 'sins of omission' are not the only reason for the dearth of teachers which we commonly encounter in the majority of our fellowships. One doesn't have to look very far in order to discover a 'sin of *commission*', one which would better account for the absence of new blood within the leadership of so many churches.

Domination within one's Denomination

Most of our preaching is about a patriarchal figure telling a submissive group of people what is good for them.

Meic Pearse

A pastor once told Liz and I that people needed to go to church and hear his sermons because there was a doctrine which he phrased as, 'Sitting under the authority of the Word.' Now I believe it's true that the Word itself does indeed possess authority, and that it is the Word of God to which all believers ought to submit; *but that's not to say that the person delivering the Word possesses authority in and of himself.* I say this because knowing the pastor as I did, perhaps I could be forgiven for thinking that what he really meant was, 'Sitting under the authority of the Pastor.'

When I asked the pastor to show me where—in the Word—the doctrine of 'sitting under the Word' was located, he was unable to do so, which struck me as considerably ironic. There was certainly no mention on his part of the desire to encourage spiritual growth or conformity to the image of Christ... ideas which *are* found in the Word; there was no discussion concerning the equipping of God's people, nor of their edification, concerning which Oswald Chambers wrote:

> 'The test for apostles and teachers is not that they talk wonderful stuff, not that they are able to expound God's word, but that they edify the saints (Eph. 4.12).' [8]

There was no suggestion of inspiring people to action as indicated in the following words, variously attributed to Francis de Sales and Billy Graham:

> 'The test of a preacher is that his congregation goes away saying, not, "What a lovely sermon!" but "I will do something."'

Of course, the idea of members of the congregation exercising any kind of initiative as a result of the pastor's sermonising is probably the last thing most pastors—at least those with a controlling disposition—would want to encourage, which brings me back to my own pastor. He gave no indication that uppermost in his thinking was that attending church might lead to an encounter with God. By comparison, Scottish preacher James S. Stewart had a particular theological test for evaluating the effectiveness of his own sermons: referring to his congregation he would ask himself, 'Did they, or did they not, meet God today?'

The harsh reality is that the core concern of many pastors often appears to lie elsewhere; Meic Pearse doesn't pull any punches when he states:

> 'Such a system encourages 'star' preachers who are strong on rhetoric and able to hold the rest of us in awe of their skills. So ministry comes to mean domination, encouraging would-be leaders in the audience to adopt

the same pattern of behaviour, while the others assume
they have nothing (even questions) to contribute.' [9]

In many churches, the reason why pressure is put on people to
attend meetings and hear the Word is not necessarily
concerned with their spiritual well-being, but rather to do with
the needs of those creating that pressure in the first place.
Underneath the genteel façade of Christian interaction, it is not
uncommon to discover a fleshly cocktail of conflicting interests
and questionable motives; present within this mix is the need
of some of those in leadership to have an audience for their
thoughts, ideas and visions, whilst at the same time
reinforcing their authority over this same group of people. It
reflects a mindset and an attitude which has bedevilled the
church from very early on in its history.

A significant and particularly troubling example of this
controlling mindset is the fact that (as we've seen) there was
enormous resistance from some within the established church
to both the translation and the publication of the Bible into
English. There were those who wanted it kept solely in Latin
to maintain the necessity of it being read to the congregation
by, of course, the priest—even if it was not understood by the
majority of the common people. With regard to this, the
chronicler Canon Henry Knighton complained in the early
1390s:

'Wycliffe translated from Latin into the language not of
angels but of Angles (Englishmen), so that he made the
Bible common and open to the laity, and to women who
were able to read, which used to be reserved for literate
and intelligent clergy.' [10]

As far as Knighton was concerned, by making the Bible
available to common men and women, 'the pearl of the Gospel
is cast forth and trodden under the feet of swine.' These are
hardly the sentiments one might expect from someone who
has assumed the responsibility for other people's soul-care.

Knighton's attitude was not an isolated one. As we saw
earlier, during the 16th century the Church of England even
resorted to the public burning of English translations of the
Bible rather than let people read the Word for themselves, inv-

oking uncomfortable comparisons with the book-burning events conducted by the Nazis in our more recent history. Both then and now, the desire to control and manage rather than equip the saints seems to be the overriding motivation amongst many of those in leadership or teaching positions. Today, as in the past, such thinking causes those in authority to jealously guard how many — if any — are permitted to join their ranks.

And so we have this 'double whammy': we have a select group of people who, whilst they are not necessarily effective teachers — partly because the methods they employ are not drawn from the Bible but from Greek oratorical tradition — at the same time also severely restrict the opportunity for others to share the responsibility. The whole flock is hamstrung purely because those in authority want to protect their own position. It's difficult to see anything other than 'regime survival' as the reason for the state of affairs which exists in the vast majority of churches; there is certainly no biblical justification for the situation in which we find ourselves.

Silence of the Lambs

Sermons remain one of the last forms of public discourse where it is culturally forbidden to talk back.

Harvey Cox

If one had to draw up a list of individual words which might describe the church experience of most Christians, then it's highly likely that 'exclusion' would be in there somewhere. Nowhere is this more evident than in the area of teaching within the church. Not only are the vast majority of Christians denied the opportunity to teach, but, as we all know, sermons consist almost exclusively of a lecture delivered from a pulpit or stage to a passive audience, with no opportunity for any kind of interaction or contribution from the 'shop floor'.

In sharp contrast, whilst Jesus — the greatest teacher who has ever lived — did sometimes teach in formal settings such as synagogues, he also taught 'along the way' to whoever happened to be present, rather than from a pulpit to a regular congregation. He was an opportunist in the best sense of the word, often stopping to use circumstances rather than a prepared speech as a means of getting over far more complex ideas. Also unlike those who give sermons today, he took questions from those gathered.

But how much, if at all, should we base our approach to Bible teaching on Jesus' methods? Were they exemplars provided for the rest of us or was his teaching style a one-off affair? Even if we allow for the fact that the context in which Jesus taught was different to the one confronting most teachers today, on the face of it, a question-and-answer format which allows for dialogue would certainly seem more productive than the traditionally accepted Sunday morning monologue... after all, schoolteachers actively encourage their students to ask questions in order to help them learn. Meic Pearse asks:

> 'Would an occasional time of questions, gently and lovingly conducted on all sides, really undermine the 'authority' of the preacher? (As if that is what mattered!) Might it not help us to move forward together, and give us a collective opportunity to 'own' what has just been said? Wouldn't it help us to really learn from the teaching in church?' [4]

Compounding the problem is the fact that the thousands of ineffective and long-forgotten sermons consume so much time and effort on the part of those few who are allowed to deliver them. One assistant pastor I knew would spend the entire week preparing a forty-five-minute sermon; his talks were interesting, witty and so on—but then considering the amount of time he put into them they ought to have been. As a Mathematics teacher, if I took a week to prepare a single Maths lesson then my students could rightfully expect it to be pretty special! Even then, as well-constructed as his sermons were, they didn't appear to have much, if any, transforming effect on those who came to hear them.

The hours devoted to preparing his sermons also meant this same man was unavailable to pastor, counsel or generally serve the body during those periods. It seems to me that he might have been far more effective if he'd scrapped his sermons and, instead, spent time during the week discipling people through the application of the truths he believed were contained within those same sermons.

In the light of all that's been discussed, we need to ask ourselves if perhaps there aren't other, more productive methods to which we might turn in order to help people learn the things of God. After all, if we are genuinely concerned that our teaching leads to a fuller understanding of the gospel — in the sense that it directly promotes genuine spiritual growth — then it certainly seems reasonable that we should consider all the possible alternatives.

Of course, practical considerations aside, the litmus test (as ever) is to examine what Scripture has to say on the subject of teaching and compare this to current practice. Ultimately, the question we have to ask ourselves is this:

> Just how biblical are the methods we use to teach biblical truths?

A Sermon on why Sermons are Wrong

If the truth were known, many sermons are prepared and preached with more regard for the sermon than the souls of the hearers.

George F. Pentecost

Since both research and personal experience suggest that the majority of sermons appear to be largely redundant in terms of personal equipping, this ought to call into question the origins of the sermon as a teaching tool. In fact the practice of sermonising, in the form we've come to know, would be hard to discover in Scripture. Whilst there are passages which talk about *teaching*, the descriptions found there seem to bear little or no resemblance to the traditional sermon. On those occasions when we do find people teaching in the New Testament, there is no evidence that this took the form of a prepared speech. So, for example, when we read in Acts 2 of Peter's message to the crowd at Pentecost, he did not deliver a ready-made three-point sermon; neither did Stephen in his address to the Sanhedrin, as recorded in Acts 7. The preaching in these cases was 'off the cuff' — or *extemporaneous* to use a fancier word — and even when we take into account the fact that these situations weren't necessarily typical, we do not find in Scripture examples of the kind of exegesis such as we find in many sermons today.

The practice of a carefully scripted sermon did not in fact come from the Word but from the world—Greek oratory tradition to be exact. It found its way into the church through gentile converts with a talent for rhetoric, such as John Chrysostom. In *Beyond Radical*, Gene Edwards writes:

> 'The sermons you hear every week are based on Aristotle's concepts of oration...In Antioch, Syria, circa 400 A.D., one of the great heathen orators of all time, John Chrysostom (John the Golden-mouth) became a believer. He brought his Aristotelian rhetoric/sermon skills into Christianity...It is John Chrysostom who not only gave us Aristotelian sermonics, but also gave us the custom of the Sunday morning sermon, that is, the tradition of a Sunday oration being delivered by the same man, in the same place, at the same time, every Sunday. Hence you see the origin of the sermon and the Sunday church services.' [5]

Chrysostom's legacy was the establishment of a scripted weekly monologue, setting a precedent that—regardless of his personal talent as an orator—would be extremely damaging to the body as a whole. Not only did the church sacrifice the opportunity for greater numbers of people to be involved, but the genuine, heartfelt and passionate teaching we find in the New Testament was reduced to the stylized, bookish and often uninspiring format which we experience to this day.

This is not to say, of course, that knowledgeable, fervent and Bible-based teachers do not exist today... but even where they do, the Greek-inspired monologue they deliver, as well as the fact that they monopolize the teaching ministry in their respective churches, is hard to justify from Scripture. As a consequence, their overall impact is much less than either they or their congregations would hope for.

The teaching methodology which has developed over the centuries and which has become the norm is that preaching and teaching has, for the most part, become a purely intellectual exercise. I heard one pastor advise a younger colleague that in order to be a good preacher one had to read a lot; it struck me that reading a lot was quite different to 'living a lot', or 'experiencing a lot', and it reminded me of Confucius' comment: 'It is better to travel ten thousand miles than to read ten thousand books.' Paul's thirty-nine lashes, shipwrecks and stoning stand in sharp contrast to the life experience of the vast majority of those who stand in our pulpits on a Sunday morning. This is not to say that only extreme hardship qualifies someone to teach, but as we shall see, the majority of early Christians — including those with the gift of teaching — at least maintained their day-to-day jobs, ensuring regular contact and relationships with the real world and the lost within it.

In stark comparison, many of those currently in 'full-time ministry' appear to exist in a kind of parallel universe, more or less 'cut off from ordinary human existence' (to borrow from Willard); as a result of their relatively cloistered existence, many of them have little to offer from their own personal experience to their brethren, who find themselves having to negotiate the obstacles and pitfalls that living and working in this world presents to those who would follow Christ. Mark Greene, Executive Director of the London Institute for Contemporary Christianity (LICC) reports:

> 'Nearly 50 per cent [of churchgoers] said that preaching and teaching were marked by a lack of relevance, depth or challenge...Indeed, it was clear that for some, it was possible to deliver an 'excellent expository sermon' that made no connection with their life...[People are looking for] spiritual wisdom to deal with the pressures and relationships of day-to-day life. What emerged most forcefully was the perception that the preacher was out of touch with people's lives.' [6]

Unfortunately, many of our Bible teachers today appear to be filled more with book-learning and head knowledge than with the Spirit; the majority of them emerge from an extended time of study in their room or office in order to deliver the essence of what other people have said. One could be forgiven for thinking that the mission statement of many teachers today might well be founded on the following version of *The Three R's*:

Read, Rehearse, Regurgitate.

In *Sermons We See* by Edgar A. Guest, one stanza reads:

> 'Though an able speaker charms me
> with his eloquence, I say,
> I'd rather see a sermon
> than to hear one, any day.'

What people need are increasing numbers of role models — living, breathing examples of faith in action — not yet another talking head. If all this seems a little uncharitable, then A.W. Tozer had some harsher words still:

> 'Too many [Bible teachers] seem satisfied to teach the fundamentals of the faith year after year, strangely unaware that there is in their ministry no manifest Presence, nor anything unusual in their personal lives. They minister constantly to believers who feel within their breasts a longing which their teaching simply does not satisfy. I trust I speak in charity, but the lack in our pulpits is real...It is a solemn thing, and no small scandal in the Kingdom, to see God's children starving while actually seated at the Father's table.' [7]

The situation we have and which has been accepted as the norm for centuries is that the sheep turn up every Sunday and a pre-packaged meal is thrown over the fence into the sheep pen. But does God *really* operate in this way? Does He sit there with a calendar, coming up with ideas and sermon series and individual talks which He then prompts someone to articulate in piecemeal fashion here on earth? Is this how we see it done in Scripture?

Perhaps now would be a good time to compare Paul's way of teaching with the professional, polished and ultimately unsatisfying performances we find in so many of our churches today.

Gifted Amateurs

The medium is the message   *Marshall McLuhan*

Compare your last Sunday sermon to the following:

> 'When I came to you, brothers, I did not come with eloquence or superior wisdom as I proclaimed to you

the testimony about God. For I resolved to know nothing while I was with you except Jesus Christ and him crucified. I came to you in weakness and fear, and with much trembling. My message and my preaching were not with wise and persuasive words, but with a demonstration of the Spirit's power, so that your faith might not rest on men's wisdom, but on God's power.'

1 Corinthians 2:1-5

Paul's words to the Corinthians are very telling: *'I did not come with eloquence or superior wisdom… My message and my preaching were not with wise and persuasive words…'* His delivery of the gospel to the unbelievers at Corinth did not rest on a cleverly worded and skilfully presented speech:

What he had to say was far too important for that.

In 2 Corinthians 11:6 Paul wrote, 'I may not be a trained speaker...' As confirmation of this, we only have to look at his reception by the Athenians in Acts 17:18: *'What is this babbler trying to say?'* And yet God used Paul to turn the pagan world upside down.

Unlike Paul, many of those who deliver our sermons today *are* expected to be trained speakers: their messages are often meticulously crafted, resulting in a final product which can be in turn sophisticated, humorous and entertaining. Unfortunately, however, the emphasis is often on style rather than substance, and consequently — also unlike Paul's comparatively amateurish efforts — these sermons too often appear *not* to demonstrate God's power, nor do they seem in most instances to be able to change the lives of those listening.

On one hand, God uses those such as Paul, a highly trained 'Hebrew of Hebrews' with a keen intellect, who nevertheless resisted the opportunity to try to persuade his listeners with skilful rhetoric; on the other hand, God not only restores but then uses Peter, an untutored fisherman, who only a few weeks before his speech at Pentecost had denied Jesus with the same lips. God also uses people like Moses, whose reluctance to be God's mouthpiece speaks volumes:

'Moses said to the LORD, *"O Lord, I have never been eloquent, neither in the past nor since you have spoken to your servant. I am slow of speech and tongue."* The LORD said to him, "Who gave man his mouth? Who makes him deaf or mute? Who gives him sight or makes him blind? Is it not I, the LORD? Now go; I will help you speak and will teach you what to say." But Moses said, "O Lord, please send someone else to do it."'

Exodus 4:10-13

Even with such assurance from God himself, it was the low view of his own abilities, rather than any opportunities there might have been for what some today call 'personal ministry', which reigned uppermost in Moses' mind. Like Paul, he did not believe he was sufficiently 'eloquent', to the degree that he felt ill-equipped to fulfil the mission God had given him. God, of course, would have none of it and the rest, as they say, is history.

When it comes to teaching, there seems to be a clear disparity between the kind of power we read about in Scripture (such as in Paul's teaching for example) and the kind of teaching we accept as the norm today. Could it be that the transition from authentic teaching like Paul's to the sophisticated but synthetic teaching of today—based as it is on Greek rhetorical style—is at least part of the reason that so much of our teaching is so fruitless? Can you imagine, for example, Paul, Peter or Moses using an 'ice-breaker' to warm up a meeting? The nearest thing to an ice-breaker found in the Bible was the one employed by John the Baptist who, clothed with camel's hair and living on locusts—and after four hundred years of silence between the Old and New Testaments—arrived on the scene shouting, 'Repent and be baptised!' at the top of his lungs. When such men of God spoke there was no need for hype. There were no rehearsed performances or tried and tested techniques for softening up an audience—instead, what they said drew upon an entirely different set of *The Three R's*:

It was Raw, it was Real and it was Relevant.

God likes to use ordinary people—those who are, in the world's eyes, the weak and the foolish—individuals who might be regarded as 'losers' in today's parlance. God seems to delight in selecting reluctant heroes like Gideon or Moses, 'oddballs' like John the Baptist or flawed characters like Samson or Jonah. Why does He like to build His house with these sorts of people rather than the confident, the well-rehearsed and the slick?

Because that way all the glory goes to the Lord rather than to the messenger.

PTSD: Post Traumatic Sermon Disorder

While we're busy about our jobs [our leaders] seek the Lord for us, and our Christian experience is nothing more than doing what they tell us.

Wayne Jacobsen

Milton Jones observes:

'Ineffective preaching points to the colour and the number of the door. Effective preaching unlocks it.' [11]

As I remarked at the beginning of this chapter, I have forgotten the vast majority of sermons that I've sat through. Having said this, one sermon in particular stands out in my memory, but unfortunately, for all the wrong reasons. It was so desperately poor, not only did it fail to provide either the colour or the number of the door, the door it led us to was in the wrong street altogether.

I was sitting alongside a good friend, and as the sermon progressed, it became clear that the speaker was going to relate a particular story with which we were both familiar, since it came from a book which happened to be a best-seller at the time. The speaker, however, didn't reveal where the story had come from, which meant that unless the tale was already familiar to the listener, he or she wouldn't know how faithful the speaker's rendition was to the original.

For our part, knowing the narrative as we did, it was distinctly painful having to sit through the retelling due to the fact that the speaker managed to almost completely mangle the story, missing the very point that it was supposed to illustrate. We both sat there in frustration, feeling that, not only was this person being paid as part of his job to read the same books that many others were having to read in their leisure time — fitting it in after a hard day at the office or taking care of the kids—but that he wasn't quoting or even understanding them correctly!

In 1523 Martin Luther wrote an essay with the rather cumbersome title:

> 'That A Christian Assembly or Congregation Has The Right and Power to Judge All Teaching and To Call, Appoint, and Dismiss Teachers, Established and Proven by Scripture.'

Unfortunately, whilst many of Luther's suggestions for reform were acted upon, the idea that the congregation ought to be able to choose who teaches them clearly never took hold. Down the centuries the vast majority of believers have been saddled, year in, year out, with the same, often self-appointed speakers, regardless of their ability; as the preceding anecdote demonstrates, not all who presume to teach in our churches are, in truth, gifted teachers. And whether talented or not, since many of those who teach appear to be more concerned with *information* rather than *transformation* then it's hardly surprising that they are largely ineffective in terms of helping their hearers to bear fruit. Revivalist Charles Finney wrote:

> 'What is growing in grace? Is it hearing sermons and getting some new ideas about religion? No, not at all. The Christian who does this, and nothing else, will grow worse and worse, more and more hardened. Finally it will be nearly impossible to rouse him.' [12]

A friend called me up one Sunday afternoon and told me that the sermon that morning had been fantastic. I have to confess that my response was deliberately provocative:

'Really?' I said, 'And how has it changed your life?'

'Well... um... I guess it hasn't...' came the reply.

'Then what use was it?'

My long-suffering friend admitted that he couldn't say exactly *what* use the sermon had been other than it had been intellectually stimulating. He wasn't at fault, of course: like the vast majority of Christians, he'd been conditioned merely to expect the delivery of a packet of information and to judge it on its erudition or its technical merits without necessarily considering its spiritual efficacy.

Paul regarded the purpose or goal of teaching in an entirely different light, summing up the situation thus: 'Knowledge puffs up', he said, 'but love builds up' (1 Corinthians 8:1). John Wesley echoed Paul's words most elegantly when he said, 'Beware you be not swallowed up in books! An ounce of love is worth a pound of knowledge.' As Blaise Pascal observed, 'The knowledge of God is very far from the love of Him.' Unfortunately, much of our preaching is concerned not even with the knowledge *of* God (let alone the love of Him) but rather with knowledge *about* Him; equipping the saints has become more to do with facts and note-taking than with spiritual formation. One has to wonder just how many more sermons and how many more visiting speakers people are prepared to listen to before they realise that perhaps not much, if anything, is changing in their lives despite the vast amount of teaching they are receiving.

Swimming Lessons on Dry Land

I hear and I forget.
  I see and I remember.
    I do and I understand.   *Chinese Proverb*

There's a story whereby the members of a church supposedly turned up for the service one Sunday morning, only to find that the main door was locked. Pinned on it was a note from the pastor which read:

'I've talked to you lot long enough.
Now go out and do it.'

Despite the fact that its authenticity is highly dubious — it's hard to imagine any real-life pastor being quite so ready to release his flock — the story challenges the commonly accepted way of doing things. The truth is many of us have far more biblical knowledge than we are walking in: the real need is how to encourage people to *walk in whatever light they already have,* rather than continually attempting to stuff their heads with more and more knowledge that neither equips nor transforms them into the likeness of Christ. Dallas Willard neatly summed up the challenge facing us:

'Imagine, if you can, discovering in your church newsletter or bulletin an announcement of a six-week seminar on how genuinely to bless someone who is spitting on you...Imagine, also, a guarantee that at the end of the seminar those who have done the prescribed studies and exercises actually will be able to bless those who are spitting on them...Imagine further, if your imagination is not already exhausted, driving by a church with a large sign in front that says, We Teach All Who Seriously Commit Themselves to Jesus How to Do Everything He Said to Do...' [13]

As it stands, the debilitating effects of the commonly accepted methods of teaching are obvious to anyone who cares to look: large numbers of saints are *not* equipped in any meaningful sense. It's hardly surprising, then, that their progression from milk to solid food is limited, when one considers that they are either kept on the bottle or fed a diet of regurgitated 'knowledge'. Exhibiting any 'fruits of the Spirit' as a direct result of sermonising becomes increasingly unlikely, with the result that the lambs are kept as lambs, rather than developing into sheep; in like manner, the sheep are kept as sheep, rather than developing into shepherds themselves. Without a fresh supply of teachers emerging from the flock, as one would expect from Scripture, the number of those in a position to exercise this gift remains small... but then again:

Some might argue that this is the whole point.

That was Then, This is Now
From the First to the Twenty-first Century

Beginning with the early church, people would have gathered in synagogues, homes and later in churches in order to receive teaching, because either they were illiterate and/or the only scrolls or manuscripts available were kept in a centralized place. Hence we find Paul writing to Timothy:

'Until I come, devote yourself to the public reading of Scripture, to preaching and to teaching.'

1 Timothy.4:13

However, the situation which confronted Paul and Timothy does not prevail today. Over time, illiteracy gradually diminished such that people no longer needed the gospel illustrated in stained glass windows. As more and more people were able to read and write, instead of having Scripture read to them once a week by a priest (or the equivalent) it became increasingly common for people to have their own copy of the Bible. As time passed, other Christian literature also became increasingly available. Yet, despite these advances, for centuries people continued to go to church, a situation which was the norm until a few years ago.

And then the Internet arrived.

If there is one single factor which might account for the fact that this generation has been the first to witness a massive departure of Christians from the church, it would be the invention of the worldwide web.

Due to the internet we are experiencing an information explosion, comparable in its effect to the invention of the printing press. In the same way that the latter was a major factor in disseminating Luther's reforms, the internet is seeding a seismic shift in the way the Christian faith is outworked. One only has to take a cursory tour of Christian websites, or browse through the wealth of available Christian literature, to recognize that more and more believers are seeking out teaching which is often excellent, and which either supplements or even replaces the teaching in their church. Today, the vast majority of believers have direct, personal access to Christian media on a scale undreamed of in times past—materials they can read, discuss, watch or listen to for themselves rather than simply wait to be taught from the front of a church building once a week.

Increasingly, people are communicating across borders and continents, encouraging one another through the sharing of ideas and visions via websites and blogs, video-links and smart phones, wrestling with what the Bible says on a host of topics—including what it has to say concerning the body of Christ. They are enjoying something denied many of them in their official meetings—and sometimes discouraged outside them too—free, open, and meaningful dialogue.

In the light of all of these developments, I believe one could argue that we do not, *of necessity*, have to turn up to a meeting in order to have someone read or expound the Bible to us in the form of a monologue. Whilst accurate teaching undoubtedly has great value, teaching *in this form* — that is, regularly turning up at a set place at a set time in order to hear the same person or handful of people deliver a lecture — is not compulsory from a scriptural standpoint, nor is it a particularly effective way of getting people to gain Bible knowledge in this day and age.

And so, when a local church leader asked me what I wanted from preaching and from sermons, I responded by saying, 'If you're prepared to send me CDs of the messages, then I'll listen to them on the way to work.' This, I imagine, would be as unacceptable to most leaders as it was to the person who asked me the question. After all, if everyone replied in the same way as I had, then there would potentially be no audience on a Sunday morning. However, if, for the moment, we put to one side the sensitivities of those who lead, it does raise an important question:

What need, if any, is there of Sunday Church?

Indeed, judging from the number of those leaving the church, many have not only asked themselves this question, they have also arrived at a conclusion.

SECTION 3: CHURCH FINANCE

Feeding the Monster

In the beginning the church was a fellowship of men and women centring on the living Christ. Then the church moved to Greece where it became a philosophy. Then it moved to Rome where it became an institution. Next, it moved to Europe, where it became a culture. And, finally, it moved to America where it became an enterprise.

Richard Halverson

14

THE SORDID TOPIC OF COIN

Fleecing the Sheep

'It is written,' he said to them, '"My house will be called a house of prayer," but you are making it "a den of robbers"'.

Matthew 21:13

In the mid-nineties a conference was hosted by a large city church, the title being *Intimacy with Jesus*; however, to my disappointment, I discovered that in order to attend a fee of £30 per person was required. At the time, this was no small amount for either myself or many of the congregation to find, and it prompted me to remark to a friend that perhaps I could a pay fiver and get a nodding acquaintance with Jesus instead.

Not only does there seem to be an ever increasing number of Christian events which charge substantial admission fees, but there's an assumption that such fees are within the means of all those who would like to attend—yet, ironically, it is often precisely those who can't afford to listen to the message who need to hear it the most.

All this raises a simple question: why are fees being charged for something which—one would think—ought to be free? How is it ever justifiable to charge for sharing the Good News?

How did money become involved?

As the church has moved away from its simple beginnings, we have unwittingly encouraged the growth of a professional class of Christians, such that today we not only have paid leaders, but in some instances we also have paid counsellors, youth workers, office staff and so on. In some denominations the word *stipend* is used to refer to the pastor's wages, although one pastor I knew was candid enough to admit that this was merely an exercise in semantics in order to sidestep the embarrassment of calling it a salary. But whatever words we choose to describe the situation, as Wayne Jacobsen puts it: 'regrettably God's army appears to be overstaffed with mercenaries.'[1]

The emergence of a professional church has resulted in a monolith that needs to be supported financially in order to maintain itself: along with footing the wage-bill of the clergy, we're also expected to finance the buildings, the programmes — the apparatus of *church-as-a-thing-in-itself.*

According to its own website, it costs the Church of England just over £1000 million *a year* to keep itself running, of which approximately three-quarters (£750 million per annum) comes from worshippers; in 2008, when these figures were published, the Church held assets of £4.4 billion.[2] Today those assets have grown to over £6 billion and one can't help thinking that the Anglican Church would do well to consider the words of Dietrich Bonhoeffer:

> 'As a fresh start, the church should give away all her endowments to the poor and needy.'

This is, of course, highly unlikely to happen since it would seem that money, rather than the Holy Spirit, is the oil needed to lubricate the cogs of the machine and stop it grinding to a halt.

Sad to say, this state of affairs is nothing new. Martin Luther's doubts about the way the Catholic Church went about its business — both theologically and financially — had been percolating in his mind for several years before he made his doubts public. But the event which caused him to nail his colours to the church door was the arrival in the Wittenberg region of a certain Johann Tetzel. Tetzel was doing the rounds in his capacity as 'Grand Commissioner of indulgences' for the whole of Germany. *Indulgences*, a completely baseless invention of the Church, enabled it to prey on fears which the Church itself had already generated through the equally groundless concept of purgatory; for a price, one could, so people were told, buy the early release of a deceased loved one from purgatory and allow them to enter heaven immediately.

The superstitious in particular were only too ready to believe this and (literally) bought into the lie; in a style which would not look out of place today, Tetzel even had his own marketing jingle:

> 'As soon as the coin in the coffer rings,
> the soul from purgatory springs.'

The invention of the indulgence was employed by the Church as a money-making scam, a cash cow which provided a very useful source of revenue. Half the money that Tetzel raised was delivered to Pope Leo X for the ongoing reconstruction of Saint Peter's Basilica in Rome; the other half was handed over to Albert, the Archbishop of Mainz, under whose authority Tetzel performed his duties. Albert subsequently used the money to pay off the debts he'd incurred in securing his own appointment to the Archbishopric. Such were the underlying 'Christian' motives of the whole enterprise, and — at least as regards money going towards church buildings and propping up sometimes questionable ministries — one has to wonder to what degree things have changed today.

Money makes the Church go round
Church plc—Business as usual

Whilst the selling of indulgences has long-since died a natural and well-deserved death, there are, nevertheless, other ways of raising finance: some are benign, such as voluntary giving by individual church members, while others — such as charging for conferences — are less so. But by far and away the most significant form of generating income is *tithing*. Given the fact that in some churches people are regularly reminded from the pulpit of the need to tithe, it is hardly surprising that tithing is an immutable doctrine in the minds of many Christians, and its practice (or otherwise) simply not up for discussion. But what if tithing was shown *not* to be a biblical principle? What would be the ramifications? These are vitally important questions, and for this reason the whole subject of tithing will be examined separately and in depth in the next chapter.

In the meantime, the following words from Rick Warren, best-selling author of *The Purpose Driven Church* and *The Purpose Driven Life* serve to underline the very real problem of the way finances are viewed within the church:

> 'About midway through last year, I stopped taking a salary from the church...I added up all that the church had paid me in the 24 years since I started the church, and I gave it all back. It was liberating to be able to serve God for free.' [3]

It's hard to know where to even start with such a statement simply because there's so much that's deeply troubling packed into it, despite its brevity. However, I need to make it clear from the outset that this is not a criticism of Rick Warren himself; it's what it says about the system he has served faithfully and the mindset it engenders which ought to cause us concern:

> *'It was liberating to be able to serve God for free.'*

The fact is, Warren could have entered into such liberty at any time; there's nothing stopping any one individual—leader or otherwise—from serving God for free in the first place; after all, *that's what any Christian worth his or her salt endeavours to do in their day-to-day lives*. It isn't necessary to go into 'full-time ministry' *and* be paid a salary in order to serve God; as we shall see, the early Christians certainly didn't adopt this practice, which is hardly surprising since it's has no place within the New Covenant.

God's Army: Join the Professionals
Robbing Peter to pay Paul

According to some, the Bible 'clearly states' that Christian leaders ought to be financially supported by the body—but is this really the case?

When talking about remuneration, there are leaders who quote Paul's words in 1 Corinthians 9, with verse 9 often being the key phrase: 'Do not muzzle an ox while it is treading out the grain' (which Paul quotes from Deuteronomy 25:4). However, Paul's application of this OT Scripture makes interesting reading in its proper context and so I will quote at length:

'Don't we have the right to food and drink? Don't we have the right to take a believing wife along with us, as do the other apostles and the Lord's brothers and Cephas? Or is it only I and Barnabas who lack the right to not work for a living?

Who serves as a soldier at his own expense? Who plants a vineyard and does not eat its grapes? Who tends a flock and does not drink the milk? Do I say this merely on human authority? Doesn't the Law say the same thing? For it is written in the Law of Moses: "Do not muzzle an ox while it is treading out the grain"...If we have sown spiritual seed among you, is it too much if we reap a material harvest from you? If others have this right of support from you, shouldn't we have it all the more? But we did not use this right. On the contrary, we put up with anything rather than hinder the gospel of Christ...the Lord has commanded that those who preach the gospel should receive their living from the gospel. But I have not used any of these rights. And I am not writing this in the hope that you will do such things for me. I would rather die than have anyone deprive me of this boast.'

1 Corinthians 9:4-15

Instead of claiming his 'full rights' concerning personal support, Paul refused to avail himself of them so as not to hinder the gospel and become a stumbling block to his brothers. Unlike those leaders who, ironically, quote Paul in order to justify the salaries paid to them by their congregations, we read that Paul sometimes made tents in order to support himself (Acts 18:3).

Consider the following passage from 2 Thessalonians 3:7-10:

'We were not idle when we were with you, nor did we eat anyone's food without paying for it. On the contrary, we worked night and day, labouring and toiling so that we would not be a burden to any of you. We did this, not because we do not have the right to such help, but in order to make ourselves a model for you to follow. For even when we were with you, we gave you this rule: "If a man will not work, he shall not eat."'

It has to be noted that Paul's gracious acts of self-denial notwithstanding, he refers to his 'right' or 'rights' several times in the preceding passages, and suggests that technically he could have expected *some* form of material support. What I hope to demonstrate, however, is that this support did not equate to a regular salary, and neither was it something to which *all* 'in ministry' have a right. Paul's example highlights the fact that when discussing the whole issue of ministry and money, an important distinction needs to be made between two groups of people:

Itinerants and Incumbents
Those who make tents versus those who set up camp

As I mentioned in Chapter 8, those in ministry could be regarded as belonging to one of two distinct groups: on the one hand there were apostles, prophets and evangelists with an itinerant ministry and on the other there were the local, resident leaders who had emerged from within their own communities. This had an important bearing on how different ministries were supported.

Taking Paul as an example, it's important to understand that he was an *apostle*—a messenger who proclaimed the gospel from place to place. However, something that many people fail to recognize is that as a direct corollary of this, not only did Paul establish Christian communities, but *he then moved on*, even if sometimes he visited them again at a later date. Some suggest that Paul may have spent as little as one month in Berea and only two to five months in many of the other places where he established fellowships; his three years at Ephesus was unusually long. He did not 'plant a church' and then, as is sometimes the case today, become a sitting pastor who expected to draw a salary.

Because of the very nature of his calling, it would have been difficult for Paul to continue to work in order to secure an income, although, as we've just seen, he did make tents now and then; so the question is, when Paul refers to his right to a 'material harvest', is he referring to some sort of financial support as many have claimed? I believe there is sufficient evidence, both scriptural and historical, to suggest that his thinking was actually more to do with board and lodging during his stay in the various communities he visited, and certainly not referring to the provision of either regular or occasional monetary income.

The *Didache* (a short, influential Christian treatise written during the early church period) states, concerning apostles and prophets:

> 'But he must not remain more than one day, or two, if there's a need. If he stays three days, he is a false prophet...And when the apostle goes away, let him take nothing but bread to last him until his next night of lodging. If he asks for money, he is a false prophet...whoever says in the Spirit, "Give me money," or something else like this, you must not listen to him.'
>
> *Didache 11.5, 6, 12*

If an apostle asked for money, he was a false prophet. One can't help thinking of those TV evangelists who seem hell-bent on storing up treasures on earth with their constant appeals for money, and who bring to mind Romans 2:4:

> 'God's name is blasphemed among the Gentiles because of you.'

Of course these high-profile figures are simply the visible, public face of a much wider, systemic problem, and merely represent the tip of the iceberg. There are too many leaders who, to varying degrees, dedicate their Sunday morning sermons to the subject of finances, which is really a subtle means of coercing the flock to pay for their own keep and, in so doing, they make their own contribution to the weakening of the kingdom.

A little further on in the *Didache*, we find echoes of Paul's words in 2 Thessalonians 3:7-10, which I quoted earlier:

> 'If he who comes is a transient, assist him as far as you are able; but he should not remain with you more than two or three days, if need be. If he wants to stay with you, and is a craftsman, let him work for his living. But

if he has no trade, use your judgment in providing for him; for a Christian should not live idle in your midst. If he is dissatisfied with this sort of an arrangement, he is a Christ peddler. Watch that you keep away from such people.'

Didache 12:2-5

Elsewhere in the *Didache,* we also find recommendations concerning the support of apostles and others with a wandering ministry; these were applied to widows and orphans as well as aliens and the poor within the community. This support, referred to as *firstfruits*, was derived from voluntary giving and provided for the basic necessities of life, but it was never distributed in any form of stipend.

A further example might serve to make this issue clear. When, in Matthew 10:10, we read that 'the worker is worth his keep', the context is very specific: it concerns the sending out of the twelve on a mission, and has no bearing on normal, day-to-day 'church' life. Jesus is talking about how they will eat during the trip, and his words have nothing to do with wages in the literal, financial sense. This fact is supported in Luke 10:7 concerning the sending out of the seventy-two, which says:

'Stay there, *eating and drinking whatever they give you, for the worker deserves his wages.'*

Church fathers such as Irenaeus and Epiphanius, certainly did not believe Matthew 10:10, Luke 10:7 or 1 Corinthians 9:7*ff* could be used as a pattern for anything other than voluntary giving and that the latter should be emphasized as a means of support.[4]

All the evidence suggests that, at least during his time of 'ministry', Paul and people like him — that is, *itinerant* workers who as a direct result of their calling could not maintain a permanent, full-time occupation — clearly did have genuine grounds for asking that they might be provided with food, accommodation and other basic necessities without having to pay for them, but nothing more. Thus, any passages in which Paul talks about support for himself should be understood in this context.

The passages considered so far refer specifically to those such as Paul who had an apostolic ministry; they have nothing to say concerning local, incumbent leaders and that being the case, it ought to be clear that one cannot extrapolate from these particular Scriptures in order to make a case for a professional clergy as many have done. We need to consider, then, whether other scriptural references exist concerning the financial support of those with a *non-itinerant* ministry – that is, local church leaders. It's time to examine possibly *the* most frequently cited passage in this regard.

Double Honour?

Time isn't always money

Some suggest that biblical support for the existence of a paid clergy can be found in books such as First Timothy. Paul is writing to Timothy who had some sort of leadership role in the church at Ephesus, and in Chapter 5, verses 17-18, we read:

> 'The elders who direct the affairs of the church well are worthy of double honour, especially those whose work is preaching and teaching. For Scripture says, "Do not muzzle an ox while it is treading out the grain," and "The worker deserves his wages."'

Whilst we have already established the fact that both, 'Do not muzzle an ox while it is treading out the grain,' and 'The worker deserves his wages' do *not* refer to clerical salaries, but rather to the provision of basic needs – there remains the question of what exactly Paul *did* mean when talking of 'double honour.' Some have suggested that the phrase has some kind of monetary implication, but this too is an unwarranted conclusion: we need to recognize that the Greek word, *tima*, translated as 'honour' actually refers to *time* and is connected to the idea of respect. To afford someone 'the time of day' is to offer respect, to afford them 'double time' even more so. Further evidence that Paul is not talking about money but literally about honour and respect, comes from the fact that shortly before these verses – in verse 3 – Paul uses the same Greek word (*tima*) when referring to the widows in the church:

'*Honour* widows that are widows indeed.' (KJV)

I know of no church teaching that suggests not only paying a salary to the clergy but to every widow too. In the same way, when Ephesians 6:2 tells us to honour our father and mother — yet again using this same Greek word — no-one takes this to mean we should pay our parents a salary either.

To confirm that 1 Timothy 5 is talking about respect rather than finances, we simply need to compare it to 1 Thessalonians 5:12-13:

> 'Now we ask you, brothers and sisters, to acknowledge those who work hard among you, who care for you in the Lord and who admonish you. Hold them in the highest regard in love because of their work. Live in peace with each other.'

Written prior to First Timothy, Paul's 'we' in the above passage refers to himself, along with Silas and Timothy. Although the word *tima* itself does not appear in the preceding verses, the sentiment nevertheless appears to be the same in both passages: the idea of respecting and loving those who tend the flock is very evident; at the same time, it becomes increasingly clear that the issue of finances has no bearing on the discussion. I would contend that both passages are simply talking in the same way about an honour and a regard that has absolutely nothing to do with the payment of a salary to anyone.

Finally, we need to remember that Timothy was a member of the same Ephesian church whose elders Paul had previously addressed in Acts 20:33-35:

> 'I have not coveted anyone's silver or gold or clothing. *You yourselves know that these hands of mine have supplied my own needs and the needs of my companions. In everything I did, I showed you that by this kind of hard work we must help the weak,* remembering the words the Lord Jesus himself said: "It is more blessed to give than to receive."'

Having given the elders instructions encouraging them to provide for their own personal needs, it would be strange then, if Paul was to subsequently contradict those instructions by saying that, rather than support themselves, elders could now expect a salary.

To those who would, even now, continue to argue that Paul's words in First Timothy are evidence for clerical salaries, one has to ask how the church at Ephesus would have been able to conceive of, let alone institute, a wage structure for elders. As we will see in the next chapter, tithing would not be practiced until a very long time after Paul's letter to Timothy, which begs the question as to where such money would have come from; the only possible source would have been from voluntary giving, but this is hardly a reliable method for providing any sort of regular, guaranteed income. And even if money could have been found by these means, would all the elders have been paid the same? After all, the verse says, 'The elders who direct the affairs of the church *well* are worthy of double honour, *especially those whose work is preaching and teaching.*' But what are the implications for those elders who *don't* do well at the job? (And how is this decided, or more importantly – by whom?) And how much or how often could those elders who *didn't* preach or teach expect to have been paid?

Of course, a time would come much later on when, in keeping with the general decline of the church, the clergy *would* be paid a regular salary – and, judging from history, they were paid simply by virtue of possessing an office and regardless of how well (or otherwise) each individual cleric fulfilled the responsibilities of that office.

Returning to Paul's letters one last time, it's inconceivable that Paul was suggesting a kind of financial arrangement for the early church – an arrangement which would only come into existence centuries after he wrote to the Ephesians, and which was only made possible due to the culmination of a particular set of circumstances, some of which have already been discussed and – as we have seen – in themselves, had no biblical warrant.

❖   ❖   ❖

Church Incorporated
The Company you keep?

Despite what most people might think, the first time Paul bade farewell to each of the Christian communities that he'd established, he left them with no 'official' leadership. This is all the more surprising when one considers that, in most cases, these communities had been formed only a few months prior to his departure: the people who were left to fend for themselves were, spiritually speaking, infants in the faith.

In each case, however, over time a leadership did indeed emerge naturally from within each group of believers. Unfortunately, as we have seen, these legitimate, organic roles gradually became formalized down the years, ossifying into offices; yet despite this particular error, at least those who occupied these offices were nevertheless expected to also hold down a regular job alongside the responsibilities which came with that office, rather than be supported financially by the body. Thomas Lindsay remarked:

> 'The idea that when men are once set apart for the function of office-bearers in the Christian Church it becomes the duty of the Church to provide them with the necessaries of life does not belong to the times of primitive Christianity.' [5]

Lindsay went on to observe that evidence exists of bishops in the early church who were shepherds, weavers, lawyers, shipbuilders, and so on. Regarding the clergy in his fourth century church, Basil of Caesarea instructed that they 'learn a handicraft and live of the labour of their hands'[6]; Basil also witnessed 'the majority of (his clergy) plying sedentary crafts, whereby they get their daily bread.'[7] Gravestones in Turkey dating from as late as the 5th or 6th century record the fact that an elder in the local church was a goldsmith, and another a master potter [8] and such examples indicate that the idea of a payrolled clergy was not universally accepted. Yet surely, if the Bible 'clearly states' that the clergy not only could but *ought* to expect financial support, as some try to argue today, one would expect this to have become the norm by this point in church history — but evidently it hadn't.

That said, as time progressed we do find instances of a salaried clergy; perhaps unsurprisingly, we also find that Cyprian — who as we saw earlier, had such a disastrous impact upon the church of the third century — was possibly the first to pay his clerical officers.[9] However, we cannot take Cyprian's example as a legitimisation of such practice today, but rather we should see that it was just one more example of the church's continued descent into error.

Some have suggested that Galatians 6:6 lends support for the existence of a salaried clergy:

'...the one who receives instruction in the word should share all good things with their instructor.'

Whilst it is perfectly acceptable for those who serve the body in whatever capacity to receive gifts — whether material, financial or other — from those who feel led to offer them as a token of appreciation, one cannot extend this to support the notion of regular salary or a paid clergy.

Ultimately, there is neither scriptural nor unequivocal historical support for the idea that leaders were (or are) expected to give up their jobs — unless they had an apostolic calling, which made full-time work more or less impossible. Even then, there is no support for the idea that *anyone*, apostles included, be paid a salary by their fellow believers in order to enter 'full-time ministry' in the way that we find many Christians doing today. Again, I quote Thomas Lindsay, writing a hundred years ago:

'A large part of the problem of ecclesiastical extension in our own days, at home and on the mission field, has to do with money. Churches and other buildings have to be erected, and a salaried ministry has to be supported. But it must be remembered that in those early days the ministry was not paid as we understand payment, and that money for buildings was not needed. Church buildings did not exist until the second century was drawing to a close, and then only in large, populous centres.'[10]

As if to confirm this, I recently came across the following article on the Chinese church in the October 2008 online edition of *The Economist*:

'Private meetings in the houses of the faithful were features of the early Christian church, then seeking to escape Roman imperial persecution. Paradoxically, the need to keep congregations small helped spread the faith. That happens in China now. The party, worried about the spread of a rival ideology, faces a difficult choice: by keeping house churches small, it ensures that no one church is large enough to threaten the local party chief. But the price is that the number of churches is increasing…The smiling Mr Zhao says finance is no problem. "We don't have salaries to pay or churches to build."' [11]

As far as the older, Western church is concerned, however, the unconscious assumption that the *ekklesia* was somehow a *thing-in-itself* was allowed to develop apparently more or less unchecked. Over a period of time this seminal error, like yeast working through a batch of dough, permeated and 'infected' the thinking of God's people; it led to the introduction of finances, the latter deemed necessary in order to prop up the whole edifice, and which, in turn, further compounded the problem.

One of the many erroneous practices that evolved is that it became perfectly acceptable for those who led this man-made institution to lay down their tools in order to enter 'full-time ministry.' Of course, for this to be possible, it became incumbent upon everyone else to provide them with a living wage.

As the organized church proliferated, so the overheads and the subsequent need for income grew correspondingly. The obvious question became:

How was all this to be funded?

As we've already seen, today's churches generate revenue through conferences and merchandising, for example. However, there's a somewhat older and more reliable method for bringing in regular revenue in order to cover burgeoning administrative costs, one to which the church turned during the Middle Ages, and something to which we turn now.

It is difficult to get a man to understand something when his salary depends on his not understanding it.

Upton Sinclair

15

PAY AS YOU GO CHURCH

In Church We Trust

My people are destroyed through lack of knowledge   *Hosea 4:6*

I remember talking after church with someone I didn't know very well; I asked him how he was doing and, as it turned out, he wasn't in a particularly good place. He and his wife were extremely stressed because of money problems; they were struggling to pay their bills and found themselves in constant debt. As the conversation continued, he mentioned that he tithed, giving to the church even though he had the bare minimum to begin with. However, rather than the financial blessing he'd been told to expect as a result of his faithfulness, he found his experience to be the exact opposite. I asked him,

'Would you be in debt if you stopped tithing?'

'No', he replied.

I looked at him and said,

'Then the solution is obvious. Stop tithing.'

He blinked for a moment, clearly not quite sure what to make of what I'd just said.

'But that would be wrong. It's biblical.'

The person I talked to is typical of thousands of Christians who have been persuaded that tithing is a principle as binding under the New Covenant as it was under the Old and a practical demonstration of faith; we ignore it at our own peril, so we're taught, not only because a failure to tithe is rebellion against God, but because by not tithing we deprive ourselves of the multiplied blessings available to those who practice it.

However, as we are about to discover, to cease paying tithes is *not* an act of disobedience for the simple reason that tithing is manifestly *not* scriptural under the New Covenant. Returning to my conversation with the person who was struggling to make ends meet, we see here a situation where false teaching blinds those who innocently assume that Scripture is being illuminated accurately, week after week, by those entrusted to expound the Word. For my part, I refrained from asking him if he really thought God wanted him to be in debt—something Scripture *does* advise against—because he was giving to the church.

For those who feel that the foregoing sentiments undermine the authority of those in leadership, the Bible itself encourages us to question what we are taught, no matter who the teacher is:

'Now the Berean Jews were of more noble character than those in Thessalonica, for they received the message with great eagerness and examined the Scriptures every day to see if what Paul said was true.'

Acts 17:11

Other than personal obedience to God Himself, which of course is a requirement of the Christian life, I do not believe that we are directed to unquestioningly obey the teaching of all who are labelled teachers; it's little wonder that accusations of cultish behaviour are sometimes levelled at Christians when we read of some things that occur because believers are not encouraged to ascertain things for themselves.

Following the example of the Bereans, then, it's time to examine the facts.

Will a Man Rob the People of God?
Guilt-edged teaching

One fact we can put money on is that, when it's time to remind the flock for the need to tithe, proponents of the latter will almost without exception quote Malachi 3:8-10:

'"Will a man rob God? Yet you are robbing Me! But you say, 'How have we robbed You?' In tithes and offerings. You are cursed with a curse, for you are robbing

Me, the whole nation *of you*! Bring the whole tithe into the storehouse, so that there may be food in My house, and test Me now in this," says the LORD of hosts, "if I will not open for you the windows of heaven and pour out for you a blessing until it over-flows."' [NASB]

Well, what can we say? Surely the passage above settles the issue of whether or not one should tithe?

Actually, *no*.

Despite what some leaders obviously regard as an ironclad argument from Malachi, there are many more —such as Derek Prince—who contend that tithing is a feature of the Old Covenant which is not binding under the New:

'In the New Testament, God never establishes a specific law, like that of the Old Testament, requiring Christians to set aside for Him a tenth of their total income. The covenant of grace does not operate through laws enforced from without, but through laws written by the Holy Spirit in the hearts of believers. In 2 Corinthians 9:7 Paul instructs Christians, "So let each one give as *he purposes in his heart,* not grudgingly or of necessity."' [1] (Emphasis in original)

Those who endorse tithing attempt to dispose of this argument by citing supposed proof-texts other than Malachi that they claim support their position. They point to Abraham giving Melchizedek a tenth of his goods in Genesis 14:20 and argue that one cannot use Derek Prince's argument against tithing — which rests on the grounds that the Old Covenant is no longer binding on Christians—since the example of Abraham and Melchizedek *predates* the Old Covenant. In other words, since Abraham's tithe occurs *before* the giving of Mosaic Law, those who support tithing argue that it must therefore be a universal principle, valid for all time.

The problem with the 'universal principle' argument is that in Exodus 16:23, we find another example of a principle which was *also* observed before the Law was given—namely the Sabbath rest:

'(Moses) said to them, "This is what the LORD commanded, 'Tomorrow is to be a day of rest, a holy Sabbath to the LORD.'"'

However, as we've already seen, Sabbath observance is not binding on us today; as Charles C. Ryrie put it:

'Not even the most ardent tither would say that the Sabbath should be observed today because it was observed before the law, yet this is the very reasoning used in promoting tithing today.' [2]

There are in fact many more counter-arguments — far too numerous to consider here — all of which undermine the claim that Abraham's practice in this area is one which we should all emulate. What follows, is simply a brief look at one or two examples which further expose the fallacy of the argument which says that tithing is for today:

Firstly, Abraham tithed from the spoils of battle, not from his pre-existing wealth or possessions, nor from some kind of wage or salary. And if people wish to use Abraham's offering to Melchizedek as a model for the rest of us to imitate, then we should tithe once and only once, for that's what Abraham did. There is absolutely no scriptural precedent in this particular passage for tithing on a regular basis.

A distinction also needs to be made between passages such as Leviticus 27:30ff — a *teaching* passage in which tithing is introduced as a practice to be observed by the Jews — and the account in Genesis 14, which is a *narrative*; the latter is simply a description of events which transpired between Abraham and Melchizedek. There is no suggestion within the text that anyone was or is necessarily supposed to emulate Abraham's behaviour in this particular regard. If one wants to press the idea that tithing *is* something we ought to practice based on Abraham's example, then we could equally justify adopting other cultural *mores* of that era such as polygamy or the taking of concubines and a lot more besides; after all, Abraham engaged in these practices too — and all, apparently, with God's blessing.

Whilst tithing did indeed become an Old Testament practice sanctioned by God, as detailed in Leviticus and Deuteronomy, one certainly cannot use the example of Abraham in support of an argument for present day tithing. This is an important point since it disposes of the suggestion that tithing is a universal principle; instead it firmly locates the practice within the Old Covenant—and as we shall see—leaves it there.

Tithing: What they *didn't* teach you in Sunday School

Preaching from the Redacted Version

Apart from references to Malachi and Melchizedek which some have misapplied in an attempt to support the doctrine of tithing, leaders are strangely silent when it comes to further developing the biblical basis for the tithes which make their own offices possible—and it's not difficult to see why.

For instance, whilst Abraham's tithe is constantly put before us as an example we should follow, interestingly, there's no record in Scripture that Isaac, Abraham's eldest son, tithed even once. Of even greater interest, however, is the fact that it's almost unheard of for pastors to preach on Genesis 28:20-22 concerning Jacob's tithe:

'Then Jacob made a vow, saying, "If God will be with me and will watch over me on this journey I am taking and will give me food to eat and clothes to wear so that I return safely to my father's household, then the LORD will be my God and this stone that I have set up as a pillar will be God's house, and of all that you give me I will give you a tenth."'

Perhaps the reason this passage is never taught in church is because of that little word *if* with which Jacob commences his vow: *'If* God will be with me...' Jacob's preparedness to tithe was *conditional*, the classic *if-then* proposition; he was not agreeing to tithe as an unconditional act of faith, something which church leaders today encourage their flocks to do.

No wonder we don't receive teaching on it.

And the problems don't end there. A more careful examination of the Old Testament reveals there was not one but three different tithes, as attested to by the book of Tobit (part of the *Apocrypha*) and by the Jewish historian Flavius Josephus.[3] The first tithe, called *the Levitical or sacred tithe* accounted for ten per cent of all one's possessions, as described in Leviticus 27:30-33, and was used for the support of the Levitical priesthood. Interestingly, according to this passage, people could redeem part of their tithe. How many people do you know who have asked for their tithes back?

In both Deuteronomy 12:17-18 and 14:23-26 we find a description of the second tithe, known as *the tithe of the feasts*. Its name comes from the fact that it was set aside for a sacred meal in a place of the Lord's choosing:

'Eat the tithe of your grain, new wine and oil, and the firstborn of your herds and flocks in the presence of the LORD your God at the place he will choose as a dwelling for his Name, so that you may learn to revere the LORD your God always. But if that place is too distant and you have been blessed by the LORD your God and cannot carry your tithe (because the place where the LORD will choose to put his Name is so far away), then exchange your tithe for silver, and take the silver with you and go to the place the LORD your God will choose. Use the silver to buy whatever you like: cattle, sheep, wine or other fermented drink, or anything you wish. Then you and your household shall eat there in the presence of the LORD your God and rejoice.'

Deuteronomy 14:23-26

Maybe if this kind of tithing were encouraged we might find more people willing to contribute!

Finally, we find reference to a third tithe, known as *the tithe for the poor*: Deuteronomy 14:28-29 (and repeated in Deuteronomy 26:12) says:

'When you have finished setting aside a tenth of all your produce in the third year, the year of the tithe, you shall give it to the Levite, the alien, the fatherless and the widow, so that they may eat in your towns and be satisfied.'

Are people encouraged today to set aside a third tithe 'in the third year'? And is the money really given to the 'alien, the fatherless and the widow' or is it primarily set aside for the maintenance of the buildings and the salaries of the church workers?

Since three tithes existed, and not just one as everyone is taught, it's possible that Jews would have surrendered anything up to twenty-two per cent of their combined wealth; [4] this is certainly not the ten per cent figure spoken of today. The fact is, the manner in which tithing is currently practiced is so far removed from its supposed biblical roots that it renders questions such as whether to tithe before or after tax completely irrelevant. Even if we felt tithing *was* something we should do, its current form of expression bears no resemblance whatsoever to that demonstrated in the Old Testament, and as we shall now see, there is no model of tithing *at all* in the New Testament.

Tithing and the New Testament
A deafening silence

Tithing is conspicuous by its near total absence as far as the New Testament is concerned. Although it is referred to in Hebrews 7, the entire point of that passage is concerned with making a comparison between the priesthood of Melchizedek and that of Jesus, and the writer is certainly *not* suggesting tithing as an application within the New Covenant. Apart from this, the following is the sum total of verses concerning the topic:

> 'Woe to you, teachers of the law and Pharisees, you hypocrites! You give a tenth of your spices — mint, dill and cumin. But you have neglected the more important matters of the law — justice, mercy and faithfulness. You should have practiced the latter, without neglecting the former.'
>
> *Matthew 23:23 and Luke 11:42*

> 'The Pharisee stood up and prayed about himself: "God, I thank you that I am not like other men — robbers,

evildoers, adulterers—or even like this tax collector. I fast twice a week and give a tenth of all I get."'

Luke 18:11-12

That's it.

Aside from Hebrews 7, in the whole of the gospels all we find is a couple of references in which Jesus addresses the Pharisees (as opposed to his followers). But even then, some have seen Jesus' words above as biblical support for present-day tithing, although it's interesting to note that teaching which promotes tithing today is almost exclusively concerned with money; I don't recall anyone suggesting handing over a tenth of one's herbs and spices!

The reason we know that Jesus' comments to the Pharisees regarding tithing are *not* commands for us to 'go and do likewise' is because the total witness of the New Testament makes it clear that the Mosaic Old Covenant—along with the practices that went with it—applied only to Israel and the Jews, and is no longer binding upon Christians. For example, in Romans 7:6 we read:

'...by dying to what once bound us, we have been released from the law so that we serve in the new way of the Spirit, and not in the old way of the written code.'

Jesus is reminding the Pharisees, as religious leaders who lived under the law (unlike us), that *if* they were truly interested in the pursuit of holiness then they needed to fulfil the *whole* law rather than just parts of it. The simple truth is that Jesus' main concern here was not the promotion of tithing but a denunciation of false piety, something that becomes increasingly evident when one continues in Matthew 23 and Luke 18. All of this serves to illustrate the dangers of isolating a verse or passage from its context and using it to support whatever it is we want it to. The simple fact is that modern-day tithing is a theologically bankrupt doctrine.

❖   ❖   ❖

The Good News: It's ~~100%~~ 90% Free

In the religion of Christ there is no taxation. Everything is of love.

Charles Spurgeon

In the Sermon on the Mount, we discover that Jesus wasn't interested so much in what people *did* as he was in their hearts. So, in Matthew 5 we hear Jesus say, 'You have heard that it was said..."You shall not murder..." But I tell you that anyone who is angry with his brother will be subject to judgment.' He goes on to say, 'You have heard that it was said, "You shall not commit adultery." But I tell you that anyone who looks at a woman lustfully has already committed adultery with her in his heart.' Jesus contrasts the Old Covenant with the New, and makes it clear that the emphasis is no longer on what we do, but on who we are, describing a righteousness which 'surpasses that of the Pharisees and the teachers of the law' (verse 20). (That's why, as others have said, we have the *Be*atitudes rather than the *Do*atitudes! And more importantly in terms of this discussion, it is why God loves someone who gives cheerfully rather than from compulsion, as recorded in 2 Corinthians 9:7.)

With the resurrection of Christ, the old system was replaced by the New Covenant, with its internal law of grace written on our hearts (Romans 2:29, Hebrews 8:10, 10:16). Despite this, from the first days of the Christian faith there were Jewish converts to Christianity who could not shake off the old ways, insisting that Gentile believers needed to adopt certain Judaistic practices. The problem became so bad that, in Acts 15, we see that Paul went to Jerusalem where a council was held in order to address the issue.

Between them, we find Paul, Peter, and the elders all agreeing to concessions and basically hammering out a deal. In a letter delivered to the Gentile believers, the leaders in Jerusalem wrote, 'It seemed good to the Holy Spirit and to us not to burden you with anything beyond the following requirements' (verse 28), going on to ask that the Gentiles observe only the following: to abstain from ritually polluted food, from sexual immorality, from the meat of strangled animals and from blood. While we do find later on in

Galatians 2:10 that Paul had been asked by the elders to remember the poor, the main point is this:

> *No mention is made of tithing or even finances in general within this central document.*

Now surely, if tithing was such an important issue that all believers were expected to practice it, then it would have appeared as a clear mandate, if not here, then at least *somewhere* in the New Testament—but the fact is, it does not.

When we read in John 3:16, 'For God so loved the world that he gave his one and only Son, that whoever believes in him shall not perish but have eternal life', do we really believe that what Christ did for us on the cross—giving himself freely so we might have eternal life—is somehow linked to a tenth of our financial worth? Can we really believe that the words of Galatians 5.1—'It is for freedom that Christ set us free'—are somehow linked to ten per cent of our income—invoking a practice that actually derives from the very law from which Paul is telling us we have been freed? Can we seriously imagine Paul ever saying the following to Gentile believers: 'Christ's work on the cross is all you need—you're free. You don't need to follow Jewish ritual and law. Oh, except that, like the Jews who continue to live under law rather than grace, you do need to give one tenth of your income.'? Having seen Paul arguing the case against the imposition of Jewish practices upon non-Jewish believers, can you imagine the response from the Gentiles? As Russell Earl Kelly comments:

> 'The silence of the NT writers, particularly Paul, regarding the present validity of the tithe can be explained only on the ground that the dispensation of grace has no more place for a law of tithing than it has for a law on circumcision.' [5]

There's no evidence in the New Testament, either explicitly or otherwise, to support any form of legalism being practiced under the New Covenant. As *The New International Dictionary of New Testament Theology* states:

> 'For the early Fathers of the Church, as for the writers of the New Testament, the tithe was a thing of the past.' [6]

That being the case—if the New Testament doesn't endorse tithing and the early church didn't practice it—then how did this throwback to the Old Covenant become reinstated in the first place, safely installed as an integral feature of many churches today?

Footing the Bill by billing the foot... along with the rest of the Body

The New Testament nowhere explicitly requires tithing to maintain a ministry or a place of assembly.

The Oxford Companion to the Bible

The following account from the *New Advent Catholic Encyclopedia Online* provides us with some of the historical background related to the development of the tithe:

'In the Christian Church, as those who serve the altar should live by the altar (1 Cor.9:13), provision of some kind had necessarily to be made for the *sacred ministers.* In the beginning this was supplied by the spontaneous offerings of the faithful. In the course of time, however, as the Church expanded and various institutions arose, it became necessary to make laws which would insure the proper and permanent support of the clergy. The payment of tithes was adopted from the Old Law, and early writers speak of it as a divine ordinance and an obligation of conscience. The earliest positive legislation on the subject seems to be contained in the letter of the bishops assembled at Tours in 567 and the canons of the Council of Macon in 585. In course of time, we find the payment of tithes made obligatory by ecclesiastical enactments in all the countries of Christendom.' [7] (Emphasis mine)

In fact, despite the claim that tithing was practiced within 'all the countries of Christendom', it's interesting to note that the Eastern Orthodox churches never accepted the idea of tithes and its members have never paid them. [8]

The role of the clergy—the 'sacred ministers'—was paralleled with or equated to that of the Levites who performed 'religious duties' on behalf of the people; since the

Levites were supported by the tithes of the people, an argument was thus made by the established church to the effect that the laity must, in like manner, support the church and its workers. And so we see that the supposed need for a clergy (as distinct from 'ordinary' believers) led, in turn, to the professionalising of the church—along with the attendant costs. In other words, the church introduced the unbiblical principle of tithing in order to support and maintain the even more dangerous and unbiblical idea of a professional priesthood—and all *these* errors evolved from the mistaken idea that God's *ekklesia* was a *thing-in-itself*. Put simply:

Church-as-a-thing-in-itself → clergy-laity → tithing

But if even a brief examination of Scripture reveals that the practice of tithing—along with a host of other commonly accepted practices—is not remotely biblical, then why wasn't the plug pulled long ago on the system as we know it? The answer is that *church-as-a-thing-in-itself* and all that goes with it has, unfortunately, been around for rather a long time and there have been (and continue to be) many people in various quarters who are more than happy to keep things just as they are. To put it bluntly, there are a lot of jobs at stake.

In order to sustain *church-as-a-thing-in-itself*, there are regular, constant efforts by some to persuade their fellow Christians that money needs to change hands in order for the church to be able to fulfil its calling: we find ourselves in a circular situation whereby we pay people in order for them to tell us, amongst other things, that we need to pay them... Consequently, tithing has been ushered in 'under the radar' — a case of *stealth and wealth* if you like. With what appears to be a disingenuous lack of comprehensive teaching on the subject, and instead a reliance on one or two well-worn passages, it seems clear that the doctrine of tithing has been 'mis-sold' by some. There is *no* biblical justification for the kind of financial support encouraged in many churches and this has to call into question the integrity of those who preach such a message. But as disturbing as all of this is, the effects of this unhealthy attitude towards finances don't end there:

There are further, deeper and more serious consequences yet.

The Enemy of Faith: Pragmatism

Money don't buy you 'appiness, but it don't 'alf cure yer nerves.

Devonshire Farmer

An elder told a friend of mine that having a guaranteed source of funds such as tithes means there's one less thing for leaders to worry about. I had a similar conversation with another elder who — whilst conceding that the practice of tithing was more or less impossible to justify from Scripture — went on to say that the positive results obtained from tithes meant that it was, nevertheless, a good practice to encourage.

I couldn't disagree more.

The problem with statements such as these is that they emanate from a mindset modelled on the world's economy and not God's — because on each and every occasion on which these regular, 'safe and dependable' sources of income are relied upon, the less people feel the need to rely on God's provision.

In *My Utmost for His Highest*, Oswald Chambers wrote:

'The great enemy of the life of faith in God is not sin, but the good which is not good enough. The good is always the enemy of the best.' [9]

The enemy of the best is not the worst — the enemy of the best is the *good*. But the question is: what might this 'best' be? Is there a 'best' which is being prevented because people tithe? Chambers has already given us the answer — the life of faith. The following example illustrates this perfectly:

George Müller, well-known for his work in Bristol orphanages, wrote the following journal entry for July 28th, 1874, when he was sixty-nine years old:

'All funds gone and 2,100 persons to be totally provided for;

All funds gone and 189 missionaries to be assisted;

All funds gone and 100 schools with 900 students to be provided for.' [10]

Müller was in great need, as his journal suggests, but we also know that God subsequently and faithfully met each of those stated needs. Twenty-two years later and one year before his death aged ninety-two, Müller was asked if God had always been faithful:

> 'Always! He has never failed me! For nearly seventy years every need in connection with this work has been supplied...Hundreds of times we have commenced the day without a penny, but our Heavenly Father has sent supplies the moment they were actually required...No man can ever say I asked him for a penny; we have no collectors, no committees, no endowment. All has come in answer to believing prayer.' [11]

Churches are supposed to be built upon the rock of faith in Christ, but I believe many churches today are built upon a raft of tithes instead. I suggested in the heading for this section that an unhealthy pragmatism can creep into our thinking and our practice; I'd also like to suggest that such pragmatism has been employed as a Trojan horse by the enemy in order to infiltrate and attack the people of God.

In sharp contrast to the faith demonstrated by Müller, I actually believe that once a church establishes tithing as a principle then it's in danger of undermining not just the faith required for finances but of diminishing faith in general, and not least amongst the paid leadership who benefit from those tithes. Recently, for example, I read this on the website of a large American church:

> 'The church doesn't exist to collect money. But if it doesn't collect money it won't be here. God instituted the tithe for a purpose.' [12]

Apart from the alarming lack of faith exhibited in this passage—the suggestion that God is incapable of sustaining something without money being available—one has to wonder how The Church managed to exist for the six hundred years previous to its decision to officially introduce tithing: the simple fact of the matter is that even within the context of an already corrupted body, the idea of a salaried leadership was far from universally accepted within the early Christian communities.

Only recently, a friend commented to Liz that he didn't hold out much hope for the long-term survival of a regular, well-known Christian conference because the leaders were already burnt out. When Liz asked why this was, the friend replied that part of the problem was that there were not enough tithes to finance the event, and the financial shortfall was placing the leaders under pressure. But surely, the burn-out of the leaders, plus the reason given for it, all point to the fact that someone, somewhere, is doing something wrong — because, as Hudson Taylor observed:

'God's work, done in God's way will never lack God's supply.'

When we move away from God's way of supplying our needs by faith, and into the world's way of working in order to sustain the edifices that we have constructed, we are on a slow road to nowhere.

The professionalising of the church has led to a paradoxical state of affairs: it's quite an irony that church structures have developed in such a way that many of its members ultimately have to pay, one way or the other — whether by tithing, conference fees or 'encouraged giving' — to hear talks on the subject of faith by those who are exercising precisely the opposite when it comes to the means by which they are rewarded for their insights. This hardly sets a positive example or precedent and does not augur well as far as effective discipleship is concerned... but of even greater concern is the fact that those who want to be discipled and grow in God are being charged for the privilege.

One occasion where we see Jesus *angry* is when he confronts the money changers within the temple courts. In his commentary published three hundred years ago, Matthew Henry made the following judgment:

'If Christ came now into many parts of his visible church, how many secret evils he would discover and cleanse! And how many things daily practiced under the cloak of religion, would he show to be more suitable to a den of thieves than to a house of prayer!'

I suspect Henry would be even more appalled by today's church than by the church in his own day. Perhaps it's time to stop the money changing, to cancel the cheques and (bank) balances, and having dispensed with such reliable means of support, to force ourselves — the entire body, leaders and led — to take the steps of faith that enable us to grow as God intended.

Perhaps it's time to...

Rise up and Walk

It is not persecution of the church in China that I fear. The church has always been able to weather persecution. My fear is love of money in the church.

Chinese pastor

In Acts 3:1-10 we read the following:

'One day Peter and John were going up to the temple at the time of prayer — at three in the afternoon. Now a man who was lame from birth was being carried to the temple gate called Beautiful, where he was put every day to beg from those going into the temple courts. When he saw Peter and John about to enter, he asked them for money. Peter looked straight at him, as did John. Then Peter said, "Look at us!" So the man gave them his attention, expecting to get something from them.

Then Peter said, "Silver or gold I do not have, but what I do have I give you. In the name of Jesus Christ of Nazareth, walk." Taking him by the right hand, he helped him up, and instantly the man's feet and ankles became strong. He jumped to his feet and began to walk. Then he went with them into the temple courts, walking and jumping, and praising God. When all the people saw him walking and praising God, they recognized him as the same man who used to sit begging at the temple gate called Beautiful, and they were filled with wonder and amazement at what had happened to him.'

Twelve hundred years after this event and during his visit to Rome, the medieval priest and scholar Thomas Aquinas is supposed to have encountered Pope Innocent IV counting out money. Looking up, the Pope remarked, 'Behold, Master Thomas, the church can no longer say, as Saint Peter, "Silver and gold have I none!"' To which Aquinas is said to have replied, 'Alas, neither can we say what follows, "but such as I have give I thee: In the name of Jesus Christ of Nazareth rise up and walk."'

Clearly, the rather inappropriately named Innocent didn't appear to place too much value on Jesus' words as recorded in both Matthew 6:24 and Luke 16:13, where we read:

> '"No one can serve two masters. Either you will hate the one and love the other, or you will be devoted to the one and despise the other. You cannot serve both God and money."'

The church isn't represented by Peter and John, as Pope Innocent suggested, *but by the crippled beggar.* For far too long those who have presumed to speak for God have been waiting by the Beautiful Gate, waylaying the people of God as they gather to enter into His presence, and asking them to pay for the upkeep of *church-as-a-thing-in-itself* through tithes as well as other means; it beggars belief that anyone can seriously promote tithing when, as we have seen, everything in Scripture militates against it. It's time for the church to do away with the lame excuses offered in support of it – to throw away the crutch provided by the re-institution of an Old Covenant practice – and to learn to lean on God instead. Only then will we begin to move in power and authority, causing the world to look on in wonder and amazement once more.

Unfortunately, however, it's highly unlikely that those who currently promote tithing are voluntarily going to revoke the practice, since, for many of them, their livelihoods depend on it. I doubt there will be a crisis of conscience on the part of those leaders who preach tithing out of vested interest and as a form of fund-raising for their own projects. Ultimately, it will be up to the people to decide for themselves whether or not they believe this practice is scriptural or not. Should they conclude that it *isn't*, they will need to make a further decision as to what, if anything, should be done about the matter.

My personal view is that, in order to see the church begin to walk in the sort of power about which we read in Acts 3, then a first, positive step forward would be if—as of this moment—all those who tithe ceased to do so. If this were to happen, one thing is certain—whole swathes of the ecclesiastical landscape would alter considerably, for if there was no income from tithes, many churches—too inflexible to cope with the change—would simply be unable to function, while others would have to dramatically restructure in order to survive. It is a hard thing to say, but I suspect that far too many ineffective ministries are being supported by tithes; the cessation of financial support would lead to the immediate removal of a lot of dead wood. More importantly, if tithing were to be discontinued then there would be a real possibility that *church-as-a-thing-in-itself* might collapse and thereby cease to obscure Christ's *ekklesia*, at long last allowing his Bride to come to the fore.

While the reality of a church without regular tithes to fall back on is a daunting prospect for those conditioned to rely on them, there's the genuine possibility that the faith level of all believers would rise—including that of the leaders. Even more importantly, God would get the lion's share—if not all—of the glory. And why?

> Because whatever happened that was good, it would be clear to everyone that it had to have been God rather than the gold that did it.

SECTION 4: CHURCH STRUCTURE

Body Building

Leading people to go to the cross and die is not easy. Until they do, there will be no growth. The cells are not the secret; it is in the crucified lives of Christians who have finally come to the end of themselves and are totally dedicated to doing the work of their Lord.

Dion Robert, African pastor

16

CHURCH WANTED... DEAD OR ALIVE

In the Beginning...
...There was no professional clergy

Whenever the topic of *church* is discussed, a word that often comes up is 'structure', but since the concept of structure is not made explicit in the Bible this makes any attempts to define it somewhat difficult. Nevertheless, if you press people to try and pin down what they mean when they use the term *church structure*, it seems they are essentially talking about, firstly, what we might call the superstructure: the public or visible features of church and which basically means *the leadership, the buildings and the meetings.* Secondly, they are talking about the behind-the-scenes structures which are judged to be necessary in order to feed into and support these outward expressions of church. Further to this and undergirding everything, there is the whole area of finances, without which it would be difficult for most of today's churches to maintain their existence.

The subjects of leadership, buildings, meetings and finances have already been examined and as we have noted, as far as the way they are generally practiced or implemented, all have fallen short in terms of any credible biblical support; it goes without saying that any subsequent or secondary structures which have developed from them are equally illegitimate.

As we observed earlier, one of the most significant errors to emerge from the initial mistake of regarding the *ekklesia* as a kind of *thing-in-itself* was the division of the *ekklesia* into two castes — the so called 'clergy' and the remaining 'laity' with all the unbiblical baggage that accompanied these terms. In terms of the deformation of the body of Christ, the damage that resulted cannot be overestimated; the clergy-laity hierarchy is, figuratively speaking, the mother of all church structures, for out of it a wider view of structure has developed which has become increasingly removed from Scripture: down the centuries, those in authority, unwittingly or otherwise, have redirected God's people away from their Maker and towards *church-as-a-thing-in-itself...* and ultimately, towards the clergy itself.

Once the *priesthood-of-some-believers* became an integral part of the fabric of Christian experience, other equally unscriptural concepts and practices followed in its wake; bespoke buildings, pulpit led meetings, the silent majority... these negative developments essentially had no biblical support and were only sustained by a handful of strong-willed individuals, some of whom bent God's original design to their own purpose, thereby helping to create something apart from the *ekklesia*: a man-made edifice, complete with its own structures and hierarchies... an institution which we humans have called *church*.

The Pressure to Produce

You people build the world's best cars... you ought to be able to build the world's best churches.

American pastor addressing German Christians

Having been appointed (or in some instances, having appointed themselves) to a position of authority, members of a professional clergy have to justify their offices and the associated salaries. Unless those in leadership are to be seen to be doing *something*, the obvious question will always arise: 'What are we paying you for?' In simple terms:

A professional clergy is under pressure to produce.

What does this pressure look like? The most obvious example is the pressure to keep the machine ticking over: officiating at weddings, baptisms, and funerals; preparing the Sunday sermon and choreographing the worship; organising the various teams, the endless meetings that *church-as-a-thing-in-itself* generates and all the note-taking and letter writing, the minutes and the emails, the bulletins and the notices... all the communications that arise from these meetings. And looming behind everything, the ever-present spectre of finances and the need to balance the books.

The pressure is probably even more acute in those churches which face competition, not from the world, but from the church next door: the one with the gifted preacher; the one with the young, dynamic worship group and the outreach programmes which seem more socially relevant; the one whose success and favour in God's eyes is apparently evidenced by the fact that they are planning to move into a new multimedia, multi-million-pound facility (if they haven't already).

Of course, many pastors will be keen to add that what I've just described is only the tip of the iceberg and that all these things don't tell half the story. Yet despite these pressures, the majority of leaders nevertheless prefer to hold onto their position with a vice-like grip, unwilling to take the risk of 'letting go and letting God'. This is hardly surprising when we consider the position of the pastor at the pinnacle of the church structure. They appear reluctant to share their elevated position, sometimes not even with God.

For this reason, those in charge do not wish to rely upon the Holy Spirit to direct affairs, preferring instead to take hold of the reins themselves; rather than exercise faith, they operate out of their own understanding and their own strength, trying to build *church* rather than allowing God to build His people instead. Unfortunately, the fruit of such labour is, more often than not, the mental, physical and spiritual exhaustion which permeates the whole human-inspired edifice, draining not only the leadership but eventually the whole body. *These are the inevitable consequences of a reality which such leaders have created, or at least helped to perpetuate.*

It also needs to be understood that (as with many things relating to the church) the pressure-to-produce represents merely the branches and leaves of a bigger root issue and is the natural outcome of a broken model. For the best part of two thousand years a situation has been allowed to develop wherein we find ourselves operating out of a grossly misguided institutional paradigm, with one of the inevitable outcomes being a continual pressure to maintain an overarching structure or edifice that God has not, in fact, endorsed. This man-made structure is, of course, *church-as-a-thing-in-itself.*

One of the ways this pressure manifests itself is in what we might describe as...

Cargo Cult Christianity
Cut and paste church

During the Second World War, the American military found itself island-hopping across the Pacific as it advanced inexorably towards Japan. Bases were established on these islands as jumping-off points, flying in tons of ordnance, supplies and all the other equipment needed to conduct a war. As one would expect, this was all something of a shock to the indigenous populations who witnessed these events; they were probably confused and amazed in equal measure as a steady train of aircraft came and went, disgorging vast amounts of *materiel*.

In time, the US, along with its allies, overcame Japan militarily and one day the Islanders woke up to find the soldiers and airmen gone. Some of them had no doubt forged friendships with individual Americans and would have missed them, but what they might have missed even more were all the 'goodies' that had arrived with these outsiders. How could the Islanders cause the influx of material blessing to resume? What could they do? *They put their heads together and came up with a plan.*

What happened next has been documented by anthropologists and classified under the label *Cargo Cults*. In order to encourage the resumption of supplies, the local people attempted to emulate what they had seen in order to reproduce the same outcome: they built mock airstrips complete with imitation control towers, inside which were radios made of sticks; some of them played the role of controllers with earphones made from coconuts; others painted *USA* on their bodies. It goes without saying that their hopes of persuading the spirit world to recommence the flow of various commodities failed to materialize.

It is, of course, not the US military which has departed from many of our churches but the Holy Spirit. In an effort to coax Him back (or at least bless us with His gifts) we have behaved in ways not unlike those Pacific Islanders. There's the temptation to look at what the Bible has to say about 'church', and rather like members of a cargo cult, strive to make a carbon copy of what we believe we've found there. By cutting-and-pasting various Bible verses people attempt to encounter God through the replication of an outward form, structure, or way of doing things—however one phrases it—without recognising that the very Scriptures they are reading (before they rearrange them) illustrate the fact that *this is exactly the reverse of how things happened in the early church.* We are endeavouring to engineer an encounter with God through the creation of particular structures, yet what we discover from our Bibles is that any structures that did develop in the early church were as a result of men's encounters with God. By manipulating the Word, we hope to manipulate God Himself into making an appearance. However, judging from His absence in so many of our churches, it seems that God will have none of it; as with the efforts of those south-sea islanders, our methodologies are simply incapable of delivering the goods. In desperation, therefore, some have looked beyond the Bible for inspiration...

Going Down to Egypt

Where there is no Mission Statement the programmes perish.

In Genesis 15, God tells Abraham he will be a father despite his advanced years and the fact that his wife Sarah is well past the age of child-bearing. If anyone felt the pressure to produce it must have been this poor woman! It becomes evident, however, that Abraham didn't seem to think that God was capable of fulfilling His promise and so he decided to help God out. This is not unlike the situation in many of our churches today: despite the fact that Jesus said he would build his body, many church leaders have decided to give Jesus a hand—if not take over altogether.

Abraham's solution—to have a child by his wife's slave—might seem strange to us, but it was the normal thing to do within his culture; however, it was not God's way. When it comes to delivering our 'baby'—which we have christened *Church*—we too, have increasingly turned to our own culture, taking our cue directly from the world rather than from God Himself. I cannot think of a more perfect example of this than the following, which I read in a report some years ago in *Renewal Magazine*. It concerned the establishment of an £8 million World Prayer Centre in Colorado Springs under the auspices of the Father of Church Growth, C. Peter Wagner:

> '[The centre will be a] strategic nerve centre for mobilising worldwide prayer...[having] state-of-the-art electronic technology for researching, processing, classifying and transmitting the information...[which] will be processed according to security classifications.' [1]

Considering the Apostles didn't even have electricity, it's a miracle that Christianity managed to get off the ground at all...

Some churches are built by employing techniques which have been transplanted directly from the world and merely given a Christian spin; there are churches whose organisation derives as much, if not more, from business models than from the Bible, with those who lead behaving more like managers than ministers. We find churches where leaders are 'head-hunted' for church offices; where individuals have *Spiritual Consultant* written on their business cards. We find churches which are led by pastors who resemble CEO's more than they do the humble shepherd; leaders who talk of 'my staff', and who refer to church workers as those whom they have the authority to 'hire and fire'. In many churches today, ministry in anything more than a minor capacity is only possible for those with certificates issued by seminaries or theological colleges, regardless of whether the Spirit of God resides within those same individuals.

Man's methods are being used, not only in an attempt to manufacture church growth and revival, but also in the everyday running of many of our churches. Demographic analyses are made, statistics are employed, charts are drawn; at the same time, skills are polished, body language is choreographed, public speaking is rehearsed and refined, whilst ice-breakers, anecdotes and jokes are field-tested.

While outwardly the fruit of such labours may occasionally look impressive, in reality, churches which employ these methods succeed only in 'creating fleshly trifles', to borrow from Tozer. A leaflet promoting a book on church growth which was circulating around twenty years ago contained the following:

> 'By viewing themselves as Chief Executives of God's business, church leaders can benefit from the lessons learned by business executives who have experienced dramatic growth in their organisations.' [2]

Interestingly, the imminent, dramatic growth for which the book was preparing churches has so far failed to materialize.

Unfortunately, many have failed to recognize that, over the centuries, the *ekklesia* has slipped its mooring and that the church is no longer firmly anchored in Scripture. One of the effects of this drift has been that instead of being *in the world but not of it*, some churches appear to be *of the world but not in it*, as evidenced by their attempts to graft man's methods onto the body. In *Church Against the World*, H. Richard Niebuhr wrote:

> '...the church is imperilled not only by an external worldliness but by one that has established itself within the Christian camp. Our position is inside a church which has been on the retreat and which has made compromises with the enemy in thought, in organisation, and in discipline...The crisis of the church from this point of view is not the crisis of the church in the world, but of the world in the church.' [3]

The world is in the church... and the excess cargo is dragging her down. Instead of talking about the *Emerging Church* as some are doing, we ought, perhaps, to be talking about the *Submerging Church*. Rather than encouraging faith in a God who beckons us to walk on water, our man-inspired structures can be seen as a lifebelt for those who are afraid of drowning without something solid and visible to cling on to.

If Scripture is anything to go by, then I suspect God is more than a little displeased by all this: on the occasions when the Jews turned to Egypt rather than God for help, they were severely chastised by Him. So, for example, we read the following in Isaiah 31:1:

'Woe to those who go down to Egypt for help, who rely on horses, who trust in the multitude of their chariots and in the great strength of their horsemen, but do not look to the Holy One of Israel, or seek help from the Lord.'

In the same way that Israel was tempted to rely on the Egyptians and their resources rather than on God, many today rely on the world instead of Him. The New Testament has more to say on the subject:

'You adulterous generation, don't you know that friendship with the world is hatred towards God? Anyone who chooses to be a friend of the world becomes an enemy of God.'

James 4:4

It's a heavy irony indeed when Christians look to the world and its methods in order to find some key with which to save that same world. One has to wonder how by becoming like the world, we hope to change it, and it ought to cause us to ask:

Who's changing whom?

The result of Abraham's attempt at a solution was Ishmael. What God had in mind—the son of the promise, the embodiment of His desire and purpose to create a new nation, a holy people—was Isaac. For our part, we need to continually resist the urge to come up with ideas that we think may help God to build His house; we've produced enough Ishmaels as it is and they all go by another name: **Church**

Ichabod—When the Glory Departs

When the Holy Spirit walks in everyone notices, but when He walks out, no-one notices.

Anonymous

In Mark 9:2-6 we read of an event commonly referred to as The Transfiguration:

'After six days Jesus took Peter, James and John with him and led them up a high mountain, where they were all alone. There he was transfigured before them. His clothes became dazzling white, whiter than anyone in the world could bleach them. And there appeared before them Elijah and Moses, who were talking with Jesus. Peter said to Jesus, "Rabbi, it is good for us to be here. Let us put up three shelters — one for you, one for Moses and one for Elijah." (He did not know what to say, they were so frightened.)'

Here we read of a special revelation of God, and yet Peter's response was to erect some kind of structure. It's often the case that when the Lord reveals something to men, sooner or later they will come up with some ideas of their own... as if they can improve upon God's intentions.

Not only does God ignore Peter's suggestion, but His response is particularly interesting:

'...a cloud appeared and enveloped them, and a voice came from the cloud: "This is my Son, whom I love. Listen to him!"' (verse 7).

But rather than listening to Jesus, for the best part of two thousand years we have not been able to hear him over the clanging and the din of our own tools as we have feverishly tried to build our own shelter in the form of the church. Verse 8 goes on to say:

'Suddenly, when they looked around, they no longer saw anyone with them except Jesus.'

Unfortunately, the pressure to produce *church-as-a-thing-in-itself* creates a blind spot which causes us to miss Jesus altogether, looking past him in order to identify something with which to build our churches. When we fix our eyes upon *church* rather than upon Jesus, the mistaken belief arises — as Tozer put it — that 'spirituality can be organized'. Elsewhere, Tozer remarked:

'Much that the church is doing today, it is doing because it is afraid not to do it. (People) take up projects for no higher reason than that they are scared into it.' [4]

The suggestion here is that much of the effort made by our churches is motivated by fear. But if so, fear of what? By way of an answer, I'd like to return to the transfiguration account where, in Peter's defence, his offer to build a shelter was due to the fact that he was understandably frightened by the presence of God; this is in stark contrast to today's leaders who build structures because they are frightened by the *absence* of God.

The Americans abandoned their pacific bases because the war with Japan came to an end, and this begs the question as to why the Spirit of God has left so many of our churches in the first place. Perhaps it is due to the fact that He feels unwanted... that, like the practitioners of the cargo cults, His people are often more interested in the gifts rather than the Giver, to the degree that some will go to considerable lengths to get what they want.

The following is an account of a leader who rather than waiting for God, took matters into his own hands; his actions mirror, I believe, those of many leaders in our churches today. It is a salutary tale, especially when one remembers that this is someone of whom David said, 'Touch not God's anointed'... yet, as a result of his attempts to try and make things happen, this is a leader whom God replaced nevertheless:

The Show Must Go On
Well, if God doesn't turn up we've got a pretty good programme anyway

In 1 Samuel 10:8 Samuel tells Saul to go to Gilgal and wait seven days for his arrival, whereupon Samuel will perform a particular sacrifice. Three chapters later we find Saul waiting in Gilgal as instructed. However, as time passes and finding himself under mounting pressure from the Philistines, Saul grows impatient. Finally, he decides to carry out the sacrifice himself, only for Samuel to arrive just as he's completed it.

'What have you done?' asked Samuel. Saul replied, *"When I saw that the men were scattering and that you did not come at the set time..."'*

1 Samuel 13:11

Like Saul, some leaders decide to take action rather than waiting for God, especially if—also like Saul—they fear that some of their members might leave:

'Most of us would prefer to spend our time doing something that will get immediate results. We don't want to wait for God to resolve matters in His good time because His idea of "good time" is seldom in sync with ours.' [5]

As far as 'doing something' is concerned, someone once warned that churches can be like butterflies, flying from one attractive flower to another in search of the 'magic programme'. The creature that comes to my mind, however, is not so delicate: until relatively recently, it was widely believed that sharks had to keep moving in order to stay alive, and it occurred to me that some churches behave more like sharks than butterflies, with many churches seeming to have an unholy terror of running out of activities with which to keep people's attention and interest. One church we attended introduced the latest ideas on church growth on a regular basis; however, as far as individual, spiritual growth is concerned, the uncertainty which constant change produces simply serves to undermine it.

Oswald Chambers observed of himself, 'The degree of panic activity in my life is equal to the degree of my lack of personal spiritual experience.' One can't help feeling that many of the activities churches dream up are driven by the same fear, writ large. Perhaps there's the fear that people will become bored, to the degree that some might even consider leaving; hence the constant introduction, in some churches, of new programmes, meetings and so on, all of which are attempts to keep the members of the church 'inspired' and thus more likely to continue attending. Other examples of efforts to keep people on board include the promise of impending revival or power if you are a Charismatic or Pentecostal Christian, or the introduction of a jazzed-up form of worship as is increasingly common in many of our churches, regardless of denomination. Not that such worship styles are necessarily invalid, of course; the question is more to do with the motivation for their introduction: in 1 Kings 18 the prophets of Baal worked themselves into a religious frenzy in a futile attempt to persuade their god to make an appearance; I can't help feeling that a degree of what passes for worship today is driven by the same motives. C.H. Spurgeon saw such things coming to pass and warned:

'A time will come when instead of shepherds feeding the sheep, the church will have clowns entertaining the goats.'

A direct consequence of continually trying to persuade the flock to turn up Sunday after Sunday is that church has indeed — in some instances — become a form of entertainment, causing God's people to degenerate from an army into an audience. This being the case:

Perhaps it's time to bring the house down.

A House Not Made With Hands
For no one can lay any foundation other than the one already laid, which is Jesus Christ.

1 Corinthians 3:11

In Psalm 118:22 we read:

'The stone the builders rejected
has become the *cornerstone*;
the Lord has done this,
and it is marvellous in our eyes'

And Ephesians 2:19-22 tells us:

'...you are...members of God's house-hold, built on the foundation of the apostles and prophets, with Christ Jesus himself as the *chief cornerstone*. In him the whole building is joined together and rises to become a holy temple in the Lord. And in him you too are being built together to become a dwelling in which God lives by his Spirit.'

The cornerstone (or foundation stone) is the first stone to be set when constructing the foundation of a building: it is of primary importance since all the other stones will be set in reference to this stone, thus determining the position of the entire structure.[6] In like manner, we are built together as God's people as we enter into relationship with His Son:

'As you come to him, the living Stone — rejected by humans but chosen by God and precious to him — you also, like living stones, are being built into a spiritual

house to be a holy priesthood, offering spiritual
sacrifices acceptable to God through Jesus Christ.'

1 Peter 2:4-5

In some translations, the word *cornerstone* is translated as
capstone. The difference is extremely significant: the
cornerstone is the first stone to be laid while the capstone is
the last, bringing to mind one of the titles of God: 'I am the
Alpha and the Omega, the first and the last, the Beginning and
the End' (Revelation 1:8 and 22:13). As far as any structures are
concerned, Jesus ought to be our foundation; he is our
cornerstone and our capstone, both the author and perfecter of
the faith of each and every member of his household.

Down the years, in both secular and church buildings, the
cornerstone has often become merely a ceremonial stone, set in
a prominent location on the *outside*; its function nowadays is
often nominal rather than one of supreme importance, and
regrettably, this is rather like what has happened to Jesus in
many of our churches. We ought to have Jesus as our
cornerstone, as our point of reference, but this is almost never
the case; since building *church-as-a-thing-in-itself* has become
our chief concern, we have overlooked Jesus' central function
such that his role has been relegated to that of the ceremonial
stone. Men take command with the result that Jesus' inclusion
in the design and construction of his own body is, in many
instances, a tokenized gesture rather than a genuine
recognition of his preeminent role in bringing everything
together and holding it in place.

This has affected the entire structure of the *ekklesia*,
causing the whole body to be out of joint. How ironic that
many have constructed their churches without including the
cornerstone — Jesus himself — who has now become the stone
that many of our builders have, to all intents and purposes,
rejected. This has happened because it is man's nature to take
control of things even when they are too big for him — and
even when God has declared that He will direct proceedings.

By demoting Jesus — valuing his presence as of secondary
importance in relation to our more pressing building
projects — the foundation of all we do in terms of fellowship
has shifted. This is evidenced in the language we use: for

example, we talk about 'planting churches' rather than about seeing people saved or making disciples... but, to borrow from Stan Firth, *people matter more than projects*; we should be focusing our attention and our efforts on human beings and not on an institution.

Regarding building projects, this would be an appropriate moment to examine one of the most famous examples found in all of Scripture:

Babel: The Tower of Power

Many people have been alienated from God by the very structure that should convey his love.

Wayne Jacobsen

Many have tried — and continue to try — to clamber up into God's presence using structures that have not been sanctioned by Him. The account of the Tower of Babel in Genesis 11:3-4 is a classic example of this, and it offers us a possible insight into the reason why there are those who appear to be so anxious to produce something:

> 'They said to each other, "Come, let's make bricks and bake them thoroughly." They used brick instead of stone, and tar for mortar. Then they said, "Come, let us build ourselves a city, with a tower that reaches to the heavens, *so that we may make a name for ourselves* and not be scattered over the face of the whole earth."'

Could it be that there are those who, albeit unconsciously, are keen to build something as much for their own glory as for God's? Is it possible that like those who attempted to build the tower of Babel, there are some who are busy erecting structures that will not only make God's name known, but their own as well?

It's interesting to note that the builders of Babel employed the regular shape and tidy conformity of the brick instead of stone because it makes for a quick and convenient *resource*; some devise church structures and *then* assign people a place within those structures, in effect viewing people as bricks. However, when it comes to the structure of His *ekklesia*, it is not in God's nature to present us with some sterile, cerebral and pre-packaged concept and ask us to use this in order to shape His Body. He's much bigger, much more exciting than that. God's creative powers are such that — unlike bricks — He has made every one of us unique rather than uniform. Like snowflakes, no two people are the same; in terms of our individual bodies, no two human beings share the same fingerprints or the same patterns in their irises; each one of us possesses God-given talents and qualities, each Christian a potential contributor to the edification of the whole body rather than merely a brick in an edifice. In sharp contrast to the way in which some of those intent on building structures might view their fellow men, each and every one of us is valuable and precious in God's sight. Unlike bricks, our form is neither rigid nor fixed but rather, as living stones, we find ourselves being shaped by God, continually formed and reformed as we are built into a house of His design.

The Babel building project was brought to nothing: that which the builders feared came upon them, its architects and labourers scattered by God Himself — and surely we don't want to make the same mistake. That being the case, what then, are the guiding principles that we should look for when it comes to structure? And is it possible to arrive at some sort of definition concerning what we mean by 'structure' in the first place? These are important questions because, until we arrive at a clearer understanding, and one which will help us all move forward, God's people will continue to be viewed as they have been for far too long: as cogs in a machine rather than human beings; as mere resources, available to serve the needs of 'the programme' rather than 'heirs of God and co-heirs with Christ' (Romans 8:17). Until that time comes, as far as *church-as-a-thing-in-itself* is concerned, to borrow from a well-known song:

All in all, you're just another brick in the wall.

It's interesting to note how little the New Testament talks about church growth, and how often it talks about 'gospel growth' or the increase of the 'word'...the emphasis is not on the growth of the congregation as a structure—in numbers, finances and success—but on the growth of the gospel...In fact, New Testament congregations, as far as we can tell, were usually small gatherings meeting in houses. They were outwardly unimpressive, and had minimal infrastructure. But God kept drawing people into them by the gospel. Or to put it another way, Christ kept doing what he said he would do in Matthew 16. He kept building his church.

Colin Marshall and Tony Payne
The Trellis and the Vine

17

GHOSTS IN THE MACHINE

Guarding a Barren Spot

Tradition is error grown old.

I recently read an account of a Russian Czar who, whilst walking in the palace grounds, came across a lone sentry standing at attention in a remote corner of the garden. Curious as to what it was exactly that the soldier was guarding, the Czar approached him and asked what he was doing there. The soldier replied that he didn't know, he was simply following his captain's orders. The Czar, intrigued, had the captain brought to him, whereupon he was informed that written regulations specified that a guard was to be assigned to that area. After ordering a search of the archives to find out the history of the regulation concerned, the Czar finally discovered the reason: many years before, Catherine the Great had planted a rose bush in that corner, and had ordered a sentry to protect it for the evening... It seemed no-one had ever rescinded the order, and the story finished:

> 'One hundred years later, sentries were still guarding the now barren spot.' [1]

In the same way, many of our traditions and structures exist in order to meet a non-existent need... far too often we discover that they are guarding a barren spot. Tozer, in both powerful and poetic tones, once wrote something remarkably apposite concerning this:

'All Christians and all churches are engaged in one of three activities: guarding the dead past, creating fleshly trifles that will perish with the flesh or working in co-operation with the Holy Spirit in the constant creation of eternal treasures that will outlast the stars.' [2]

Much of what the older churches are doing is guarding the dead past. They simply perpetuate the traditions of the elders, working assiduously to maintain the structures they have inherited, often without pausing to consider what purpose—if any—they fulfil. On the other hand, many of our younger churches are, in truth,

'directionless...[supporting] the new and spectacular, regardless of whether or not it is in accord with the Scriptures and the revealed will of God.' [3]

Much of what they are doing is merely creating fleshly trifles that will perish with the flesh. In sharp contrast, what God *has* called us to do is to work with the Holy Spirit to create not yet another church structure, but rather, 'eternal treasures that will outlast the stars.' There is a world of difference between the carnal and the celestial. In *Mere Christianity*, C.S. Lewis said, "Aim at heaven and you will get earth 'thrown in': aim at earth and you will get neither."[4] I'd like to borrow from this in order to suggest the following:

Aim at Jesus and you will get the ekklesia 'thrown in':
Aim at church and all you will get is church.

Unfortunately, aiming at church is precisely how many people direct their time and energy—especially those who appear to think that Jesus and Church are synonymous.

structure versus *STRUCTURE*

Making sure not to put the cart before the horse

As I mentioned earlier, legitimate structures did exist in the early church and we must therefore be careful not to throw the baby out with the bathwater; it's important that we identify any biblical principles with which we can discern those structures that are valid and those structures that are not.

The first accounts of any structural developments within the *ekklesia* are found in the Book of Acts, where we find that a sort of Christian commune had begun to flourish. In Acts 4:34-35, for example, we read:

> 'There were no needy persons among them. For from time to time those who owned lands or houses sold them, brought the money from the sales and put it at the apostles' feet, and it was distributed to anyone as he had need.'

The practicalities of living together in this new way were negotiated as and when problems arose. In Acts 6, for example, we read of a grievance that was brought to the attention of the apostles: the Hellenistic Jews had complained that their widows were being overlooked by those Hebraic Jews who were responsible for distributing food. Whilst the apostles rightfully saw their primary task as feeding people through the Word, they also recognized the physical needs of the people—the importance of feeding people through both word and deed, one might say. Thus, gathering the other disciples together, the apostles gave the following instructions in order to deal with this particular grievance:

> '"It would not be right for us to neglect the ministry of the word of God in order to wait on tables. Brothers, choose seven men from among you who are known to be full of the Spirit and wisdom. We will turn this responsibility over to them and will give our attention to prayer and the ministry of the word." This proposal pleased the whole group.'

> *Acts 6:2-5*

We see here the development of a specific structure which hadn't existed before, but—in case anyone is tempted to anticipate where this is going—I am not about to talk of a *leadership* structure: those anxious to justify a top-down church hierarchy claim that this passage describes the introduction of the office of deacon in the New Testament church, and that the picture it paints is one of a leadership team deciding to create a new layer of 'middle-managers', so to speak. However, as

I. Howard Marshall points out in his commentary on the Book of Acts:

> 'It is not necessarily suggested [in Acts 6] that serving tables is on a *lower level* than prayer and teaching; the point is rather that the task to which the Twelve had been specifically called was one of witness and evangelism. The solution of the problem was the appointment of a new group of leaders to serve tables…it is noteworthy that Luke does not refer to the Seven as deacons; their task had no formal name.' [5]

This passage is *not* concerned with church governance, but more with the fact that a group of men was agreed upon whose responsibility it was to make sure that food was distributed to a number of people who had inadvertently been overlooked. This was a new structural development and it is extremely important to note that *this structure emerged solely as a response to a need,* and whatever else we can say about any structures that might exist, it seems clear that *they are supposed to be there for the support and benefit of the believers.*

From this initial example I would thus like to offer a tentative definition of a legitimate structure:

Structures are a response to a need
for as long as that need exists.

But if structures are indeed a response to a need or needs, what might these needs look like? Whilst need presents itself in a multiplicity of forms, ultimately, the most important is the legitimate need for believers to be spiritually fed. This is hardly surprising when one remembers that the *ekklesia* is a living *body,* Christ's body.

That's not to say that our current structures don't already feed certain needs, but the question is *whose?* Ostensibly they exist in order to feed the flock; however, I believe a case can be made that *church* serves the clergy as much — if not more — than the laity. Indeed, one can't help feeling that, in reality, our structures are often designed by at least some of those in positions of authority primarily *to feed their need to lead.*

Changing the Structure of our Hearts

You are saved–seek to be like your saviour.

Charles Spurgeon

It is, of course, insufficient (if not to say potentially dangerous) to produce a definition of structure based upon only one example; it would, therefore, be helpful at this point to take a look at another case.

In Chapter 11, we looked at the Corinthian church and examined Paul's solution regarding the way they conducted themselves when they gathered together. By appealing for order in the Corinthian church, Paul was calling for some degree of *structure* to be put in place with regard to their meetings. However, we saw that his concern was not so much about having orderly meetings *per se*, but it had more to do with mutual edification. Paul's overarching aim — not only with the Christians at Corinth but with regard to all the Christian communities with which he was involved — is found in Galatians 4:19 where he writes:

> 'My dear children, for whom I am again in the pains of childbirth *until Christ is formed in you…*'

In a similar vein, in Colossians 1:28-29, we read:

> 'We proclaim him, admonishing and teaching everyone with all wisdom, so *that we may present everyone perfect in Christ*. To this end I labour, struggling with all his energy, which so powerfully works in me.'

As the preceding verses indicate, Paul was interested in inner transformation and this would have been difficult to achieve under the circumstances which prevailed in Corinth.

By way of analogy, I can say from personal experience that it's difficult, if not impossible, to help school children learn if the classroom environment is noisy or disorganized; as a teacher, I require order as a precondition for the main goal — that of personal and intellectual growth. In the same way that a noisy classroom prohibits learning, if a Christian gathering is without any structure then it stands to reason that any potential spiritual growth that might be obtained from being present at that meeting will be limited at best.

In the same way that the solution to the food problem in Jerusalem was a response to a need, *Paul's instructions regarding the structuring of the meetings at Corinth were also a response to a need*: not the need to physically feed people this time, but the need for people to be fed spiritually. Paul was concerned *with the most important need of all: that of spiritual growth.*

Unfortunately, there is scant evidence today that all of those who have assumed Paul's role have these same objectives in mind. In their book, *The Trellis and the Vine*, Colin Marshall and Tony Payne warn that we have become preoccupied with church structure at the expense of our true goals. They argue that:

> '...structures don't grow ministry any more than trellises grow vines...most churches need to make a conscious shift—away from erecting and maintaining structures, and towards *growing people who are disciple-making disciples of Christ.*'[6] (Emphasis in original)

Growing people who are disciple-making disciples of Christ sounds very much like what Dallas Willard called a 'curriculum for Christ-likeness', and I'm sure Paul would have identified with the preceding sentiments; individual and collective transformation were the goals which he was pursuing, and I believe that this ought to be the ultimate purpose of any so-called structures that do exist and the ultimate point of all 'church activities'. One thing certainly needs to be made very clear:

> Order for order's sake can limit spiritual growth almost as much as unbridled chaos.

Flat Pack Churches
God's People — Ready to Assemble

It would appear that many in positions of authority are as susceptible as the rest of us to *Golden Calf Syndrome*—the human condition which causes many to fabricate a God-substitute, something comprehensible to the natural man. This tendency, combined with the pressure to both justify their position in the eyes of the flock whilst at the same time controlling it, causes many of those in charge to trawl through the Bible in search of some sort of template that might help them to build, or at least maintain a made-to-measure church. Due to a preoccupation with form rather than substance, those who adopt this approach are so busy looking through the Bible for a formula that they fail to recognize that there *is* no formula. Instead, they approach sections of the Bible in the same way that they would an *IKEA* manual, and it's difficult not to feel that some churches are assembled in similar fashion to the way one puts together a piece of inanimate furniture. The *ekklesia*, however, is a very different kind of assembly: it is the *qâhâl*, the assembly of the people of God, the gathering together of His children in unique forms and structures, all of which reflect the fact that each of them is fearfully and wonderfully made.

We often find that those who have assumed the responsibility of caring for the flock, both invent and implement structures without considering the actual people involved: in so doing, they thus betray a mindset that appears to be more concerned with their own needs than those of the sheep... in other words, we find structures designed *by* leaders *for* leaders. And yet, since it is *the people and their needs* from which any structures should derive, then this approach actually undermines the very purpose for which these same structures are supposedly created. Wayne Jacobsen illustrates this well:

> 'No-one told the early church to form a community. I can't imagine the disciples gathering on Pentecost evening trying to figure out what to do with 3120 people. Can you see Peter trying to suggest an idea like this?

> "Let's have everyone meet together on Sunday mornings and we'll organize home groups for mid-week. Andrew and Nathanael find us the natural leaders out of this group and take them on a retreat this weekend. They'll lead groups for us. Thomas, draw up some guidelines for participation and we'll have people sign them. We'll require attendance and the rich to sell their property to help the poor..."' [7]

Whilst many today are preoccupied with the topic of church structure I doubt whether a phrase like this even entered the minds of the early Christians; the disciples did not draw up a list of structures and hierarchies and *then* invite people to join them—I expect they were too busy fellowshipping with the Creator of the Universe to worry about planning and organising. This is not to say that structures didn't begin to evolve within the early Christian communities—because as we've seen, clearly they did—but as the pattern of the early church was gradually lost to more and more of God's people, slowly but surely, the living water of the gospel became dammed up by redundant structures and dead traditions. One can observe the long-term effects of this in the following passage which describes Pope Gregory's efforts to evangelize the English around the turn of the 6th century:

> 'Pope Gregory's letters to his mission team are very revealing. As well as dealing with questions of everyday living, he also gives clear instructions about the way to structure a national church... it does, at times, feel as if the cart is leading the horse. Establishing a hierarchy seems to be everything. This is in stark contrast to the Celtic missionaries who set up monasteries as centres of spirituality and encouraged natural communities to grow up around them.' [8]

Too many of our church structures are founded on church rather than on the rock of faith to which Jesus referred when he addressed Peter. Hence the structures which we develop are formed very differently and with little in common with Peter or Paul's way of thinking, with the result that many of them prohibit rather than encourage much in the way of genuine spiritual growth. Historically, the end product has been a large number of spiritually immature and needy believers, programmed to be dependent on the church and its leadership rather than on God.

❖   ❖   ❖

welcome2themachine@church.org

Organized Christianity has probably done more to retard its founder's ideals than any other agency in the world.

Richard Le Gallienne

If, either by accident or design, Jesus' called-out ones — the *ekklesia* — are perceived as a 'thing', then the natural human inclination is to roll up one's sleeves and try to build that thing. To put it another way, mistakes can occur if people come to see the body as an *organisation* rather than an *organism;* indeed, this is exactly what has happened, with disastrous consequences. The *organism-organisation* comparison is not a new thought on my part — others have made the same comparison — but it's nevertheless important to explore this idea since it is particularly relevant to the whole discussion concerning church structure.

The problem, however, is that one immediately encounters difficulties when trying to discuss the idea of the *ekklesia* as an organism, particularly with those who hold to a traditional view of the church. The attitude towards those who describe the church in organic terms appears to be that the 'body' metaphor is simply being pursued too far. Whilst some might concede that the whole organic perspective is an interesting idea, ultimately their view is that unless *someone* makes the decision to 'get practical', then the church will start out chaotically, become totally dysfunctional and finally collapse in a heap. The problem with this argument is that it is based upon the unwarranted assumption that as soon as anyone uses a word like 'organic' when discussing the church, he is in the same breath saying he doesn't believe in or see a need for *structure.*

Of course, the simple answer to this is that any living organism clearly has need of a structure if it's going to both survive and develop — a person only has to consider his or her own body to see the truth of this. In the same way, there's no contesting the fact that *some* sort of structure should exist within any body of believers; however, if we observe a foetus as it develops in the womb, we find the whole body — flesh and bone — developing together, and it seems reasonable to suggest that we should expect to see Christ's body develop in similar fashion. What we *don't* see (in the womb or anywhere else) is a fully formed skeleton first and *then* the rest of the body gradually materialising around it. Yet this is exactly how some people try to build church: they build a skeleton—a structure—from selected Scriptures and then they try to put flesh on it, usually in the form of other Christians who are prepared to outwork their ideas.

As Christ's *ekklesia* has come to be understood as a *thing-in-itself*, the concept of *structure* has taken on a meaning and a significance not anticipated by early Christians. The *ekklesia* was conceived, *not* because someone took it upon himself to build and organize it first, but rather, it was because '*In the beginning was the Word*'. People met Jesus, and through him they were born again into the kingdom of God, receiving eternal life. Everything that developed or grew flowed out from this encounter. Like the 'formless and empty' world of Genesis 1:2, if we allow the Holy Spirit to hover over us, then as with the *ekklesia* of the New Testament, we too will find ourselves knit together into authentic, meaningful community, taking shape and form as the Spirit directs.

The main stimulus for the formation of the earliest Christian communities was a shared love of Jesus and the fact that when they gathered together, God was in their midst. Their continued growth and development was due to exactly the same reason. The early believers did not get together out of a sense of duty or because someone talked to them about the need for commitment; they met together because they *wanted* to, not because they had to.

Regrettably, as generations passed, it would appear that the number of people who possessed this natural enthusiasm and zeal gradually diminished as, slowly but surely, a reductionist view of the body of Christ took hold. Looking back, one can observe the historic failure to see the *ekklesia* for what it is—a living, breathing, Spirit-filled body rather than as an abstract theological concept. Christ's *ekklesia* is an organism; *church-as-a-thing-in-itself* is an organisation. Comparing the two is like comparing DNA with an instruction manual: one is God-breathed and alive; the other is man-made and dead. The *ekklesia* is Spirit-led and moves in the supernatural; *church-as-a-thing-in-itself*, the product of man's organisation, rarely moves beyond the superficial. Christ's body is a flesh-and-blood creation of God rather than the bricks-and-mortar, Babel-like imitations engineered by men. God's structures engender individual and corporate growth; man's structures engender individual and corporate control, the fruit of the latter too often being a dry and relatively ineffective body of believers. The designs we use in order to create our structures make total sense *if* we are trying to manufacture *church-as-a-thing-in-itself...* but they have absolutely no application to organic, God-inspired, Spirit-filled, Jesus-centred community.

In the meantime, the search continues for a biblical blueprint which will bring power or revival, or produce a 'successful' church — but as the practitioners of the cargo cults of the Pacific discovered, it is an exercise in futility. Whatever successes we may have seen — if indeed they are *genuinely* successful from the point of view of those other than the leadership — are, by default, a result of God's sovereign power and grace rather than our methodology. Those who continue to try and construct the *ekklesia* in the teeth of all this are reminiscent of those described in Colossians 2:19:

> 'They have lost connection with the head, from whom the whole body, supported and held together by its ligaments and sinews, grows as God causes it to grow.'

Instead of the Bride of Christ we have created something much more like the Bride of Frankenstein; we gather what we think are all the right parts dug up from Scripture, and then stitch them together. But despite our efforts to generate a lightning bolt in order to spark life into this monster — introducing the latest teaching from best-selling authors, importing programmes from mega-churches, incorporating new worship styles — our fleshly attempts to create life in the laboratory have failed.

Life flows from the Head to the body: life cannot flow from the body to the body, and yet this is precisely the result that many church leaders are attempting to achieve... it is, therefore, little wonder that so many, including themselves, are uninspired and lacking in vitality. No structure, plan or organisation has the ability to impart life into the body of Christ... only Christ himself is able to do such a thing. As A.W. Tozer observed:

> 'One hundred religious persons knit into a unity by careful organisation do not constitute a church any more than eleven dead men make a football team. The first requisite is life, always.' [9]

One's attention can be diverted by issues of 'church life' which in turn can lead to spiritual death. Or, to put it another way:

If you focus on the body rather than the Head
you will end up with a corpse.

The man-made structures which are the natural by-product of *church-as-a-thing-in-itself* are the frame on which the body is hung, and I use the word hung deliberately... our structures are more like strictures, strangling the life out of the very thing they are meant to support:

It's time to cut the body free before it chokes to death.

CONCLUSION TO PART 2

Jesus and his Bride:

The State of the Union

It is a constant of church history that new, lively, growing movements in the church have a habit of getting everybody involved. They tend to have plural leadership and very little hierarchy. In real revivals, every-member ministry is the norm. Only when a movement starts to stagnate does the amount of structure increase, both in terms of the conduct of meetings and in church government. Eventually the movement gravitates back to one-man leadership, and the church is once more dependent upon some great leader preaching up a storm to bring about revival...Always the pattern is the same. As movement grows into machine, and finally into monument, liturgy squeezes out life, structure squeezes out substance, anointing succumbs to administration, and gifting to good order.

Meic Pearse
Who's Feeding Whom?

18

ARRESTED DEVELOPMENT:
The Result of Outgrowing Scripture

The Body that Fell to Earth
Approaching Terminal Velocity

It's hard to believe, when we stop to think about it, that the earth is hurtling through space at tens of thousands of miles an hour, and all the while revolving at the same time. Instead, it feels perfectly stationary, as if fixed in place on a solid foundation. Clearly, though, our senses aren't giving us a true picture of this particular reality.

Throughout this book I've endeavoured to demonstrate that—due to a fundamental misconception concerning the body of Christ—when it comes to most of our practices, the vast majority of our churches have little or no biblical foundation with which to undergird them. As a result, and rather like our world, the church has been in free fall for most, if not all of its existence—although, like the seemingly motionless earth, you wouldn't know it—and as a result, far too many have a false sense of security when they should be groping for the ripcord of a parachute. It's time, however, for us to face the facts and (if you'll forgive the pun), acknowledge the gravity of the situation. The ground is already rushing up to meet denominations such as the Anglicans, the Presbyterians and the Methodists, whilst the failure of the church in general has contributed to the plummeting spirituality of the Western world. The only reason the church at large hasn't crashed and burned already is because God, in His mercy, has seen fit to sustain and bless so many of His people working within the walls of *church-as-a-thing-in-itself*.

We need to appreciate that being in free fall isn't free: it has already cost us too much and is set to continue doing so unless something is done to arrest the descent.

And then again... we talk of letting go and letting God: perhaps *God's* plan is to ultimately let go and drop the whole thing—maybe a time is coming where He will let the church hit the ground and break apart upon impact in order to build something new. Certainly, something earth-shattering has to happen in order to break the cycle in which so many have been and continue to be trapped.

History Repeating Itself

What has been will be again,
  what has been done will be done again;
    there is nothing new under the sun.

Ecclesiastes 1:9

I hope by now that a convincing argument has been made to the effect that much of what happens as part of 'church' on any given Sunday is scripturally insupportable, even if not necessarily 'wrong' in and of itself.

I also hope to have provided an insight into the historical background as to how and why at least some of these practices managed to become established within *the* church... within *your* church. I mention this because recently it occurred to me that the history of the first church I ever attended was very much a microcosm of church history as a whole:

When I first became a Christian I joined a newly established church which had been created by the amalgamation of a small group of spiritually on-fire university students with two or three other local fellowships in the area. As time passed, this newly-formed group attracted an increasingly large following and as more and more people joined—not just students, but people from other walks of life—they began to meet in homes. In due course, a leadership group emerged which primarily consisted of the 'founding fathers'; this proceeded to further stratify into pastors and elders. Sunday meetings began to be held in a local school, but as numbers grew, the meetings were relocated to the medical building of the University.

As time progressed, money became an item for discussion and tithing was subsequently introduced, not only to pay the rent for the building but also in order to support some of the leaders who felt God had called them into 'full-time ministry'. Eventually the church moved out of rented accommodation and into a large church building with a correspondingly large mortgage. More full and part-time administrative and pastoral staff were added and consequently, more and more money was needed.

Looking back, it's fascinating to observe that these events, which spanned no more than twenty or twenty-five years, mirrored two thousand years of church history, briefly summarized as follows:

The Christian faith started out with a handful of people who were excited about God; they initially met in homes and, as time went on, were looked after and guided by more mature, seasoned believers who shepherded them because they were pastorally minded and servant-hearted by nature. Over time, however, and as we have seen, there evolved from within this group a hierarchical, top-down form of leadership which would, in turn, lead to a minority moving into full-time ministry. As more time passed, the early church—just like mine—started to meet in buildings rather than homes. Meetings became increasingly ritualized as a handful of Christians gradually took over greater responsibility for the proceedings. Church finances, particularly in the form of tithes, were introduced in order to keep the whole thing running.

Sadly, but inevitably, the parallels between my own church and the historical church don't end there.

Initially, the trajectory of my church, just like that of the early church, was heavenwards; it was aiming at God rather than at simply sustaining itself. I remember there was a buzz about the whole thing in those early days... there was a sense of awe and reverence, of excitement, hope and expectation. But that was many years ago now. As a result of the changes outlined above, the trajectory of my spiritual *alma mater* gradually flattened out, just like the experience of countless other churches before it, stretching back centuries. As time went on, the passion of many of the original members of my church seemed to wane, the love of many appeared to grow cold. That's not to say there weren't—or aren't—fervent Christians still in the congregation... but just that the numbers of those who were frustrated, bored, or disillusioned started to grow.

Judging from history, the decline which I observed in my church seems to be almost inevitable, regardless of the passion with which many a fellowship begins; at some point, the refreshing, spontaneous presence of the Holy Spirit is elbowed out in favour of the latest brainchild of those who lead.

Today, a variety of methods are employed in an attempt to inject some adrenaline into a flagging body: the response within some circles is to preach relentlessly on impending revival, for example. On the other hand, some denominations, such as the Anglican Church, appear to be more concerned not with revival, but simply *survival*. The church at large, however, needs something more akin to a Second Reformation. Luther's words half a millennium ago are as relevant today as they were then:

> 'The Church needs a reformation. And this cannot be the work of a single man, as the pope—but it must be that of the whole world.'

Luther was certainly correct when he identified the need for us all to be involved as agents of change, as he himself most certainly was; the fruit of his own labours in this regard—his contribution and its impact—is incalculable. However, some would argue that his reforms didn't go far enough. In *Ever Feel Like Quitting Church?* Jim Rutz writes:

> 'The Reformation was a great start on fixing the church, but it fell way short in regard to our structures. It

succeeded marvellously in getting back to sound doctrine: *sola Scriptura* (placing the Bible above the Church), *sola gratia* (salvation by grace), and *sola fide* (through faith, not works).

But it never got us back to the New Testament church pattern that we see in Paul's letters. It simply exchanged the priest for a minister and put a sermon in place of the Eucharist.' [1]

I submit that Luther's vision for reformation stopped short because of the failure to make one vital observation: as Sir Ken Robinson put it when referring to education, 'Reform is no use any more, because that's simply improving a broken model. We need a revolution'.

I believe the same could be said about the church: regardless of terminology — whether it be revival, reformation or revolution — there needs to be a root and branch review of the whole set-up. One certainly cannot fix the 'problem of church' simply by changing a few practices here and there. To fix an error of this magnitude, and to repeat a phrase I used at the beginning of this book:

It would require something of biblical proportions.

Coming up for Air

Hoping for change from within? Don't hold your breath.

Church-as-a-thing-in-itself has more in common with the Old Testament than the New, such that we have reverted to religious practices centred upon the temple and the priesthood in everything but name. As Arthur Wallis observed:

'To put the New Testament church — which God had intended to be a dynamic, liberated community — into an Old Covenant strait-jacket was the master stroke of the devil.' [2]

Church-as-a-thing-in-itself is an impostor which is not, and never has been, fit for purpose; it has tried to dress up the Good News in the garb of the Old Testament, something Jesus explicitly warned against:

'No one sews a patch of unshrunk cloth on an old garment, for the patch will pull away from the garment, making the tear worse. Neither do men pour new wine into old wineskins. If they do, the skins will burst, the wine will run out and the wineskins will be ruined. No, they pour new wine into new wineskins, and both are preserved.'

Matthew 9:16-17

However, despite two thousand years of burst wineskins and torn garments, people don't seem to have learned, and it will take a new breed of Christian to reverse the human tendency to systematize the free relationship with God which He offers us. We take God's gift, put it in a box, tie it up with a pretty ribbon and hand it back to Him, saying, *'There — we thought it would look nicer like this.'* We continue to try and force-fit the gospel into the mould of our preconceived and woefully inadequate ideas of what the *ekklesia* ought to look like — but the fact is, the Good News is heady stuff, and like a good wine, we need to give it an opportunity to breathe. It's time to throw off the dead weight of *church-as-a-thing-in-itself* which has crushed the life out of far too many of God's people, stifling their joy and suffocating them spiritually.

It's time to come up for air.

PART 3

WHERE DO WE GO FROM HERE?

SECTION 1

STAYING ON MESSAGE

The pain of loneliness arises from the constitution of our nature. God made us for each other. The desire for human companionship is completely natural and right. The loneliness of the Christian results from his walk with God in an ungodly world, a walk that must often take him away from the fellowship of good Christians as well as from that of the unregenerate world. His God-given instincts cry out for companionship with others of his kind, others who can understand his longings, his aspirations, his absorption in the love of Christ; and because within his circle of friends there are so few who share his inner experiences he is forced to walk alone.

A.W. Tozer
Man — The Dwelling Place of God

19

THE VALLEY OF DECISION

Getting off the Beaten Track
Wake up, Sleeper... time to cause a train wreck

A missionary friend of mine once said that trying to change *anything* within one's church—no matter how small—is like trying to pull a locomotive with a rope over your shoulder. The changes we need to confront today are not about what colour to paint the church door... or to what day the Mother and Toddlers' group should be moved... the challenge we face concerns the very fabric of The Church itself. By constructing *church-as-a-thing-in-itself* and then perceiving this to be the norm, we've committed an error of incalculable proportions, the consequences of which cannot be overestimated.

Church-as-a-thing-in-itself is an idea so entrenched in our psyche that any attempts at reform on our part are almost certainly doomed to failure. Like a locomotive, the church as we know it possesses such a tremendous degree of inertia that it seems nothing and no-one can either stop it or move it in a different direction; people have tried and then given up in exhaustion as it thunders along the tracks, heading—I believe—in entirely the wrong direction.

The freedom to follow the guidance of the Holy Spirit has been and continues to be denied by the constraint of the rails which have been laid down over hundreds of years and which represent the beliefs, traditions, attitudes and structures that have evolved down the centuries and are generally—and incorrectly—accepted as being grounded in Scripture. These restraining features are all outcomes of having a false view of the *ekklesia*: it is this misguided train of thought which has ultimately led to the existence of *church-as-a-thing-in-itself*, and has, in turn, helped to derail the Christian mission. *Church-as-a-thing-in-itself* represents a way of thinking which has hindered and is continuing to hinder real growth in the body rather than encouraging it. In fact, growth has not only been brought to a standstill, but—with a few exceptions—churches everywhere are in actual decline.

I have the sense that in order to undo centuries of outworked error, God actually wants the church to go right *off* the rails—but for that to happen, we need to take this ancient, rusty and wrongly oriented track and break it up. I also believe this could be achieved, except for one thing—the existence of large numbers of Christians who unquestioningly accept the status quo and don't recognize the problem. What feature of a railway track holds the rails together? The *sleepers*.

The harsh reality is, short of blowing up the tracks, this train isn't stopping.

The question is: *what are you going to do about it?*

The Road Less Travelled?
Every journey begins with a single step

The jury's in: there is no longer any doubt that there exist millions of Christians who are unhappy with their own church situation, with statistics indicating that many have already slipped out through the back door as a result; however, far from taking the road less travelled—as many assume they have—it turns out that they have actually chosen a well-worn path, and one that is becoming increasingly so. But were they right to choose this alternative? And what are the realities of making such a decision?

These are important questions, since I think it's logical to assume that many more consider following suit, but are yet to be convinced that it's the correct course of action. And finally, are there actually alternatives to church as we know it, or are exile and possible isolation all that remain?

A popular fridge-magnet quotes Reinhold Niebuhr's words, 'God grant me the serenity to accept the things I cannot change, courage to change the things I can, and the wisdom to know the difference.' If this advice is followed then what, if anything, should one do?

On the face of it there would appear to be three choices, each of which will be discussed in turn. However, what follows probably offers only a partial insight—if that—regarding the potential consequences of pursuing any one of them; it is merely the first tentative step towards a complete, coherent solution, to both an individual situation and to the wider questions raised by *church-as-a-thing-in-itself*. Moreover, it needs to be recognized that each of these options comes with a potential cost.

Option 1. Rocking the Boat
Finding a port in a storm or stirring up a storm in the port?

How do you remove the cork from a champagne bottle? Shake the bottle and wait for the pressure to force the cork out. It's a course of action adopted by some when they wish to instigate the kind of change which they feel is long overdue. They agitate. But how effective is it? (If the champagne's flat, which it often appears to be, then I would suggest, not very.) More importantly, does this approach have any place amongst God's people?

Whilst it's usually possible to challenge the status quo, it needs to be recognized that to call for any sort of change always provokes resistance in almost every sphere of life, and the church is no exception—in fact, it is probably more impervious to change than any other institution in the world, as church history clearly demonstrates. For example, in *Where Do We Go From Here?* by Ralph Neighbour, we read:

'If you are a church staff member or a church member, I would frankly like to say to you that you should not attempt to bring change to your church.' [1]

This is a statement made by a leader for, one suspects, the benefit of the leadership rather than the led, and it gives an indication of the kind of opposition to be expected should one even *think* of suggesting that something might be in need of reform.

There exists an unhealthy conservatism amongst God's people (and not only amongst leaders, but 'ordinary' believers as well) which causes them to resist change rather than be prepared to embrace it, even when there's a recognition on everyone's part that something is genuinely wrong.

This inbuilt tendency to oppose any sort of reform is compounded by the commonly held belief that any questioning of the church or its leadership is an implied form of criticism and thus inherently 'un-Christian', even if offered in a humble and Christ-like spirit. However, as we see in Galatians 2 where Paul openly rebukes Peter for hypocrisy, we have to acknowledge that criticism isn't always inappropriate; we need to be prepared to say it like it is, but also remember that we're to speak the truth in love: *to say our piece without losing our peace.* At the same time, we need to recognize that no matter how gently or tactfully we deliver our observations, people aren't necessarily going to accept what we have to say; indeed, concerning the church, it's highly probable that they *won't.*

The stronghold of tradition, combined with church politics in general, means that any attempt at serious reform—even in the smallest churches—is a lost cause; quite simply the odds are stacked against those who suggest any kind of genuine, corporate self-analysis. Trying to bring change is like trying to steer the Titanic away from the iceberg by leaning over the side with a paddle, as many have discovered to their cost. For example, a good friend of mine, a God-fearing man who was well respected by others, remained in his church for twenty-six years while many others left; he believed he could affect the kind of positive change that would encourage people to remain in the church. But he was wrong, and after a quarter of a century of loyal service, he joined the ranks of the already departed. Apart from notably rare exceptions in church history, for every person who makes a difference there are hundreds, if not thousands of people—also with good intentions and with legitimate concerns—who are ignored, their suggestions for reform coming to naught. Ultimately, like my friend, they are faced with the choice of either accepting the situation or leaving altogether.

There are some who manage to make waves to such a degree that the decision is made for them: like the prophet Jonah, they end up being thrown overboard by their shipmates and the boat continues on without them; or they're accused of mutiny by the ship's captain, and consequently find themselves walking the plank out through the church door...

The fact of the matter is, trying to change anything but the most superficial features of most, if not all churches is doomed to failure—even when the change concerns trying to align one's church more closely with the Word of God. Since the very foundations of church in general are wrong, then any change achieved will be at best cosmetic—the proverbial rearranging of the deck-chairs on the Titanic.

Option 2. Be prepared to go down with the ship
Sink or Swim

The second choice is to accept the situation and remain in one's church, recognising that no fundamental change within it is likely to take place, and coming to terms with the fact that this is probably as good as it's going to get.

This need not consign anyone to a passive role, but rather, each and every individual can try to work within and according to the system, aiming to grow personally and, perhaps, helping to mentor and develop those around them. But this, I admit, is easier said than done. During our time in various cities, countries and churches Liz and I, like many others, served where and when we felt we could, according to our abilities and in light of what we felt were our gifts; frustration, however, was ever-present as we tried to meet the expectations and demands of church while hungering for a deeper reality that was not met through attending the requisite meetings or signing up for the appropriate duty rota. We discovered that it is very easy to become spiritually dry when feeding the flames of *church-as-a-thing-in-itself.*

If you *are* going to remain in your particular church situation you must, as far as possible, be determined not to allow anyone to make your own personal walk with Christ dysfunctional, for whatever reasons. We may have no control over what's 'out there' as far as church is concerned, but we do have control regarding our own attitudes. What God holds each one of us responsible for is our own personal relationship with Him regardless of how anyone else is doing. The depth and quality of that relationship is significantly affected by the degree to which we look to God as our source rather than to anyone or anything else, including the church. As Christians, we ought not to allow anyone or anything—be it leaders or *church-as-a-thing-in-itself*—to usurp Christ's place or role in our lives.

I also think it's important to be honest as to one's motives for staying: whilst many genuinely feel called by God to remain in their church situation, I have the feeling that there are those who justify their reason for not leaving under the guise of a variety of positives such as loyalty or commitment, but whose real reasons for staying are otherwise. For example, although most people would not admit it—and as we've already seen—it is too easy to view church as a vehicle with which to advance one's 'personal ministry', and some stay with the hope of fulfilling just this.

Others stay because their friendship group is in the church and this is something they don't want to lose; I remember talking to several individuals whose reason for remaining— even though they were unhappy with their respective fellowships—was precisely this. Whilst understandable, a reluctance to move out of one's comfort zone is hardly going to move forward the kingdom of God; such people have little credible ground for complaint about their church situation.

There are other negative reasons for remaining in a church: a misplaced sense of guilt, or fear, or simply indecision represent some of these; and whilst one's church might have serious problems, being part of it can nevertheless offer relative security. The problem is, the kind of people for whom church (as opposed to God) represents a safe-haven are also the kind who are easily threatened by those who express publicly what the former might only consider privately. Since their security is primarily rooted in the church rather than in God, they are often shaken by those who not only consider leaving but who voice their concerns at the same time. The attitude of some of those who choose to remain seems to be, 'If I'm going to be stuck in this church, then the last thing I need is to hear your criticism of it.' Their response to others' adverse comments or concerns can be quite aggressive, but we need to remember that, since much of their security lies in church rather than in God, their reaction is rooted in fear and insecurity.

Usually such people attempt to put a gloss on the situation in an effort to convince themselves that all is OK; but as I've observed in the lives of some of those who choose to remain for the wrong reasons, often all that happens is that they gradually dry out, as they cling on to the hope that some sort of sea change will take place within their church one day. However, those who remain on board would be well advised to steel themselves to the following ineluctable fact:

That day will almost certainly not arrive.

Option 3. Abandon Fellow-Ship?
Man Overboard

Most people are familiar with the fact that in the early church, along with the cross, other symbols such as the dove and the fish were used amongst believers. Not so well known is the fact that both the ship and the anchor were also used for a time, the ship representing the church with its cargo of human souls. Its usage derives from the story of Noah's ark, which is said to prefigure the church as a refuge from the world for the saints of God, floating on the sea of unbelief. Unfortunately, some have seized upon this metaphor and used it to frighten people back on board: at the *First Vatican Council*, the Roman Catholic Church went so far as to state, 'It is an article of faith that outside the Church no one can be saved... Who is not in this ark will perish in the flood.' Presumably, anyone who subscribes to this point of view must have felt that Christian philosopher Søren Kierkegaard was playing with fire (or rather, a very large volume of water) when he took the decision to leave the Danish Church. James Houston, in his book *Joyful Exiles*, wrote:

'Kierkegaard claimed to be a "prophet of the second Reformation," setting himself against the national Danish church to advocate that Christendom needed to die if the reality of true Christianity was going to be reborn. But he would have told you that if you were called to be such a prophet, you would need to place yourself outside the establishment and be ignored. All favours and rewards of ecclesial life must be resigned by anyone who would call it to repentance. You cannot be a leader and a reformer of the church at the same time. John the Baptist had to accept being a voice in the wilderness to lead the renewal of God's people. This was his exercise of the hidden life in order to proclaim the advent of the Messiah. Dying away to religious life means being rejected – and hidden indeed. Kierkegaard had longed to be a parish priest in the Danish church; instead he never preached his sermons, he only wrote them.' [2]

Kierkegaard clearly felt that rocking the boat from within wasn't a viable course of action: *'You cannot be a leader and a reformer of the church at the same time.'* Consequently, there are those who – like Kierkegaard – decide to throw *themselves* over the side of the ship. The kind of people who choose voluntary exile are not looking to *church* to provide them with meaning; they are not looking to *church* to enable them to *be someone*. Those who, in order to be true to their own principles, walk away from all that the church offers in terms of personal recognition or ministry are following the example of Jesus, who 'made himself nothing' for the sake of God's glory. By the grace of God, such people *also have the strength to be nothing,* echoing the words of John the Baptist when talking about Jesus: 'He must increase, but I must decrease' (John 3:30). They have come to understand that:

Ministry is about making God's name known, not ours.

As one who made the decision to leave the established church many years ago, what I can offer to those considering following suit is simply my own personal testimony. But one thing I can say immediately is that it is not a decision for the faint-hearted, and anyone considering whether or not to 'slip over the side' needs to be clear about what this involves. After all, stepping out of the boat and onto the water proved to be terrifying for Peter — who are we to think it will be any different for us?

You'll Never Walk Alone?

How to acquire The Cloak of Invisibility: Leave Church

That there are increasing numbers of people who are placing themselves outside of the church establishment is beyond doubt, and I think it's safe to assume that at least some of them might be searching for like-minded people who are also outside of 'normal' church — those for whom *God* is enough, as opposed to *God-and-church-as-a-thing-in-itself.* But while the number of such people appears to be growing, it doesn't mean there are any near you right now, and you need to accept that encountering such individuals isn't guaranteed. It's common for people who leave their churches to go through extended periods of isolation simply because everyone else around them is still 'going to church' and as a consequence, those who have left find it difficult to locate and connect with people who think the way they do. Making the decision to come out of one's fellowship can result in a lonely existence and ought not to be taken lightly.

It's been my experience and that of others with whom I have talked, that if or when someone stops going to church it is both surprising and disappointing how quickly it seems that they cease to exist. What I mean by this is that contact with many of those with whom one previously fellowshipped dries up very quickly, no matter how positive the relationship might have felt beforehand. It's as if you fall off the map, which of course raises the question as to how real or meaningful the fellowship was in the first place. In *So You Don't Want to go to Church Anymore?* Jake Colsen writes:

'Institutionalism breeds task-based friendships. As long as you're on the same task together, you can be friends. When you're not, people tend to treat you like damaged goods.' [3]

If you *do* make the decision to walk away from your church, you have to be prepared for the fact that you will almost certainly be misunderstood by those either happy with or resigned to the system and you will probably be accused of a number of things: of rebellion or having a problem with authority; of selfishness and pride; of having a negative or critical spirit — and this is to name just a few.

It is a bitter pill to swallow and I have deliberately not sugared it. The fact of the matter is, if you come out of your church, there is the distinct possibility that both accusation and isolation lie ahead of you: the essential question is whether or not this is something for which you are prepared.

Hit over the Head with Hebrews

Using the Bible as a blunt instrument rather than a double-edged sword

If you *do* stop attending church meetings, as surely as night follows day it's only a matter of time before someone challenges you with Hebrews 10:25:

'Let us not give up meeting together, as some are in the habit of doing, but let us encourage one another — and all the more as you see the Day approaching.'

On the face of it, those who rebuke others for ceasing to attend church do seem to have a very good case: after all, the message here to not give up meeting together seems pretty clear. However, the problem lies not in whether we should meet or not, *but in our understanding of the form those meetings should take*. One cannot simply lift this verse out of context in order to herd people back into the kind of unbiblically orchestrated meetings which we find in most churches today. Wayne Jacobsen has this to say:

'I don't know of another Scripture that has suffered more abuse than this one. It is often quoted as the reason people must file into a religious institution on

Sunday morning, sit in rows and submit to a music performance and a lecture that others have put together for their benefit...The above passage from Hebrews was never intended to be a proof-text to demand people sit through a programmed 'service' every week...I think we make a critical error if we assume that's all the writer had in mind.' [4]

As we've seen in earlier chapters, the first Christians met informally in homes, rather than formally in a church building, so when the writer says, 'Let us not give up meeting together', he is not actually talking about the kind of meetings most people think of today when they read this passage. For one thing, the fact that the author of Hebrews exhorts Christians to meet in order to *encourage one another* indicates participation on *everyone's* part—something which doesn't happen in a traditional Sunday morning service. In addition, in Hebrews 3:13, the author tells his readers to 'encourage one another *daily*', a practice recorded in Acts 2:46 which says that the believers met every day. Clearly, the writer is not envisioning organized weekly meetings when discussing this. Consequently, to link Hebrews 10:25 to more or less compulsory attendance of Sunday meetings, in which there is little or no opportunity for participation, is a gross misapplication of Scripture. In truth, many employ this verse as a scourge with which to drive the sheep back to the fold — not the green pastures of Psalm 23, however, but rather the 'dry and weary land where there is no water' of Psalm 63.

Many of the meetings in our churches are formulaic and predictable, even in supposedly Spirit-led Pentecostal or Charismatic congregations where we find carefully organized spontaneity, or 'praise on rails' as one friend put it. Combined with the lack of opportunity to contribute, for many Christians a large proportion of meetings are ultimately boring and/or ineffective. This is precisely because the meetings do *not* resemble the way the early Christians met and because Sunday Church has virtually no connection to Scripture. As a direct result, far from going to meetings where they can both encourage others and be encouraged themselves, many Christians file out of a church building every Sunday feeling *discouraged*: instead of being sharpened they are dulled; instead of feeling liberated they feel confined and frustrated.

Some of those who become dispirited by such gatherings make the often difficult decision to move to another church in an effort to find a place where they can grow spiritually, but they are then accused, unfairly, of being church-hoppers, or 'ecclesiastical hitch-hikers'[5], yet such criticisms are often made by the very people who have helped to drive them away in the first place.

Still others, out of despair, simply give up fellowshipping altogether, abandoning any hope of finding meaningful community. They are assumed by everyone else to be loners who are deliberately isolating themselves from church for reasons which are almost always interpreted in the least positive light. Once again:

Are you prepared to face an *Out-of-Body Experience*?

Setting the Record Straight

Many whom God has, the church does not have; and many whom the church has, God does not have.

Augustine

Before going any further, I need to make it abundantly clear that whilst I have tabled the idea of withdrawing from one's church as an option, I am most certainly *not* encouraging people to stop *fellowshipping*: as far as the latter is concerned, nothing could be further from the truth. I don't mean by any of what's gone before that we shouldn't gather together; I don't mean we give up on teaching or worshipping collectively or discipling one another — far from it.

During our time in Japan, Liz and I found ourselves in fellowship with a handful of other Christians who, though small in number, were to have a dramatic effect on our lives. One cold winter's evening we were in the middle of bundling our three young children into the back of the car before heading out for a time of fellowship with our friends, when another couple of friends — who were not believers — happened to pass by. We stopped to chat briefly and then continued to throw in the sleeping bags and strap in the children, causing the husband to remark, 'Well, it must be some special meeting for you guys to be going to all this trouble.' I remember to this day, our one-word reply:

'Absolutely!'

Thinking back to that time, it strikes me that any Christian *who is serious about his or her faith* has a natural desire to meet with other believers with whom they can share their journey and in whose company they can encounter God. This is hardly surprising when one considers that the Godhead is a community of three, and since we are made in God's image, those who genuinely thirst after Him are essentially hard-wired for Christian community or fellowship.

With this in mind, I find it troubling that those who condemn others when they give up going to church so often fail to recognize that if sincere Christians go against their nature and stop attending church, then there has to be a good reason—one which those who express concern would do well to identify and reflect upon.

If and when people stop going to church, paradoxically it's not necessarily because they don't want to meet with anybody any more, neither are their actions incontrovertible evidence that they are giving up on God—in fact, often it's the opposite. I think the majority of these 'misfits' actually hunger for fellowship—but real, meaningful fellowship, not the *ersatz* variety on which many are currently forced to subsist: *they're fed up with not being fed*; at the same time, they are equally frustrated at not being allowed opportunities to feed others by virtue of the gifts God has bestowed upon them. They're tired of being starved and then rebuked with the charge of being Consumer-Christians should they, like Oliver Twist, have the temerity to ask for more. John Milton could have been describing this situation when, in his poem, *Lycidas*, he penned the following words:

'The hungry sheep look up and are not fed.'

The desire of a minority to control everyone else has led to the spiritual malnourishment of the masses; God offers us a table in the wilderness, a banquet feast—yet in stark contrast, we often find that the only thing on offer on Sunday's menu is boiled potatoes. It may sometimes be dressed up as *duckling a l'orange,* with all the trimmings—great music, energetic speakers, and so on—but in terms of genuinely feeding the body, when all's said and done, it's still boiled potatoes and nothing more. Why? Because regardless of how many 'bells and whistles' are in evidence (and in some churches this is literal rather than metaphorical), virtually all church meetings are about a minority producing a show whilst the role of the majority is merely to provide the audience.

The result has been that many committed Christians have simply given up on the man-inspired and humanly directed structures as a way of ever deepening their faith and relationship with God. They lament the lack of awe, power and majesty which is the state of affairs we find in too many churches today; the actual presence of God has been replaced with a one or two-hour performance, presented once a week by a handful of individuals fortunate enough to be able to exercise their gifts. However genuine the latter may be, the truth remains that many of the rest—those who constitute the 'laity'—remain moribund, quietly becoming less and less passionate with each and every passing Sunday.

And Now for Something Completely Different

It's easier to see the mistakes of others than it is to lead forward oneself along the right path.

Karl Barth

Returning to the three choices as outlined in this chapter, namely: to try and bring about change; to accept the situation and do one's best within it; or to leave altogether: I'd like to conclude by introducing a fourth, and perhaps more important option by way of the following story:

A tourist driving through Ireland, realising he's lost, pulls over to ask for directions from a passer-by:

'Excuse me… can you tell me how to get to Dublin?'

The local scratches his head for a moment before replying:

'Well, you definitely don't want to start from here.'

We cannot point church in the right direction by starting out from it, taking it from where we perceive it to be now to where we think it should be; this is simply because 'the church', in the normally accepted sense, ought not to exist in the first place.

Ultimately, we need to recognize that our mission isn't actually to rectify the problems in our churches: the choice facing us is not a question of saying *No* to church as we know it; rather it's to do with accepting the call to a bigger *Yes*. A sentence from *The Wisdom of the Sands* by Antoine de Saint-Exupery captures this sentiment beautifully:

> 'If you want to build a ship, don't drum up people together to collect wood and don't assign them tasks and work, but rather teach them to long for the endless immensity of the sea.' [6]

The problem we face, and one which God wishes us to confront, is simply this:

> *Too many people seem to be interested in ship building rather than actually sailing the sea.*

The antidote is not to do with rocking the boat, or deciding whether or not to jump ship... it's about setting the course of one's own life in the direction of Jesus and seeing where he takes us. And if where we're headed looks attractive enough to others, who knows?

Perhaps it might inspire some to lower the lifeboats and paddle after us, whether we are in or out of church.

Finally, our position is in the midst of that increasing group in the church which has heard the command to halt, to remind itself of its mission, and to await further orders.

H. Richard Niebuhr
The Church Against the World

20

A WORD OF WARNING

Escape from the Troglodytes

Beware that you do not lose the substance by grasping at the shadow.

Aesop

In his *Republic*, Plato presented the following allegory:

Imagine a group of people who have spent their whole lives imprisoned inside a cave, their feet and necks chained in such a way that they cannot turn around to see what's behind them. Instead, they have spent their entire existence staring at a wall at the back of the cave.

Imagine next that a fire burns permanently behind them, illuminating the wall; imagine further, that between the cave dwellers and the fire, a raised walkway (also behind their backs and therefore out of their line of sight) has been constructed, along which a steady stream of people move, carrying figures of men and animals, and of other things besides. The fire would cast the shadows of these objects onto the wall at the back of the cave. Those trapped in the cave are unaware of all these goings-on; they would form a captive audience as they watched — not the actual objects themselves — but their shadows.

Plato asked the following questions: what sort of perception of reality would these people have? Would they not believe that the *shadows* were real rather than merely representations of real objects? He argued that people in this sort of situation could not possibly grasp the true nature of reality.

He went on to consider what would happen if one of the inhabitants was set free: turning around, his eyes would initially be blinded by the fire, and even once they'd adjusted, when eventually he was able to look at those things that had produced the shadows, it would take a long time for him to comprehend what it was he was seeing and to be able to make the connection between shadow and object.

The difficulty would be magnified if the former prisoner were then taken outside the cave altogether, where the sun would blind him yet again and in even greater measure than before. After a while, however, his eyes would adjust once more, allowing him to see an increasing number of things. By the end of the process, he would have a completely different and more complete picture of reality.

Plato finally asks us to consider what would happen if the freed man chose to return to the cave and its inhabitants: what sort of reception might he expect from the others if he tried to explain to them that what they thought was real was in fact only a projection of the real? Plato argued that the returnee would be treated as a madman.

In terms of our understanding of *church*, Plato's allegory neatly sums up the situation in which we find ourselves today. Church as we know it is merely a shadow of a deeper reality — it is not, itself, the reality that Jesus was referring to when he talked about his *ekklesia*; but, like the cave-dwellers, we have been conditioned to see it as such. And should anyone try and point to a life beyond the cave — to the possibility of a life or an existence in the very light which creates those shadows — like the individual in Plato's allegory, he too will be treated as a madman.

Those conditioned to the cave — to *church-as-a-thing-in-itself* — regard those who point to the mouth of the cave and encourage people to at least stick their head outside and take a look around, as a threat to be disposed of. They prefer the safety which the cave offers, despite its confines; like prisoners, they have become institutionalized to the degree that they cannot imagine life on the outside. Plato might have been describing these people when he said, elsewhere:

'We can easily forgive a child who is afraid of the dark; the real tragedy of life is when adults are afraid of the light.'

Like the visionary in Plato's story, those few who believe they have 'seen the light' concerning the church are often surprised that, rather than being welcomed with open arms, they experience rejection instead; they are viewed as wild-eyed fanatics and written off as such.

Jesus talked about another group of people who bear a striking resemblance to such individuals:

'A prophet is not without honour except in his own town, among his relatives and in his own home.'

Mark 6:4

Those individuals who have experienced life outside *church-as-a-thing-in-itself* find it increasingly hard to contemplate a return to 'the cave', and indeed many never return. Those who—for whatever reasons—do go back, find the re-adjustment extremely difficult since any attempt to discuss their experience is, at best, met with disinterest or in-comprehension, and at worst, outright antagonism.

But it's no longer just those who are perceived as 'oddballs' (or worse) who set themselves adrift from the mother ship. Increasing numbers of 'ordinary' people—people who have, up to now, remained in their churches—want to experience God rather than 'the programme', causing many of them to at least consider departing from their churches in search of authentic fellowship... however, for those who do make the actual decision to leave, this is, as many of them have discovered, often harder to find than one might expect.

In the absence of discovering an alternative fellowship, a logical thought is to create one's own, especially with other like-minded people who share the same opinions on how things should be done. This is a fairly reasonable idea in the circumstances—but it is not always as simple as it seems, and it is a path beset with dangers, as we shall now see.

Organising Meetings: Going the way of all Flesh

You wanna be startin' somethin'   *Michael Jackson*

It would appear that part of the psychological makeup of all human beings, Christians or otherwise, causes them to see Meetings—with a capital M—as the default setting when establishing any kind of group. In other words, as far as Christians are concerned, *starting a new fellowship usually equates to starting meetings.*

Both those on the inside and on the outside of such 'new-starts' often refer to them as splinter groups; however, the problem with splinter groups is that they share the DNA of the parent from whom they are trying to separate, and thus they carry exactly the same genetic disorder from which those involved are trying to free themselves—such groups are literally chips off the old block.

Within these groups there are often those who see for themselves an opportunity for leadership and attempt to organize the new meetings in a way that will provide a platform for their own pet ideas; this, of course, is no different from the situation which many experienced in their previous church and one of the very things from which they had escaped in the first place. As a result, it's been my experience that, more often than not, meetings of believers which form in this way don't tend to last very long before the whole idea is abandoned... or worse, they rumble along interminably, serving no positive purpose. These sorts of groupings are aptly named because, like splinters, they often end up being simply irritating at best or, at worst, downright painful for all concerned.

Many years ago, Liz and I were invited to attend the first meeting of a newly assembled Christian home group which, as we very rapidly discovered over our mugs of tea, had been formed for all the wrong reasons; it had been put together by a number of people as a reaction to their parent church, which, they felt, wasn't accommodating their views. There had been no discussed 'agenda', but Liz and I began to sense that there was a plethora of hidden ones, and we waited with more than a hint of apprehension to see how things would unfold.

Eventually, one of those present made the decision to start proceedings, but it quickly became evident that his main intention that evening was to make all of us aware of the need for Christians to send aid to our brethren in Eastern Europe. Whilst being a worthy aim, it was certainly *not* what anyone had expected as an opening to this inaugural meeting. We all sat with frozen expressions of what we hoped passed for interest, as he then proceeded to play a muffled and interminably long cassette tape about the work in some place that, to be honest, I doubt most people in the room had ever heard of.

No sooner was this over than another of those present took it upon himself to inform us — at length — that *he* believed that socialising, with a view to 'developing friendships of the order of David and Jonathan', should be the main purpose of our group. He then tried to organize a barbecue but, as a result of his insistent tone and presumptuous demeanour, the whole idea failed miserably as everyone in the room came up with reasons why they couldn't possibly make it on *any* of the dates he suggested. And so it went on. Most people never went again.

Of course, not all groups have their origins in some sort of discontent; many develop as the result of more positive intentions, but even so, this does not guarantee their success. Many years after the above experience, Liz and I were living in a different part of the country where we had joined a local church. Gradually we became established, and as time went by we found ourselves enjoying times of fellowship over a coffee, tea or glass of wine in our kitchen with several other Christians whom we'd met since our arrival. The conversations were open and natural and we all seemed to benefit from lively and meaningful talks about many aspects of our personal walk with God and about faith in general. What marked those times was that they were, more often than not, completely spontaneous; there was no 'reason' to meet other than a desire on each person's part to offer fellowship and — by extension — encouragement to everyone else.

However, this was all to change when the church asked Liz and I to lead a midweek post-*Alpha* group at our house which was to be comprised of these same people, along with some others who had come through an *Alpha* group which I'd led not so long before. At the time, post-*Alpha* groups were a new idea and one which both Liz and I felt had a lot of potential. Unfortunately, it didn't take long for us to realise that our initial optimism was not well-founded.

At our first gathering, it became evident that each individual was now coming to 'the meeting', with a checklist of things that he or she felt should feature in any Christian assembly, no matter how small. One person wanted to 'open in prayer' every week, whereas someone else wanted to start with 'a time of worship' instead. Could we perhaps sit in a circle and hold hands to pray? Could we use a prayer book, or a certain prayer to begin? And so it went on.

We continued to meet for several months, but the informal and yet spiritually productive atmosphere we'd enjoyed in our kitchen on Saturday afternoons failed to manifest itself in our living room on Wednesday nights. What had been a relaxed and positive spiritual environment rapidly deteriorated into a series of dry and awkward evenings which, unsurprisingly, eventually fizzled out. The project ended up as just another failed idea for a meeting, resulting in disappointment and ultimately the loss of true fellowship which we had been experiencing with some of these same people only a short time before.

However, as demoralising at it was, this experience did provide both of us with some unexpected and valuable insights. We came to realise that people have expectations concerning a lot of things—including meetings in particular—and that often these expectations are unconscious such that they are not even recognized *until they are not met*, and it's at this point that frustration sets in, usually being directed towards whoever's leading The Meeting.

The main lesson we learned from the post-*Alpha* group was, to put it simply, that there is a world of difference between genuinely fellowshipping and 'holding a meeting'. When we meet casually, there are not the same expectations and therefore not the pressures one finds when people gather together formally, and this allows things to develop in a more natural, unforced and productive way. The message seems to be:

Meet together — *but don't hold meetings.*

Are we doing Church yet?
When the cure is the disease

For those intent on starting afresh with the aim of 'doing it right', Wayne Jacobsen provides us with a salutary tale and one which resonates entirely with our own experience with the post-*Alpha* group:

> 'I remember when my parents and their friends first discovered God's reality. People flocked to our home every Friday night to sing, pray, and share what the Lord was doing in them, often going late into the night. Excitement abounded. Eventually those people were forced out of their church and started their own. No more Friday night meetings; now it was services Sunday morning, Sunday evening, and midweek. Boards were elected and programmes planned — and the excitement quickly vanished.' [1]

Initially believers meet because they want to experience the shared joy they have found in Christ, but at some point organisational 'needs' press in, and before long, instead of encountering the Living God, they find themselves engaged in meetings about who's going to bring the biscuits.

Jacobsen's experience also leads me to the following point. Many people are familiar with the phrase *Institutional Church*, and there are numerous books and discussions regarding the problem or danger it represents. The perceived antidote to institutional church is, as one might expect, to build 'non-institutional church' which currently exists under a variety of names — house church, cell church, emerging church, to name just a few. But it seems to me that people see the word 'institution' as the problem, when in fact the difficulty lies with the word 'church' instead, and ironically, it is *this* that has led to the institutionalising of the body of Christ in the first place. In fact, when people talk about institutional church, my question is — *can 'church' ever exist in any other form?*

All of the 'movements' listed above and many more besides have that word *church* tacked on the end, and as I hope to have demonstrated by now, it is this relatively short word (or rather what the word implies) which has caused huge problems for God's people and helped to undermine our mission in this world.

I believe that attempting to build non-institutional church as the obvious solution to the problem of institutional church is a dangerous mistake. As the example from *The Naked Church* illustrates, this mistake will ultimately cause any newly established 'non-institutional' church to revert back to the very thing from which it is trying to escape — *church-as-a-thing-in-itself.*

As things stand, *knowing God* has, in some quarters, been reduced to *going to church.* God requires faith, but church merely requires one to attend. Put another way, you can 'do' church, but you can't 'do' Christianity. The simple fact of the matter is:

Finding new ways to do church will never do.

The antidote to institutional church — to *church-as-a-thing-in-itself* — is *not* some attempt at non-institutional church:

It is Christ himself.

Rise and Shine!
Restore to me the joy of your salvation   *Psalm 51:12*

Whilst there's an increasing amount of literature that recognizes that there *is* a problem within the church at large, generally speaking the solutions simply offer a Plan B for 'doing church' differently, which I think misses the central point. People — believers as well as non-believers — don't need a different set of ideas about church — they need Jesus. The world needs to see Christians who have Christ first and Christ alone as the foundation of their lives, both as individuals and as communities. People do not need more ideas so much as living examples. Gandhi put it succinctly when he said, *you must be the change you wish to see in the world.* You effect change in those around you by being changed yourself, from the inside out, and ultimately, the only person who can produce the necessary changes in you is Jesus.

Whether you 'stick or twist' regarding your current church situation, a subtle danger is that the idea of *changing things* can take the place of God in your life. There can be a temptation to redirect your passion for God towards converting people to a better understanding of *church,* and this mission in itself can easily become an idol in your life. If this happens, there's the very real danger that you will go 'off message', becoming nothing more than 'a resounding gong or clanging cymbal'. You will not be modelling that which is needed most of all — Christ; instead of being rooted and established in love, you place yourself at risk of becoming a root of bitterness about which the writer to the Hebrews warns us (Hebrews 12:15).

It is to my great regret that there have been times where I've allowed such bitterness to become a feature of my life, and it is something I have needed to repent of and constantly guard against. It is imperative that we check our motives as far as we are able, since as Jeremiah 17:9 warns us, 'The heart is deceitful above all things and beyond cure. Who can understand it?' Or, as someone else put it, the heart of the problem is the problem of the heart. We need to adopt David's attitude when he said:

'Search me, O God, and know my heart; test me and know my anxious thoughts. See if there is any offensive way in me, and lead me in the way everlasting.'
*Psalm 139:23-24*1

The bottom line is simply this: unless we're offering the people around us a changed life rather than merely a different ecclesiology, we are not offering what's truly needed. *How* we go about things will be just as important as *what* it is we try to do. But whatever decision one makes — whether to remain in one's church or leave it — it is vital to keep Jesus front and centre and not lose sight of him. Anything else is building on sand.

If enough people build on the rock of faith in Jesus, making the fulfilment of the greatest commandment their primary goal — loving God, rather than *church* — then I believe genuine body life will be an increasingly common experience once more. E.M. Bounds said, 'The Church is looking for better methods; God is looking for better men.' Michael Jackson was wrong:

It's not about starting something.

It's about being something.

SECTION 2

GROUND ZERO

Jesus does not supply harvest fields of ministry in order to help his disciples feel fulfilled by labouring in them. On the contrary, Jesus sees a world full of need, likens it to a harvest field, and consequently calls upon his disciples to go and work in them. But we postmodern Westerners tend to put self first: I have a need to do something—or to feel that I'm doing something; I need to be needed; I need an outlet for my abilities. Fulfilling a ministry will provide all of this. This is the opposite of Jesus' priorities.

Meic Pearse
Who's Feeding Whom?

21

CHURCH DISMEMBERSHIP

The Valley of Dry Bones

O God, You are my God; I shall seek You earnestly;
My soul thirsts for You, my flesh yearns for You,
In a dry and weary land where there is no water.

Psalm 63:1

In his publication, *On the Babylonian Captivity of the Church,* Martin Luther condemned the Catholic Church's control of the Mass by means of which it held hostage the people of God. But although Protestantism modified the role or influence of the Eucharist within the church, a ruling clergy and the abuse of authority that came with it, nevertheless remained.

As the centuries have passed, the legacy of this controlling spirit is that each generation has seen an increasing hardening of the heart towards the church from those outside it, and by association, towards Christianity and the gospel itself. The church has been rejected — and tragically, along with it, so has God Himself.

But while the world clearly has a long track record of turning its back on the church, this is almost certainly the first generation which has seen *Christians* also rejecting the church on such a large scale; while they may have given up on the church, however, they have not given up on God. Indeed, many are leaving the church not because they have given up their faith, but in order to preserve it. In simple terms:

They want less of Church and more of God.

Many have discovered, though, that life outside the church walls is no walk in the Garden of Eden. It's quite likely that a good proportion of these individuals are unaware of the existence of others like themselves within their own locality and with whom they could potentially meet and enjoy fellowship. As a result, I suspect almost all of them are convinced that they are part of a tiny minority—yet as we have seen, *those who do not go to church are, in fact, in the majority.* They are part of a vast and growing population of displaced persons—they just don't realise it: as a consequence, such people remain isolated from those others who have also made the often painful decision to come out of their respective churches.

In the meantime, whilst some exiles are engaging in 'eChurch' via the internet, they are also discovering that there is no substitute for face-to-face fellowship, and corporate worship in particular. They thus find themselves trapped in a no-win situation, facing the prospect of spiritual dryness whether inside the church or out of it. Even then, it is noteworthy that the majority of those who shake the dust of church from their sandals apparently view self-imposed exile as preferable to a return to the fold and the renewed prospect of slow spiritual death, as evidenced by how many Christians leave and then remain outside the church.

Interestingly, the current situation mirrors to some degree that found in the book of Ezekiel which was addressed to another group of exiles—the Jews who were held captive in Babylon:

> 'The hand of the LORD was on me, and he brought me out by the Spirit of the LORD and set me in the middle of a valley; it was full of bones. He led me back and forth among them, and I saw a great many bones on the floor of the valley, bones that were very dry. He asked me, "Son of man, can these bones live?" I said, "Sovereign LORD, you alone know."...Then he said to me: "Son of man, these bones are the people of Israel. They say, 'Our bones are dried up and our hope is gone; we are cut off.'"'
>
> *Ezekiel 37:1-3, 11*

In fact, not only did God restore hope and life to His people, rescuing the children of Israel from captivity in Babylon, but He later came down to earth and dwelled among us in order to offer the hope of salvation and eternal life to the whole world. What a tragedy, then, that His body has been so squeezed and drained of life that Ezekiel's vision of a valley of dry bones applies to us just as much now as it did to God's people two and a half thousand years ago. It would be no exaggeration to say that a large part of the responsibility for this state of affairs can be laid squarely at the feet of those in authority who, throughout the history of the church, have sought to rule rather than to serve.

Big Brother Isn't Watching You

I wish they'd remember that the charge to Peter was Feed my sheep; not Try experiments on my rats, or even, Teach my performing dogs new tricks.

C S Lewis

In John 21:15-17 we read the following:

> 'When they had finished eating, Jesus said to Simon Peter, "Simon son of John, do you love me more than these?" "Yes, Lord," he said, "you know that I love you." Jesus said, "Feed my lambs." Again Jesus said, "Simon son of John, *do you love me*?" He answered, "Yes, Lord, you know that I love you." Jesus said, "Take care of my sheep." The third time he said to him, "Simon son of John, do you love me?" Peter was hurt because Jesus asked him the third time, "Do you love me?" He said, "Lord, you know all things; you know that I love you." Jesus said, "Feed my sheep."'

John 21:15-17

This passage teaches us two things about pastoral care:

The first is that the primary qualification for any kind of pastoral role is not a degree in Theology but a passion for Jesus. The second thing is that the role of a pastorally inclined believer is to feed the sheep... to have a passion for God's people. In short, leadership and ministry are rooted in a love for God and for His Body.

True leaders are not self-promoting but self-sacrificing, not concerned to feed their own needs (or their own egos, as Meic Pearse suggested) but to feed God's sheep. Philippians 2:3 reminds us:

> 'Do nothing out of selfish ambition or vain conceit. Rather, in humility value others above yourselves, not

looking to your own interests but each of you to the interests of the others.'

This outworks itself as putting to death one's own desire for recognition and applause and in so doing, modelling some of the most important features of the Christian faith. Jesus said,

'I am the good shepherd. The good shepherd lays down his life for the sheep.'

John 10:11

Leadership is not about laying down the law:
Leadership is about laying down one's life.

Despite this, it would appear that many churches seem to be led by those who appear to be more in love with their status and their ministry than with God. Clive Calver, former director of the *Evangelical Alliance* once said, 'I feel there are few Christian leaders today who are deeply in love with the Lord Jesus.' Calver went on to say:

'It is easy for us to love Christ's work, to love the ministry opportunities we have through our churches; to love the way he uses and blesses us. And yet how vital it is to remind ourselves — especially at a time of relative "success" — that ultimately it is not what we do, but who we are.' [1]

Unfortunately, our current ideas of leadership seem to be more concerned with running church than with loving God. This lack of passion for Him extends to the way many leaders regard His people too: there are career Christians who enter the pastorate for many different reasons, but, sadly, having a love for their fellow man isn't necessarily one of them. Despite the fact that Proverbs 27:23 says, 'Be sure you know the condition of your flocks, give careful attention to your herds', *church-as-a-thing-in-itself* has made it possible for someone to enjoy the title of *pastor* without the need for them to have a pastoral heart; indeed, I have talked with some leaders who freely admit they are not pastorally-minded. Evangelist Charles Finney had some strong words for people such as these:

'It is wrong to neglect to watch over your brothers and sisters in Christ...How little do you know or care about the state of their souls?...What have you done to become acquainted with them? With how many of them have you taken enough interest to know their spiritual state?' [2]

Of course, such intimate knowledge of each and every individual is more or less impossible in today's large churches (and yet another reason for keeping fellowships small) but this doesn't alter the fact that there is so often a lack of concern for the soul-care of the flock, regardless of context or setting.

In sharp contrast, we find Jesus who,

'...saw the crowds, (and) had compassion on them, because they were harassed and helpless, like sheep without a shepherd.'

Matthew 9:36

If those in a pastoral position do not have at least some measure of love for God's people — if he or she does not share Jesus' compassion for the sheep — then they cannot possibly do what's best for those in their care, but are much more likely to do what's best for themselves. They will be motivated by personal ambition, no matter how much they seek to cloak their intentions in religious jargon. They persuade themselves that they are doing God's work, reasoning — as Oswald Chambers put it — that 'God intends me to be here because I am so useful.' Elsewhere, Chambers offered the following important reminder:

'The lodestar of a saint is God Himself, not estimated usefulness. It is the work that God does through us that counts, not what we do for him.' [3]

These words notwithstanding, the harsh reality is that rather than exercising genuine pastoral care, many shepherds have instead abandoned the sheep in pursuit of their own ministries; indeed, there are those who appear to regard the church as a vehicle for supplying their own needs rather than the needs of the flock.

Lost, Found and Forgotten

Rejoice with me; I have found my lost sheep   *Luke 15:6*

In the preceding verse, Jesus reveals the joy in heaven when a sinner repents and enters the kingdom of God. Sadly, it would appear that many of those who are brought into the fold are then neglected while the shepherds busy themselves with reinforcing the fences. In Ezekiel 34 we read the following:

'The word of the LORD came to me: "Son of man, prophesy against the shepherds of Israel; prophesy and say to them: 'This is what the Sovereign LORD says: Woe to you shepherds of Israel who only take care of yourselves! Should not shepherds take care of the flock? You eat the curds, clothe yourselves with the wool and slaughter the choice animals, but you do not take care of the flock. You have not strengthened the weak or healed the sick or bound up the injured. You have not brought back the strays or searched for the lost. You have ruled them harshly and brutally. So they were scattered because there was no shepherd, and when they were scattered they became food for all the wild animals. My sheep wandered over all the mountains and on every high hill. They were scattered over the whole earth, and no one searched or looked for them' (vv. 1-6).

God was clearly unimpressed with those leaders who were more than happy to enjoy the benefits that came with the role of shepherd, but who did not fulfil their own pastoral responsibilities. By putting their own interests ahead of those of the flock, the shepherds of Israel were responsible for allowing the sheep to scatter across the hills—rather like the bones that were strewn across the valley floor in Ezekiel's vision. This sounds a lot like the situation confronting us today: as was the case with Israel's leaders, genuine pastoral care continues to be turned on its head, with the flock being used to supply the needs of the clergy rather than the other way around.

Instead of overseeing the sheep,
Many shepherds have overlooked them instead.

This being the case, it's surely no surprise that so many Christians have wandered away from the church. It's time for those who have assumed the mantle of authority to exercise genuine wisdom and humility; to relinquish control and release God's people into their God-given gifting and their unique calling — that, or risk losing many of them anyway, as is already the case. Such an act demands a laying aside of personal ambition, replacing it with a desire to see God's people set free. If Moses was with us today, I imagine his words on God's behalf — but directed to church leaders this time — would once again be:

Let my people go!

We must be prepared for the possibility that it might be the will of God eventually to destroy the ancient churchly framework of the *Ekklesia* or at least—as is now already happening—to complete it by structures of a very different order.

Emil Brunner

22

FLESH AND BONE

Fanfare for the Common Man

I will tear down the wall you have covered with whitewash and will level it to the ground so that its foundation will be laid bare.

Ezekiel 13:14a

At the outset of this book I referred to the fall of a wall — the Berlin Wall — of which French film director Luc Besson had this to say:

> 'It's always the small people who change things. It's never the politicians or the big guys. I mean, who pulled down the Berlin Wall? It was all the people in the streets. The specialists didn't have a clue the day before.'

While Besson was clearly overstating the case insofar as much of our history has, as we all know, been shaped by 'the politicians and the big guys', he was correct in noting that the common man has also had — and will have — his day too.

It's my belief that the walls which have protected *church-as-a-thing-in-itself* for the best part of two millennia are going to be demolished by God Himself, and that, in His mercy, He also desires to involve 'the small people...the people in the streets' in the process... in other words, people like you and me. If it's true that God uses 'the weak and the foolish', then I, for one, am eminently qualified to take part.

Nehemiah built walls to protect Jerusalem and some have drawn parallels from his example, suggesting that Christians should help build the walls of the church. But our 'Jerusalem' has fallen a long way from her original estate, and I believe we are going to play a part more in keeping with Joshua's role at Jericho than with Nehemiah's at Jerusalem: by this, I mean we are going to help bring walls down, walls which have hemmed God's people in and kept God out. The streams of living water which ought to have flowed out from His Body and into the world have for too long been dammed up by those whose desire has been to control both God and men, with the result that God's people have been allowed to stagnate while the parched world beyond is dying from thirst. The *ekklesia* certainly needs to be rebuilt as a vessel fit for His purposes, and I believe this is exactly what God is in the process of doing, bringing to mind the words of Isaiah 43:19:

> '"See, I am doing a new thing! Now it springs up;
> do you not perceive it? I am making a way in the
> wilderness and streams in the wasteland."'

As far as our role in this process is concerned, Ecclesiastes 3:3 tells us that there's 'a time to tear down and a time to build':

> I believe the time for this may well have arrived.

In these final pages, I would like to offer a picture of how the body of Christ *might* look if we were able to dispense with *church-as-a-thing-in-itself*, thereby releasing God's people to function as the *ekklesia* instead. What follows is an exploration of the 'what if's'; a thought-experiment motivated by the desire to encourage at least a consideration of the amazing possibilities that I believe exist for the *ekklesia* and which—if we stand back and let God have His way for once—we could actually see come to fruition.

While I strongly believe in the possibility of this picture becoming a reality—not least because I'm convinced it is more closely aligned with a biblical description of the *ekklesia* than any of our current expressions of Christ's body—I do not claim that it is prophetic; it is simply a vision borne out of hope, a vision of the sort of things that *could* happen rather than what *will* happen.

However, the darkest hour is before the dawn: before we can begin to appreciate what God might have in store for us, any rebuilding process must be preceded by a tearing down, and it is to this we must turn one last time.

Wars and Rumours of Wars

My centre is giving way, my right is in retreat; situation excellent. I shall attack.

Marshal Ferdinand Foch

Eighty years ago, H. Richard Niebuhr, Professor of Christian Ethics at Yale University Divinity School, wrote the following:

> 'In the crisis of the world the church becomes aware of its own crisis: not that merely of a weak and responsible institution but of one which is threatened with destruction. It is true...that the church will probably survive in some form in any circumstances...the real question is whether it will survive as a reliable witness to the Christian faith.' [1]

Church-as-a-thing-in-itself has indeed been able to survive the onslaught of the enemy for hundreds of years, somehow managing to stagger on in its own strength. But while Niebuhr questioned whether it could continue as a 'reliable witness to the Christian faith', one has to ask: has it *ever* been a reliable witness to the Christian faith? I would argue that the church has for most of its existence been guilty of presenting *itself* as much, if not more, than the gospel of Christ. It is only through the grace of God manifested in the lives of godly individuals — members of the true *ekklesia* working within the institutional church — that God's message has ever managed to shine through. I would argue that there has always been a witness, not because of, but in spite of *church-as-a-thing-in-itself.*

Not only has the lack of a scriptural foundation been a major factor in the church's diminishing influence in the world, but it has also had a negative impact on successive generations of God's people who have been progressively weakened and incapacitated. The result has been what we might call *The Insufficient Church*, populated by those who have been dulled and blunted through years of neglect:

We have sown a harvest of potatoes: not couch potatoes, but row after row of church potatoes — or, perhaps more aptly — pew potatoes.

By failing to equip 'their' congregations, many leaders have hindered the spiritual development of multitudes of Christians, thereby rendering a large proportion of God's army ineffective. In turn, this has diminished the impact of the Christian community on a lost world, limiting its ability to go out and make disciples. The self-serving attitude of many in authority has meant that, collectively speaking, God's people are punching well below their weight; at the same time, they are ill-equipped to deal in the long term with the kind of attacks with which they are already being confronted. We need to realise that such attacks will only grow in intensity — particularly those of militant atheism and radical Islam. We are in a war, the scale and intensity of which I doubt any of us fully understands or appreciates.

Recently, I listened to a radio broadcast of what can only be described as a well-meaning but — at the risk of sounding uncharitable — rather naïve sketch performed by Christians in a church somewhere in Middle England; a few days earlier the American journalist James Foley had been murdered in the most horrific fashion by religious extremists, and the contrast between the two worlds could not have been greater. Many Christians (certainly in the comfortable West) are engaged in a Phoney War but they have persuaded themselves that it is the real thing; they are, in effect, playing a game of *Risk* in the middle of the Battle of the Somme, seemingly oblivious to the explosions and slaughter taking place around them. It's time to face reality: this is not a game; whether we like it or not, we are embroiled in a conflict with a relentless, implacable and utterly malevolent foe and we need to engage it with the weapons at our disposal: Ephesians 6:11-12 tells us to,

'Put on the full armour of God, so that you can take your stand against the devil's schemes. For our struggle is not against flesh and blood, but against the rulers, against the authorities, against the powers of this dark world and against the spiritual forces of evil in the heavenly realms.'

The ancient structures are crumbling: too inflexible to cope with such levels of assault, the old order is gradually being swept away. In places like Britain and Europe—and with America looking set to follow suit—the observable Christian perimeter is shrinking. Large sections of *church-as-a-thing-in-itself* look set to end, not with a bang but a whimper.

But while all might appear lost in terms of what most people see as the Christian witness in the world today, we must keep in mind the essential truth that I hope by now has been made clear: the church and the *ekklesia* are not the same thing. Despite the ferocious attacks that Satan has launched upon the body of Christ down the centuries—not least of which has been the shackling of a once free and healthy body with chains wrought from the pride and self-interest of those who would raise themselves above others—God's people *will* prevail. Whilst church as we know it might collapse, we need to remember Jesus' proclamation: 'I will build my *ekklesia*, and the gates of Hades will not overcome it.' We can be confident in the knowledge that the ultimate outcome is assured. Nevertheless, there are still battles ahead, leaving no room for complacency; most regrettably, one of the biggest battles is going to be overcoming the legacy of *church-as-a-thing-in-itself.*

The Good, the Bad and the Ugly

God holds the shepherds primarily responsible for the state of the flock. Church failure is invariably leadership failure.

Arthur Wallis

Earlier in the book I recounted the story of an elder who seemed overly enthusiastic about identifying the members of his church for the primary purpose of disciplining them. 'Accountability' is a word which is often employed by people like this, those who are keen to engender subordination in their brothers and sisters—but I firmly believe there are people in positions of authority today who themselves will be held accountable by God for misrepresenting the heart of the gospel—those who 'exercise authority' but who fail to model genuine leadership. We have already seen how Ezekiel prophesied against the shepherds of Israel who were failing to care for His people; perhaps those who fit this description today would do well to consider the subsequent judgment pronounced on their forerunners:

'"Therefore, you shepherds, hear the word of the LORD: As surely as I live, declares the Sovereign LORD, because my flock lacks a shepherd and so has been plundered and has become food for all the wild animals, and because my shepherds did not search for my flock but cared for themselves rather than for my flock, therefore, you shepherds, hear the word of the LORD: This is what the Sovereign LORD says: I am against the shepherds and will hold them accountable for my flock. I will remove them from tending the flock so that the shepherds can no longer feed themselves. I will rescue my flock from their mouths, and it will no longer be food for them."'

Ezekiel 34:7-10

Alarming as it may be to some, I am convinced that a key element in the rebuilding and bringing together of God's people today would include the removal of the professional clergy; too many of these hired hands have usurped God's authority and placed themselves as the cornerstones of structures they have designed and built, primarily with their own interests in mind.

But if the shepherds *were* removed as Ezekiel 34 describes, then what of the sheep? In our present-day context, who would take care of them? The passage continues, providing an answer which applies just as much now as it did in the time of the Israelites:

'"For this is what the Sovereign LORD says: I myself will search for my sheep and look after them. As a shepherd looks after his scattered flock when he is with them, so will I look after my sheep. I will rescue them from all the places where they were scattered on a day of clouds and darkness. I will bring them out from the nations and gather them from the countries, and I will bring them into their own land...There they will lie down in good grazing land, and there they will feed in a rich pasture on the mountains of Israel. I myself will tend my sheep and have them lie down, declares the

Sovereign LORD. I will search for the lost and bring back the strays. I will bind up the injured and strengthen the weak, but the sleek and the strong I will destroy. I will shepherd the flock with justice"' (vv. 11-13b, 14b-16).

This passage offers the hope, for the thousands, if not millions of disconnected believers dispersed around the world today — followers of Christ who are searching for something better than the half-life offered by *church-as-a-thing-in-itself* — that there may well be light at the end of the tunnel and that their search might be coming to an end.

Speaking to the same exiles through the prophet Jeremiah, God offered the following message of encouragement to those cut off from their spiritual home — and I believe it's a message for us too:

'For I know the plans I have for you," declares the LORD, "plans to prosper you and not to harm you, plans to *give you hope and a future.'*

Jeremiah 29:11

The good news for the lost and the strays is that God has not abandoned His people. A time is coming when God Himself will take up His rightful place as Chief Shepherd in order to bring His sheep into good pasture.

Vital Signs

Then the LORD God formed a man from the dust of the ground and breathed into his nostrils the breath of life, and the man became a living being.

Genesis 2:7

Despite Jesus' promise in John 10:10, that he came so that we 'may have life, and have it to the full', we find instead that his body is on life support and has been for quite some time; and whilst there are many out in the world who are only too eager to administer the Last Rites, it's also true that too many church-going Christians have been living in the shadow of the valley of a near-death experience for far too long.

Like Lazarus, many congregations are, in spiritual terms, prostrate, lifeless corpses. Too many of our 'church bodies' have flatlined, but it has to be stressed that this condition is not necessarily anyone's fault in particular. The truth is, *church-as-a-thing-in-itself* works against spiritual life, opposing the efforts of those who long for God's presence in their midst.

On the other hand, some churches are indeed zombie brides, led by blind guides... by dead men walking. Authoritarian leadership has provided the boulder with which to seal off the tomb, shutting out both light and oxygen, with the result that countless Christians are kept in the dark, wrapped in the burial cloths of ritual and church traditions. Ironically, the only person who can rescue these living dead is the one person we forgot to invite to the party and this is the reason why so many of our churches are lifeless in the first place. That person, of course, is Jesus, who, at Lazarus' tomb, declared:

'I am the resurrection and the life. The one who believes in me will live, even though they die.'

John 11:25

While the terms reformation, revival, restoration and revolution have all been used throughout this book when discussing potential remedies for the failing health of the church, over and above all these things the body is in desperate need of *resuscitation*. Just as God breathed life into the first body—Adam—we need now to stand well back, allowing God to administer the kiss of life and breathe into Christ's body... we need Him to fill it—to fill *us*—with his Holy Spirit. It has happened before—it can happen again:

'This is what the Sovereign LORD says to these bones: I will make breath enter you, and you will come to life. I will attach tendons to you and make flesh come upon you and cover you with skin; I will put breath in you, and you will come to life. Then you will know that I am the LORD.'"

Ezekiel 37:5-6

My fervent hope is that God, through His Spirit, is going to resurrect and rebuild the body, reconnecting the scattered bones—His people—according to His thoughts and His ways. My prayer is that He will build His body the way He intended it to be built the first time—that is, until man got in the way and took over, almost killing it in the process. This is not to say that God won't involve His people again—He just won't use the kind of shepherds who helped dismember the body of Christ in the first place...

Battle Stations: On your feet, Soldier

For if their purpose or activity is of human origin, it will fail. But if it is from God, you will not be able to stop these men; you will only find yourselves fighting against God.

Acts 5:38-39

H. Richard Niebuhr wrote:

'[The church] has seen enough of the indifference or hostility of the world, and of the defeats of some of its component parts, to realise that its continuance in the world is by no means a certainty. It knows the ways of God too well not to understand that he can and will raise up another people to carry out the mission entrusted to it if the Christian community fail him.' [2]

Is it possible that God is even now in the process of doing just this—raising up another people in order to fulfil His purposes? Returning once more to the valley of dry bones, we read the following:

'Then he said to me, "Prophesy to these bones and say to them, 'Dry bones, hear the word of the LORD!'"...I prophesied as he commanded me, and breath entered them; they came to life and stood up on their feet—a vast army.'

Ezekiel 37:4, 10

There is, I believe, the possibility that a growing ragtag army—of a kind not seen since the early Christians who prevailed against the might of Rome—is slowly but surely coalescing under the guidance of the Holy Spirit into a fighting force that will rattle the gates of hell.

Such an army—if it indeed exists—would be composed of Christians whose desire to follow God has overridden their natural inclination to remain within their comfort zones. Some of them are currently languishing in churches scattered all over the world while many more are without any fellowship at all, but what they all have in common is the fact that they are better constituted to face the future—somewhat like the pioneers who left Europe for the New World despite all the risks. This new generation of Christians will be enlisting in an army that consists of those who are not prepared to stick their heads in the sand anymore and ignore the obvious fact that clearly, 'something is rotten in Denmark'; they will be a people who, if it comes to it, would rather be ostracized than an ostrich, as some of them have already demonstrated.

These Christian foot-soldiers would form an underground army, one which would look quite unlike anything either the church or the world has seen for a very long time, with two of the most tangible differences being the absence of a clergy and of designated buildings.

Some will say that the church *has*, in fact, operated along similar lines in the past in places like Russia or China, for example, and this is indeed true, but what makes the scenario I have outlined here different, is this: on the occasions where God's people have had to exercise discretion in order to survive, they have understood the underground church to be an adaptation of 'real church,' forced upon them by circumstances; in contrast, the kind of situation described above would have the chance—for the first time in centuries— to be recognized not as a make-do alternative, but as *the real thing*.

Disorganized Religion

If you can explain what's going on, then God didn't do it.

Warren Wiersbe

Some will ask how any Christian community could possibly survive in the long term without the traditionally accepted structures of *church-as-a-thing-in-itself*. For such people, the 'Brave New World' of the liberated Christian body, with no building and no clergy, is too frightening to even contemplate. But if the body existed once like this, then who's to say it shouldn't do so again? And if God kept to his vow of removing the shepherds once—as in Ezekiel 34—then who's to say that He won't do it again? Lest we forget, God is perfectly capable of looking after His sheep and does not need the assistance of any human agency.

Crucially, the absence of an official clergy would *not* mean the absence of *leadership;* in fact, I believe quite the opposite — that a greater and more effective, *God*-ordained, Spirit-led leadership would emerge *if* the barrier of a professional, mediating priesthood were to be removed. Rather than having people with titles such as *Bishop, Pastor* or *Elder* in charge, the people would be taught, encouraged and led by those 'who *seem* to be leaders'; by brothers and sisters who have never been interested in seeking ecclesiastical office or looking for ways to 'exercise their ministry' as some put it; rather they would be individuals whose constant priority is to seek first the kingdom of God.

We would see the emergence of servant-leaders who command respect and have genuine authority, not because someone gave them a label, a title or an office on the strength of a qualification obtained in a seminary — or because they went through an ordination process — but because of the authority that comes with the in-dwelling presence of Christ. In other words:

Office-bearers would be replaced with Light-bearers.

Just as the absence of a professional clergy does not equate to the absence of leadership, so the absence of church buildings would not mean that the body lacked a physical presence. If buildings were locked and the keys given away, we would most likely see a return to the home as the primary setting for fellowship gatherings: this, in turn, would engender a greater Christian witness at the local level, affecting those who surround us in our homes — the neighbours we are called upon to love — believers and unbelievers alike.

The resultant emphasis on events on one's doorstep — offering the possibility of a common ground in terms of both fellowship and evangelism to Christians who live just a few houses apart — would surely serve to increase dialogue between believing neighbours who formerly attended different churches, or even no church at all... people who, as things stand, might as well live on opposite sides of the world.

The basis for fellowship would cease to be defined or restricted by one's church or denomination — or even on the grounds of whether one is 'churched' or 'de-churched'; this would allow for the real possibility of previously disconnected believers coming together, enabling them to combine as a much more effective fighting force. Slowly but surely, the fragmentation and black-hole effect caused by the existence of church buildings would be reversed.

As Christian insurgents we would have the opportunity to engage in guerrilla warfare so that rather than large, expensive and labour-intensive programmes and rallies, we would fight street by street, from house to house, rescuing one family at a time. Kierkegaard anticipated the future rules of engagement thus:

> 'It is in the living room that the battle must be fought, not imaginatively in church, with the pastor shadowboxing and the listeners looking on.' [3]

Those saved out of the world in this way would find themselves becoming not simply part of a new church world with its myriad insular activities, but part of a body which looks very different: as Alan Knox puts it,

> 'Today, the church focuses so much on doing church-stuff at church-times in church-places with church-people...But, there's so much more to following Jesus Christ.' [4]

One of the more radical characteristics of this new community would be that while gatherings might retain some aspects of current practice, they would not be limited to set places at set times; teaching and fellowship would not take place in buildings 'somewhere else' but rather, as I mentioned earlier, the focus would be much more centred in homes, in people's own streets and neighbourhoods. Fellowship would no longer be restricted to a few hours of very limited participation on a Sunday with perhaps a few more hours in the middle of the week; instead, people would have the opportunity to exercise their God-given gifts more fully and effectively, making a dramatic difference in the lives of those around them.

The Christian life — both its outward form and the changes wrought within it by the freedom now available — would take on a new shape: There would be the potential for all sorts of gatherings in all sorts of places, with all sorts of combinations of people at all sorts of times. However, these people would not be meeting for meeting's sake, or out of 'Christian duty', as some seem to understand passages such as Hebrews 10:25; instead, they would meet in a natural, unforced way in order to encourage one another, exactly as the author of Hebrews intended.

Time spent in fellowship would, comparatively speaking, take place on an industrial scale, and yet it would still leave plenty of room for essential interaction with the world; there would be far less chance of repeating the collective failure to move out of the disengaged subculture which the limiting, divisive influence of *church-as-a-thing-in-itself* has helped to create. Meaningful, edifying fellowship would energize, motivate and equip increasing numbers of Christians to be salt and light, enabling them to shine like stars in the darkness. A fragmented world that is witnessing the inexorable break-down of family and society as a whole is crying out for the sort of community that is possible within a Christ-centred *ekklesia*: more importantly, much of the world is crying out for the gospel message of love, hope and truth which would once again have the opportunity to spread organically through the type of relational living that Jesus exemplified and the early Christians modelled.

Now, imagine *this* being repeated in every neighbourhood, in every village, in every town and in every city throughout the world.

Making Mistakes in a Good Direction

Jesus does not give recipes that show the way to God as other teachers of religion do. He is Himself the way.

Karl Barth

While the future possibilities for the *ekklesia* are exciting to explore, the predicament of both the churched and the de-churched remains very much an issue in the here-and-now.

With regard to the scattered sheep in particular, there is as yet no real cohesion within the ranks of those who have drifted away from their churches:

'Like every revolt in its early stages, the Christian revolution of today is uncertain of its ends and vague in its strategy. It seems to be a sentiment and a protest rather than a theory and a plan of action. It is a matter of feeling, in part, just because the situation remains unanalysed.' [5]

The current state of affairs, then, is exactly as one might expect it to be, although I also believe that things will gradually become clearer as God leads and directs. However, what *is* clear, is that there are increasing numbers of people from all denominations for whom church as we know it clearly isn't enough anymore; they simply want God for His own sake, without all the 'church-stuff' that gets in the way. Ironically, more and more people are making the decision to *move out of church-as-a-thing-in-itself in order to move on in God.*

Should you decide to come out of the existing set-up—not because you're 'rebellious', or because you have a 'problem with authority', but because you firmly believe that institutional church does not square with the Scriptures—then be confident, and take strength from the fact that you are not the first to take such action and you certainly won't be the last. Indeed, pray that more people who feel the same way will have the courage, the faith, and a level of desire and love for God that will cause them to step outside the confines of *church-as-a-thing-in-itself* and into the freedom that God promises to those who fellowship with Him. For,

'...the Lord is the Spirit, and where the Spirit of the Lord is, there is liberty'.

2 Corinthians 3:17 [NASB]

In terms of the number of Christians currently disengaged from the church, there most certainly exists the potential for a critical mass with which to bring about change. However, I suspect that some of these 'dry bones' are still pursuing the chimera of 'proper church' and constantly running down dead-ends as a result. At the same time, I imagine there are others who have resigned themselves to the idea that their faith will remain a personal, private affair, an individual rather than a corporate faith. My guess is that few of the people in either group have considered the possibility of a third way: a return to the *ekklesia*.

Any coherent, God-inspired movement that might currently exist within this large, amorphous body, may be only 'a cloud the size of a man's hand' and thus not be in a position to make its presence felt... but I'm cautiously optimistic that there is a coming deluge. Two thousand years ago, and starting with just twelve men, the Christian faith prevailed against the Roman Empire: what might a handful of people, moving in the power of God and within the context of the true *ekklesia*, achieve today?

In the meantime, it is my sincere hope that by adding weight to the argument against *church-as-a-thing-in-itself*, this book will not only encourage those who are exhausted from carrying all the excess baggage that comes with the institution, but it will also help swell the ranks of those Christians who are prepared to step out in faith and discover Christ on Christ's own terms, free from the encumbrance of church. I also hope it will increase the likelihood of us all having true fellowship with more and more of those who have decided to risk living outside the city walls: those who simply want to grow in God rather than merely go to church.

Inevitably, some will be led up blind alleys as they grope towards both a better understanding of what Christ meant when he referred to his *ekklesia* and the way it is outworked in community. Errors will occur, but let's remember one thing: *church-as-a-thing-in-itself* is the most far-reaching and grievous mistake ever made by the people of God, and we can hardly do worse than that. And as long as we remain open to God, if we do make mistakes, then—to borrow from Japanese mathematician Goro Shimura—we will make mistakes in a good direction.

There will be those who, even now, want more detail as to how things are supposed to develop and greater clarity on where all this might be heading—those who would ask, '*What next?*' But it's important to recognize that it was and continues to be a desire such as this—the desire for a kind of route map, emanating from a need for fleshly reassurance rather than from the exercise of faith—which has led God's people to wander in the wilderness for a second time, and for the best part of two millennia.

We must not run ahead of God. Instead, we need only refer to the example of Abraham: God called him out of Ur but did not reveal to him the final destination. He wanted Abraham to literally walk by faith and trust that He would take him exactly where he needed to be and precisely when he needed to be there. So it is with us. As Oswald Chambers observed:

'Faith never knows where it is being led, but it loves and knows the One who is leading.'

It's time to learn how to take things one step at a time, placing our confidence in Jesus rather than in our own efforts, and seeing where he takes us. As Wayne Jacobsen put it:

The Word of God doesn't offer us a map.

It offers us a Guide.

We shall not cease from exploration
And the end of all our exploring
Will be to arrive where we started
And know the place for the first time.

T.S. Elliot
Little Gidding

23

REDISCOVERING THE ANCIENT PATHS

The Way Home

This is what the LORD says: 'Stand at the crossroads and look: ask for the ancient paths, ask where the good way is, and walk in it, and you will find rest for your souls.'

Jeremiah 6:16

It's highly likely that many reading this book have at some time walked past a cathedral or church at night, and if the building was particularly grand or famous, it's quite probable that it would have been illuminated by floodlights. It occurs to me that in a sense, this is what we Christians have done for centuries—we have illuminated our own creation, redirecting the world's attention away from the Son of God and fixing it instead on *church-as-a-thing-in-itself*.

But enough is enough: we need to turn our eyes away from the institutional church and return our focus to the person of Jesus Christ; to cultivate the same sort of desire which King David expressed when he wrote the following words:

'One thing I ask from the LORD,
this only do I seek:
that I may dwell in the house of the LORD
all the days of my life,
to gaze on the beauty of the LORD
and to seek him in his temple.'

Psalm 27:4

In His mercy, God has not remained within the inert walls of the temple in which David yearned to dwell. *God* has come to dwell inside and amongst *us*, 'For we are the temple of the living God' (2 Cor. 6:16), the living, breathing body of Christ.

The only structure that has ever been truly intended is one built by Him—entirely devoid of walls and instead composed of living stones: '*You* are God's field, God's building', Paul reminds us in 1 Corinthians 3:9.

But while planted and tended by God, for far too long His people have found themselves hedged in and living in the shadow of *church-as-a-thing-in-itself*—a man-made edifice which has blocked God's life-giving light, producing shrivelled and stunted plants, pale and malnourished believers.

It's time to uproot and to tear down—just as Solomon wrote in Ecclesiastes 3: it's time to demolish this monument to ourselves in order to reveal Jesus, and see him bring to life and build his body once again. If we open ourselves sincerely and fully to God, then just as a plant or a flower bends naturally towards the light, so we will bend towards Him; in so doing, not only will we find ourselves leaning in towards one another, but more importantly we will all be leaning on the beloved described in *Song of Songs*. We will find ourselves growing and coming together in new ways—not in order to 'do church right this time', but simply in order to gaze on the beauty of the Lord. We will mature as disciples of Christ, knowing the truth and having that truth set us free—free from the strait-jacket of *church-as-a-thing-in-itself*, allowing us to truly experience and enter into the abundant life promised as we pursue the Son of the Living God.

Together, we will learn to tread the ancient paths…
to walk in the good way once more, and, at long last,
to find rest for our souls.

Bibliography

Already Gone: Why your kids will quit church and what you can do to stop it by Ken Ham (Master Books, 2009)

An Hour with George Müller: The man of faith to whom God gave millions, edited by A. Sims (Moody Press Chicago)

Balancing the Christian Life by Charles C Ryrie (Chicago, IL: Moody Press, 1969)

Bible: The Story of the King James Version by Gordon Campbell (Oxford University Press, 2010)

Blessing or Curse by Derek Prince (Word UK Ltd, 1990)

The Best of A.W. Tozer, compiled by Warren Wiersbe (Christian Publications Inc. 1978)

Beyond Radical by Gene Edwards (The SeedSowers, 1999)

The Church by Hans Kung (New York: Sheed and Ward, 1967)

The Church and Ministry in the Early Centuries by Thomas M. Lindsay (Cosimo, originally published 1902)

Classic Christianity by Bob George (Harvest House, 1989)

Cyprian and Roman Carthage by Allen Brent (Cambridge University Press, 7 Oct 2010)

Decision Making and the Will of God by Gary Friesen and J. Robin Maxson (Multnomah Press, 1980)

The Divine Conspiracy by Dallas Willard (Fount, 1998)

How To Choose a Bible Version by Robert L. Thomas (Mentor, 2000)

Excellence in Leadership: The pattern of Nehemiah by John White (Inter-Varsity Press, 1986)

How to Experience Revival by Charles Finney (Whitaker House, 1994)

I believe in the Church by David Watson (Hodder & Stoughton Religious, 1985)

The International Bible Commentary, General editor F.F. Bruce (Marshall Pickering/Zondervan, 1986)

Introducing Early Christianity: A Topical Survey of Its Life, Beliefs & Practices by Laurie Guy, IVP Academic (September 28, 2011)

Introduction to Psychology and Counseling by Meier, Minirth, Wichern & Ratcliffe (Baker Academic)

The Joyful Christian by C.S. Lewis (April 1st 2000 by Broadman & Holman)

Joyful Exiles by James Houston (IVP, 2006)

The King James Bible: A Short History from Tyndale to Today, by David Norton (Cambridge University Press, 2011)

Letters to Malcolm; Chiefly on Prayer by C S Lewis (San Diego: Harvest, 1964)

Mere Christianity by C S Lewis (Fount)

The Misunderstanding of the Church, Emil Brunner (Lutterworth Press, 2003)

The Naked Church by Wayne Jacobsen (Body Life, 1998)

Our Brilliant Heritage by Oswald Chambers (Oswald Chambers Publications Association and Marshall, Morgan & Scott, 1929)

Priest and Bishop: Biblical Reflections by Raymond E. Brown (Geoffrey Chapman, 1971)

The Pursuit of God by A.W. Tozer (Christian Publications, 1982)

The Radical Christian by Arthur Wallis (Kingsway, 1981)

Should the Church Teach Tithing? By Russell Earl Kelly (Writers Club Press, 2000)

So You Don't Want to go to Church Anymore? By Jake Colson (Windblown Media, 2006)

The Story of Christianity: 2000 Years of Faith by Michael Collins and Matthew A. Price (Dorling Kindersley, 1999)

The Trellis and the Vine by Colin Marshall and Tony Payne (Matthias Media 2009)

Where do we go from Here? by Ralph Neighbour (Touch Outreach Ministries, June 1990)

Who's Feeding Whom? by Meic Pearse (Solway, 1996)

Who is your covering? by Frank Viola (Present Testimony Ministry, Aug 2002)

The World Treasury of Physics, Astronomy, and Mathematics Edited by Timothy Ferris (Back Bay Books, 1991)

Notes

Introduction
1. Werner Heisenberg, quoted in *The World Treasury of Physics, Astronomy, and Mathematics*, p.822

Chapter 1. A View from the Pew
1. A.W. Tozer, *The Pursuit of God,* Preface
2. http://www.telegraph.co.uk/news/religion/10062745/Christianity-declining-50pc-faster-than-thought-as-one-in-10-under-25s-is-a-Muslim.html
3. http://www.bbc.co.uk/news/world-us-canada-23774334.
4. http://www.eauk.org/church/research-and-statistics/church-membership.cfm
5. http://www.telegraph.co.uk/news/religion/8633540/Ageing-Church-of-England-will-be-dead-in-20-years.html
6. http://www.wnd.com/?pageId=100324; Quoting Ken Ham, *Already Gone: Why your kids will quit church and what you can do to stop it.*
7. Ken Ham, *Already Gone: Why your kids will quit church and what you can do to stop it,* Chapter 1, p.22
8. http://www.whychurch.org.uk/trends.php
9.Josh Packard, *Exodus of the Religious Dones,* Group Publishing, Inc. (August 3, 2015)
10. A.W.Tozer, *Of God and Men*, Chapter 34
11. Ralph Neighbour, *Where do we go from Here?* p.340
12. Mike Yaconelli, *Dangerous Wonder*, p.24
13. Thom & Jess Rainer, *The Millennials,* Broadman & Holman (1 Jan. 2011), p.244
14. John Stott. *IFES Review 25.* Motives for Mission
15. Bob George, *Classic Christianity,* p.18
16. Arthur Wallis, *The Radical Christian*, p.97
17. Meic Pearse, *Who's feeding Whom?* P.97

Chapter 2. Church-as-a-Thing-in-Itself
1. Emil Brunner, *The Misunderstanding of the Church*, p.10-11
2a,b. Michael Ramsey; quoted from *I believe in the Church*, by David Watson, p.18
3. C.S. Lewis, *Mere Christianity,* p.45
4. Ralph Neighbour, *Where do we go from here?* p.180

5. Dallas Willard, *The Divine Conspiracy*, p.222
6. Francis Frangipane: http://messages.frangipane.org/cgi-bin/gx.cgi/AppLogic+FTContentServer?GXHC_gx_session_id_FutureTens eContentServer=3552312a4e0aae75&pagename=FaithHighway/Globals/ DisplayTextMessage&PROJECTPATH=10000/1000/728&sermonid=textse rmon_1231704539407&customerTypeLabel=Weekly&sermontitle=Find %20God!
7. Source not found.

Chapter 4. Body Language
1. E.W. Goodrick, *Do It Yourself Hebrew and Greek: Everybody's Guide to the Language Tools*, Zondervan/Multnomah, 1980, p. 9:4
2. F.F. Bruce, *The Spreading Flame*, p.71
3. James D.G. Dunn, *The Theology of Paul the Apostle*, p.540

Chapter 5. Upon this Mistranslation we will build our Church
1. http://www.graftedinfellowship.org/uploads/5/7/3/3/5733440/ the_word_church.pdf
2. M.G. Easton, *Illustrated Bible Dictionary,* p.244 Third Edition, published by Thomas Nelson, 1897. http://www.ntslibrary.com/PDF%20Books/Eastons%20Bible%20Dictiona ry.pdf
3. http://www.alanknox.net/2007/07/ekklesia-and-kuriakon/
4. Smith's Bible Dictionary,1884, p.452
5. Ibid
6. http://www.bartleby.com/81/3556.html
7. *Pope Gregory's letter to Mellitus.*
8. http://www.alanknox.net/2007/07/ekklesia-and-kuriakon/
9. Gordon Campbell, *Bible: The Story of the King James Version,* p.14
10. Robert L. Thomas, *How To Choose a Bible Version,* p.26
11. Quoted from *The King James Bible: A Short History from Tyndale to Today*, by David Norton, Cambridge University Press, 2011, p.87

Chapter 6. Worshipping what our Hands have Made
1. A.W. Tozer, *The Knowledge of the Holy*, p.8
2. A.W. Tozer, *This World: Playground or Battleground?* p.37
3. Wayne Jacobsen, *The Naked Church*, p.14

Chapter 7. A Tragedy of Errors
1. Arthur Wallis, *The Radical Christian*, p.94

Chapter 8. Shepherds and Hired Hands

1. http://www.bbc.co.uk/history/ancient/romans/social_structure_01.shtml
2. Raymond E. Brown, *Priest and Bishop: Biblical Reflections,* p.10-13
3. Hans Kung, *The Church,* p.366
4. Raymond E. Brown, *Priest and Bishop: Biblical Reflections,* p.13
5. Arthur Wallis, *The Radical Christian,* p.95
6. Although some translations render 'leader' as either 'teacher' or 'instructor', the basic principle remains: function is not the same as office.
7. See for example, Ignatius of Antioch, *Letter to the Trallians;* (http://www.newadvent.org/fathers/0106.htm)
8. Thomas M. Lindsay, *The Church and Ministry in the Early Centuries,* p.270
9. The role of evangelist is mentioned only 3 times in the NT and is virtually absent from subsequent literature; it seems to have been equivalent in function to that of an apostle, the difference being that the individual had not physically seen Christ at any point.
10. In some denominations, particularly Pentecostal and Charismatic churches, the ministries of apostle and prophet have reappeared, but this is a limited and relatively recent phenomenon. It's also difficult to say to what degree these present day ministries correspond to those found in the New Testament and early church.
11. Lindsay, p.273
12. http://www.internationalstandardbible.com/M/ministry.html
13. Tertullian, *On Baptism*, Ch.17
14. Laurie Guy, *Introducing Early Christianity: A Topical Survey of Its Life, Beliefs & Practices*, p.93
15. Lindsay, p.299
16. Cyprian, Epistle 66
17. Lindsay, p.307, 309
18. Allen Brent, *Cyprian and Roman Carthage,* p.328
19. http://www.fourthcentury.com/index.php/imperial-laws-and-letters-involving-religion-ad-311-364/
20. Michael Collins and Matthew A. Price, *The Story of Christianity,* p.65
21. C.A. Volz, *Pastoral Life and Practice in the Early Church* p.44; cited in *Introducing Early Christianity: A Topical Survey of Its Life, Beliefs & Practices*, p.98, by Laurie Guy.
22. Lindsay, p.357
23. Robert L. Thomas, How To Choose A Bible Version, p.117

Chapter 9. Brought to Book

1. Robert L. Thomas, *How To Choose a Bible Version*, p.19
2. *Christian Monthly Standard*
http://www.christianmonthlystandard.com/index.php/looking-at-the-bible-versions-kjv-1611/
3. Gordon Campbell, *Bible: The Story of the King James Version*, p.82
4. Frank Viola, *Who Is Your Covering?* p.55
5. Frank Viola, *Who Is Your Covering?* p.48
6. Emil Brunner, cited in *The Church: Sacraments, Worship, Ministry, Mission*, by Donald G. Bloesch, p.52
7. John White, *Excellence in Leadership: The pattern of Nehemiah*, p.83
8. A.W.Tozer, *This World: Playground or Battleground?* p.19
9. This is a significant passage when one considers how, hundreds of years later people would nevertheless retroactively confer ultimate ecclesiastical authority and power upon the apostle.
10. Lindsay, p.59-60

Chapter 10. The Sabbath

1. http://www.jewfaq.org/shabbat.htm
2. Arthur Wallis, *The Radical Christian,* p.165-6
3. James Cardinal Gibbons, Archbishop of Baltimore, *The Faith of Our Fathers,* 88th edition, page 89. Originally published in 1876, republished and Copyright 1980 by TAN Books and Publishers, Inc., pages 72-73.

Chapter 11. Meeting Expectations

1. F.F. Bruce et al, *The International Bible Commentary*, p.1379
2. Thomas M. Lindsay, *The Church and Ministry in the Early Centuries*, p.49
3. Laurie Guy, *Introducing Early Christianity*, p.25-26

Chapter 12. House of God or House of Cards?

1. According to the Schaeffer Institute, the United States Census Bureau of Records – backed up by denominational reports and the Assemblies of God U.S. Missions
2. Wayne Jacobsen, *The Naked Church*, p.172, 176
3. Gene Edwards, *Beyond Radical*, p.19
4. http://en.wikipedia.org/wiki/Constantine_the_Great
5. Michael Collins and Matthew A. Price, *The Story of Christianity*, p.64
6. Howard Wilson*, Rome for the modern pilgrim, 3: Constantine's building programme.*

http://www.pilgrimstorome.org.uk/Rome%20for%20the%20modern%20pilgrim%20Part%203.pdf
7. Laurie Guy, *Introducing Early Christianity*, p.24-25
8. Gene Edwards, *Beyond Radical,* p.22
9. Brother Andrew, *Gods' Smuggler,* p.270
10. Wayne Jacobsen, *Living in the Relational Church-Part 2. BodyLife*, September 1999
11. Chuck Colson, *Loving God*, p.200

Chapter 13. Talking Heads
1. Søren Kierkegaard, *Concluding Unscientific Postscript to Philosophical Fragments*, p.465
2. Meier, Minirth, Wichern & Ratcliffe, *Introduction to Psychology and Counseling.*
3. Dallas Willard, *The Divine Conspiracy*, p.48-49
4. Meic Pearse, *Who's Feeding Whom?* p.72
5. Gene Edwards, *Beyond Radical*, p.26, 27
6. *Idea* magazine, November/December 1998, p.6-7
7. A.W.Tozer, *The Pursuit of God*, p.2
8. Oswald Chambers, *Our Brilliant Heritage*, p.42
9. Meic Pearse, *Who's Feeding Whom?* p.72
10. Gordon Campbell, *Bible: The Story of the King James Version,* p.9
11. Milton Jones, *Even More Concise 10 Second Sermons*, p.69
12. Charles Finney, *How to Experience Revival*, p.11
13. Dallas Willard, The Divine Conspiracy, p.344-5

Chapter 14. The Sordid Topic of Coin
1. Wayne Jacobsen, *The Naked Church*, p.118
2. https://www.churchofengland.org/about-us/funding.aspx
3. Interview with Jim Dailey for *Decision Magazine*, Nov 1st 2004 http://www.billygraham.org/articlepage.asp?ArticleID=483
4. *Zondervan Pictorial Encyclopedia of the Bible, Vol. 5*
5. Lindsay, p.203
6. The 87th canon of Basil; cited in Thomas M. Lindsay, *The Church and Ministry in the Early Centuries*, p.203, footnotes
7. Cited in Laurie Guy, *Introducing Early Christianity*, p.95
8. Lindsay, p.203
9. Cyprian, *Epistle xxxvii. (5).2*
10. Lindsay, p.201
11. http://www.economist.com/node/12342509

Chapter 15. Pay as You Go Church

1. Derek Prince, *Blessing or Curse*, p.91
2. Charles C. Ryrie, *Balancing the Christian Life*, p.88
3. Flavius Josephus, *Antiquities,* Book 4, chapter 8, section 22.
4. Gary Friesen and J. Robin Maxson, *Decision Making and the Will of God,* p.357
5. Russell Earl Kelly, *Should the Church Teach Tithing?* p.173
6. *The New International Dictionary of New Testament Theology, Quoted* in *Idea* Magazine, p14, June/July/August 1998
7. *New Advent Catholic Encyclopedia Online*
http://www.newadvent.org/cathen/14741b.htm
8. http://www.britannica.com/EBchecked/topic/597211/tithe
9. Oswald Chambers, *My Utmost for His Highest*, p.121 (reading for May 25th)
10. A. Sims (Editor), *An Hour with George Müller: The man of faith to whom God gave millions,* p.7
11. Ibid
12. http://www.crossroadschristian.org/blogs/blog/12691797-thirty-one-days-of-quotes-on-tithing-giving

Chapter 16. Church Wanted... Dead or Alive

1. *Renewal Magazine*, late 1990's?
2. Julian Watts, *God's Business; Preparing the Church for Dramatic Growth*
3. H. Richard Niebuhr, Wilhelm Pauck and Francis P. Miller, *The Church Against the World.*
  http://www.religion-online.org/showchapter.asp?title=412&C=194
4. A.W.Tozer, *This World: Playground or Battleground?* p.19
5. Oswald Chambers, *My Utmost for His Highest*
6. http://en.wikipedia.org/wiki/Cornerstone

Chapter 17. Ghosts in the Machine

1. http://www.actsweb.org/articles/article.php?i=1285&d=2&c=5
The article quotes Murray Raphel, from his book *Mind Your Own Business*
2. A.W.Tozer, *This World: Playground or Battleground?* p.37
3. A.W.Tozer, *This World: Playground or Battleground?* p.55
4. C.S. Lewis, *Mere Christianity,* p.111
5. I. Howard Marshall Acts, Tyndale New Testament Commentaries, p.126

6. Colin Marshall and Tony Payne, *The Trellis and the Vine*, p.17
7. Wayne Jacobsen, *The Naked Church*, p.187
8. Reference not found.
9. A.W.Tozer, *Man-The Dwelling Place of God*, p.41-42

Chapter 18. Arrested Development
1. Jim Rutz, *Ever Feel Like Quitting Church?*
http://www.wnd.com/index.php?pageId=41026
2. Arthur Wallis, *The Radical Christian*, p.95

Chapter 19. Valley of Decision
1. Ralph Neighbour, *Where Do We Go From Here?* p.356
2. James Houston, *Joyful Exiles*, p.45
3. Wayne Jacobsen and Dave Coleman writing as Jake Colson, *So You Don't Want to go to Church Anymore?* p.96
4. Wayne Jacobsen, *Living in the Relational Church – Part 2*; BodyLife, September 1999.
http://dev.lifestream.org/sites/default/files/bodylife_living_in_the_relational_church_part_2_0.pdf
5. R. Kent Hughes, *Disciplines of a Godly Man*, p.151
6. Antoine de Saint-Exupery, *The Wisdom of the Sands*

Chapter 20. Word of Warning
1. Wayne Jacobsen, *The Naked Church*, p.190

Chapter 21. Church Dismembership
1. Clive Calver, *Idea Magazine*
2. Charles Finney, *How to Experience Revival*, p.22
3. Oswald Chambers, *My Utmost for His Highest*, entry for August 29

Chapter 22. Flesh and Bone
1. H. Richard Niebuhr, *Church Against the World*
2. H. Richard Niebuhr, *Church Against the World*
3. Søren Kierkegaard, *Concluding Unscientific Postscript to Philosophical Fragments*, p.465
4. http://www.alanknox.net/category/blog-links/
5. H. Richard Niebuhr, *Church Against the World*

16494135R00192

Printed in Great Britain
by Amazon